WORKING MEN'S COLLEGE.

LIBRARY REGULATIONS.

THE FIRST ROMANTICS

Also by Malcolm Elwin:

THE LIFE OF LLEWELYN POWYS
SAVAGE LANDOR
OLD GODS FALLING
DE QUINCEY (Great Lives)
VICTORIAN WALLFLOWERS
THACKERAY: A Personality
CHARLES READE: A Biography

COLERIDGE IN 1799

(*from the original portrait in the possession of Mrs. Walter Cam.*)

THE
FIRST ROMANTICS

by

MALCOLM ELWIN

"*To reach the essence of a great poet's work
it is necessary to consider his physical nature, his
normal character, his average being, independently
of his peculiar type of intellect and imagination.*"

JOHN COWPER POWYS
The Pleasures of Literature

LONDON
MACDONALD & CO., (Publishers) LTD.

First published 1947

MADE AND PRINTED IN GREAT BRITAIN BY PURNELL AND SONS, LTD.,
PAULTON (SOMERSET) AND LONDON

To

JOHN COWPER POWYS

one of the great romantics of his generation

CONTENTS

PART ONE

WORDSWORTH IN PRELUDE

PART TWO

COLERIDGE'S PRELUDE

PART THREE

THE YOUTH OF SOUTHEY

PART SEVEN

THE APOSTATES

ILLUSTRATIONS

WORDSWORTH IN PRELUDE

I. THE MAKING OF A MALCONTENT

As young Victoria's aged Laureate and a man of property, wrapt in the respectability of high Tory associations, Wordsworth discovered the interest in ancestry common among aspirants to gentility. An admirer presented him with an almery, made for a William Wordsworth in 1525, which he cherished as a family heirloom. But the name, variously spelt, was common for centuries in Yorkshire, where its bearers, like the Forsytes in Dorset, were rather " small beer," mostly yeomen farmers or tradesfolk. Wadsworth was a frequent variant spelling of the name, and as the maternal ancestors of Henry Wadsworth Longfellow emigrated from Yorkshire, possibly the authors of *Hiawatha* and *Peter Bell* sprang from the same root in the unrecorded past.

Early in the eighteenth century, Richard Wordsworth migrated from Yorkshire to Westmorland, married a Miss Robinson of Appleby, was made superintendent or bailiff of the Lowther estates, and officiated as receiver-general of the county during the '45 Rebellion. His second son John, born in 1741, became an attorney at Cockermouth and in 1766—on his advantageous marriage to Ann, daughter of William Cookson, of Newbiggin Hall, Penrith—was appointed by Sir James Lowther, " steward of the manor and forest of Ennerdale," a post which he held till his death seventeen years later. Also of Yorkshire stock, the Cooksons had no more distinction than the Wordsworths, William Cookson being in trade at Penrith as a mercer. But he had married the sister and heiress of the last Crackanthorpe of Newbiggin, an old Westmorland family—a Crackanthorpe of Cockermouth had been high sheriff *temp.* Henry IV—and his

13

eldest son Christopher assumed the surname and arms of Crack-anthorpe.

Ann Wordsworth bore five children—Richard on 19th August 1768, William on 7th April 1770, Dorothy on Christmas Day 1771, John on 4th December 1772, and Christopher on 9th June 1774. Aged only thirty-one, she died in March 1778, in consequence of a chill caught from sleeping in the "best bedroom" of a friend's house. Her memory is celebrated with filial piety in *The Prelude*, where it appears that, with simple faith in providence, she believed in allowing her children's characters to develop without much moulding by discipline. On her deathbed she confided to a friend a feeling of anxiety for William alone of her five children; she believed that he would be "remarkable either for good or for evil," on account of his "stiff, moody and violent temper."

In old age Wordsworth remembered how, in a passion of resentment at some indignity he had been made to suffer, he fled to the attics of his grandfather's house with the intention of destroying himself; how, again, as a gesture of defiance, he struck his whip through the canvas of a family portrait. "From some want of judgment in punishments inflicted," he declared, "I had become perverse and obstinate in defying chastisement, and rather proud of it than otherwise."

Lacking the mollifying influence of an understanding mother's gentle tact, his sensitive resentment of injustice engendered the instincts of a rebel. But the spirit of rebellion inspired in him no such fiery outbursts as in Walter Savage Landor, whose intransigeance caused a lifelong conflict with authority, incurring his removal from school and university, frequent expensive litigation, and three times exile from the home of his choice. Wordsworth in rebellion was not the man to set up his standard of revolt in the market place, but rather the malcontent, nourishing grievances in silence, who supplies apt material to the agitator. Sullenly he submitted to unjust punishment, his demeanour doubtless exasperating his elders to further impatience; and seeking refuge outdoors from a disapproving household, he laid the foundation of that lifelong habit of solitary

contemplation and communion with Nature which supplied
the mainspring of his genius.

> " *Ere I had told*
> *Ten birthdays, when among the mountain-slopes*
> *Frost and the breath of frosty wind, had snapped*
> *The last autumnal crocus,* '*twas my joy*
> *With store of springes o'er my shoulder hung*
> *To range the open heights where woodcocks run*
> *Along the smooth green turf. Through half the night,*
> *Scudding away from snare to snare, I plied*
> *That anxious visitation.*"

To read autobiography in a poet's, as in a novelist's work,
is to skate on treacherously thin ice. *The Prelude* describes " the
growth of a poet's mind," but Mr. Herbert Read has justly
observed that " the poet is conceived, not merely as William
Wordsworth, but as an ideal character progressing towards a
state of blessedness in which he shall be fit to write that great
philosophical poem conceived by Coleridge in the early years
of their poetic faith." Wordsworth's memories of his own past
were frequently untrustworthy, and he consciously wrote *The
Prelude* for the critical appraisal of Coleridge, whose fervent
admiration he was then anxious to preserve unimpaired. Recalling to his mind's eye the well-loved scenes of boyhood, he
saw them with the poet's vision cultivated in company with his
sister and Coleridge at Racedown and Alfoxden, and suggested
that his sensitive susceptibilities were already awakening in the
schoolboy. In a revealing passage of *The Prelude*—revealing alike
as autobiography and as an example of his habitually uncertain
groping in introspection—he wrote:

> " *So feeling comes in aid*
> *Of feeling, and diversity of strength*
> *Attends us, if but once we have been strong.*
> *Oh! mystery of man, from what a depth*
> *Proceed thy honours. I am lost but see*
> *In simple childhood something of the base*
> *On which thy greatness stands; but this I feel,*

> *That from thyself it comes, that thou must give,*
> *Else never canst receive. The days gone by*
> *Return upon me almost from the dawn*
> *Of life: the hiding-places of man's power*
> *Open; I would approach them, but they close.*
> *I see by glimpses now; when age comes on,*
> *May scarcely see at all; and I would give,*
> *While yet we may, as far as words can give,*
> *Substance and life to what I feel, enshrining,*
> *Such is my hope, the spirit of the Past*
> *For future restoration."—*

In the schoolboy was "something of the base," but not yet the feeling that awakened sympathetic communion with Nature. Wordsworth as a boy possessed none of the precocity and outstanding brilliance of Coleridge or Landor. Nor, when he sought solitude to nurse his sullen moods, did he seek refuge in a world of fancy created by a romantic imagination, like De Quincey— for, among great poets, Wordsworth signally lacked invention. De Quincey, who knew him more intimately than any man save Coleridge, shrewdly remarked that "Wordsworth's intellectual passions were fervent and strong; but they rested upon a basis of preternatural animal sensibility diffused through *all* the animal passions (or appetites)"—a criticism endorsed by the above-quoted passage of *The Prelude,* and supplying the key to the problems of his personality and intellect. Physically strong and healthy, he loved to be out of doors, and his pleasures were the normal boyish practices of birds'-nesting, snaring, and boat-racing on Windermere. He knew the thrill of well-being felt by every healthy person at seeing the summer sun rising to a cloudless sky, the exultation of fresh rain driven against stinging cheeks, the satisfaction in the peace of a glowing sunset after an active and tiring day; he learned also much about birds, beasts and plants—practical knowledge of value when he came to associate emotions with ideas.

After his mother's death, Wordsworth and his elder brother Richard were sent to the grammar school at Hawkshead.

Dictating in old age his autobiographical notes to the adoring Miss Fenwick, he had " little to say " of his schooldays " but that they were very happy ones, chiefly because I was left at liberty then and in the vacations, to read whatever books I liked." To his feminine adorers Wordsworth wished to suggest that, as a schoolboy, he had an instinctive love of books, just as he desired Coleridge and readers of *The Prelude* to infer that he had felt instinctively the inspiration of Nature. He never cared for reading, read only for instruction in subjects occupying his mind, and in later life advertised the weakness of his eyes as an excuse for the poverty of his reading. " I have read nothing this age, nor indeed did I ever," he wrote to a college friend in November 1791. To Miss Fenwick he mentioned Fielding's works, *Don Quixote, Gil Blas, Gulliver's Travels,* and *The Tale of a Tub* as boyhood favourites; the fifth book of *The Prelude*, though devoted to " Books," adds to this list only a " slender abstract " of the *Arabian Nights*. He declared himself " much indebted " to one of the Hawkshead ushers for teaching him " more of Latin in a fortnight than I had learnt during the preceding years at the school of Cockermouth," but an eight-year-old boy's knowledge of Latin may be easily increased. In the same letter of November 1791 he lamented how he knew " little of Latin, and scarce anything of Greek."

Hawkshead was a small school, and Wordsworth never knew the loneliness of a small boy among seven hundred, like Coleridge at Christ's Hospital. The sons of country parsons, local tradesmen and farmers, his schoolfellows were all of the same fustian pattern; without effort, his superior intellectual powers won obvious distinction in such company, so satisfying the self-esteem which was a decisive, and frequently disfiguring, feature of his character. They were " left at liberty " for plenty of outdoor play:

> " *A race of real children; not too wise,*
> *Too learned, or too good; but wanton, fresh,*
>
> . . . .
>
> *Mad at their sports like withered leaves in winds.*"

B

For the headmaster, William Taylor, was a bluff countryman, with a love of fun and games profounder than his scholarship.

> "*The sighs which Matthew heaved were sighs*
> *Of one tired out with fun and madness;*
> *The tears which came to Matthew's eyes*
> *Were tears of light, the dew of gladness.*"

By his zest for the sunshine and " the breathing air," this " honoured teacher of my youth " contributed to building " something of the base," and with vivid recollections of the tired, happy feeling at the end of a hard day's play, Wordsworth wrote candidly:

> "*a boy I loved the sun,*
> *Not as I since have loved him, as a pledge*
> *And surety of our earthly life, a light*
> *Which we behold and feel we are alive;*
> *Nor for his bounty to so many worlds—*
> *But for this cause, that I had seen him lay*
> *His beauty on the morning hills, had seen*
> *The western mountain touch his setting orb,*
> *In many a thoughtless hour, when, from excess*
> *Of happiness, my blood appeared to flow*
> *For its own pleasure, and I breathed with joy.*"

Nor were the Hawkshead boarders herded together in dreary dormitories; they lodged with cottagers near the school. Here again Wordsworth was lucky in finding a childless landlady, Anne Tyson, who lavished her maternal instincts on her young lodgers. She was the first of the women in Wordsworth's life on whose faithful service and tender care he utterly depended; to her, in learning to win her favour by fetching and carrying, by considerate attentions which perhaps earned such rewards as an extra ration of favourite cake, he served an apprenticeship in the art of pleasing women that proved of advantage to his comfort. For years her cottage was home to him, and to " my old Dame, so kind and motherly " he hurried on vacation from

Cambridge, when " she perused me with a parent's pride." Of her gossipping tales, related by the fireside on winter's nights, many remained in his memory all his life, like the history of the Jacobite and the Hanoverian related in the sixth book of *The Excursion*. Through her he became intimately acquainted with the Cumberland peasantry, and in describing the Pedlar in *The Excursion*, he drew largely upon his schoolboy memories, supplemented by anecdotes recounted by his wife and his sister; for, as a man, his awkward, aloof manner did not inspire friendly confidence in the dalesfolk—" he was not a man as folks could crack wi'," said Hartley Coleridge's landlord, " nor not a man as could crack wi' folks . . . eh, dear! quite a different man from li'le Hartley."

The careless freedom and happiness of his home with Anne Tyson emphasised his dissatisfaction with the chill disapproval of his relatives. In December 1783 his father died, leaving little provision for his children, beyond claims against his employer, Sir James Lowther, an unscrupulous Tory politician, whose wife was a daughter of George III's first Prime Minister, Lord Bute, and who earned, by money, influence, graft with his betters, and oppression of his dependants, the earldom of Lonsdale in 1784. Sir James had not only withheld payments due, but neglected to refund to his agent moneys paid out on his behalf. For years John Wordsworth's representatives conducted fruitless litigation against the earl; only after Lonsdale's death in 1802, his successor paid to the Wordsworths £8,500 in discharge of the debt and interest accrued.

John Wordsworth left his children to the joint guardianship of his elder brother, Richard Wordsworth of Whitehaven, and his wife's elder brother, Christopher Crackanthorpe. The former fulfilled his duty by sharing the financial administration and inviting his wards for an occasional visit, but he had a family of his own. " Uncle Kit " Crackanthorpe, on the other hand, was a middle-aged bachelor, living with his parents, who were naturally expected to provide a home for their orphaned grandchildren. The old couple lived over the mercer's shop at Penrith. Formerly they had doubtless lived there for old Cookson's convenience in conducting his business; they continued to live there because they had reached an age disinclined to change, and because they still kept querulous watch on the shop and its takings. Uncle Kit's situation was not calculated to achieve serenity or satisfaction. As heir of his mother's ancient family he had surrendered the Cookson name for that of Crackanthorpe, but instead of enjoying a squire's dignity at Newbiggin Hall, he had to forget his gentility to follow his father's trade as a shopkeeper. Apparently the old man kept him so close that he was unable to marry, for old Cookson died in December 1787 and eight months later Kit Crackanthorpe married Charlotte Cust, who had been for years a favoured caller on his mother.

Even if he did not feel hostility towards his nephews as possible rivals for the old people's affections and money, self-pity for his own situation inspired him to regard his wards as a tiresome infliction. He lost no opportunity of grimly reminding the boys of their dependence, often in the hearing of the servants, who, disposed to resent the extra work created by schoolboys' careless habits, took their cue from the future master of the house, and were " every one of them so insolent to us as makes the kitchen as well as the parlour quite insupportable." The head manservant, a " particular favourite " with Uncle Kit, discovered that he could insult them with impunity; he would echo his master's reminder that they were dependent upon their grandfather, and when they required such services as shoe cleaning, grumbled insolently that they required " as much waiting upon as any *gentlemen.*"

Doubtless on account of his sullen temper, Wordsworth was especially disliked by his uncle; hence, he probably suffered a proportionately larger share of insolence from the servants. Just as the man was not one " as folks could crack wi'," so the boy lacked charm to engage the sympathy and affection of inferiors. He resented their insolence while despising their dislike, and contrasting his treatment at the hands of these over-fed sycophantic, servile dependants of their betters, with the freemasonry he enjoyed from the homely peasant friends of

Dame Tyson, he became receptive material for the revolutionary vapours wafted across the Channel from the boiling cauldron of France. It is important to remember that Wordsworth, unlike Landor and Shelley, was no aristocratic intellectual inspired by the fine principles of liberty, equality and fraternity ; he was no enthusiast for an idealistic philosophy, like Coleridge; he was a malcontent, resentful of the repression he had himself suffered, ready tinder for kindling by any agitator suggesting a change from existing conditions of injustice.

2. NOT VERY WILD OATS

On her mother's death in 1778, the only daughter of John and Ann Wordsworth had been sent to live with a first cousin of her mother's, Elizabeth Threlkeld, at Halifax. She was then only six years old. At Halifax she was brought up in exclusively feminine society, lavishing dutiful affection upon her " Aunt ", as she called Miss Threlkeld, and bestowing her confidence in her close companion, Jane Pollard. In the spring of 1787, when she was fifteen, she was adjudged old enough to be done with schooling and to make herself useful as companion to her grandmother.

To Penrith she came, impressionable, warm-hearted, emotional, eager, full of girlish curiosity about the brothers from whom she had been separated for nine years, and prepared to love each with all the strength of an ardent temperament. But she was quick of perception and comprehension, and her lively intelligence appreciated intellectual gifts in others. She was delighted to find that William and Christopher showed promise of exceptional parts. She liked good, honest John, too, but he was " not so bright as either William or Christopher "; he was shortly to be a sailor in the East India service, to which he was preferred by the influence of a powerful family connection, Mr. John Robinson, successively M.P. for Westmorland and Harwich, whose daughter became Countess of Abergavenny and who

himself declined a peerage offered in just reward for long service
as secretary to the Treasury.

She was least favourably impressed by her eldest brother;
Richard was "equally affectionate and good," and though "far
from being as clever as William," he was "very diligent and
far from being dull." But the truth, which could hardly be
frankly confided to Jane Pollard, was that Richard naturally
showed less interest than his brothers in their fifteen-year-old
sister. He was nineteen, with his way to make in life. Till this
time he had been William's closest companion; together they
had gone from the dame's school at Cockermouth to Whitehaven; together they had journeyed to and fro for holidays,
jointly contending with difficulties of transport when Uncle Kit
neglected to send horses for them; together, too, they had
enjoyed the boyish sports and rambles remembered in *The
Prelude*.

> "*Happy time! more dear*
> *For this, that one was by my side, a friend*
> *Then passionately loved; with heart how full*
> *Would he peruse these lines! For many years*
> *Have since flowed in between us, and, our minds*
> *Both silent to each other, at this time*
> *We live as if these hours had never been.*"

It has been suggested that these lines refer to one or the other
of two schoolfellows, Fleming and Farish, who both became
parsons. But their early intimacy and subsequent relations
indicate that Wordsworth was thinking of his eldest brother.

Richard was that most fortunate of creatures, the average
person, who makes no bones about accepting his allotted circumstances and doing his best to adapt them to his own comfort.
Good-natured and easy-going, he refrained from invoking his
uncle's hostility by displays of resentment; while necessity
required his residence at Penrith, he made the best of a bad job,
but with equal realism he determined to make the earliest
possible escape from a disagreeable environment. He elected to
be a lawyer, because his father's connections and Mr. Robinson's

influence would prove useful in that profession, and soon after his sister Dorothy's arrival at Penrith, he departed to take up his studies at Staple Inn. For many years he rarely returned to the scenes of his boyhood. But he maintained close touch with his family. Whenever his brothers were in London, they saved their pockets by free lodgings at his rooms. On his coming of age, his uncles willingly surrendered to him the management of his own, his brothers', and his sister's affairs, together with the complicated claims against Lord Lonsdale. As his sister admitted, he had "all the plague" of prosecuting the Lonsdale business to a profitable conclusion, and the negotiations were fraught with peril as well as anxiety when Lonsdale was disposed to use repressive measures, permitted by a reactionary government to loyal patriots against revolutionist sympathisers, to rid himself of personal "annoyancers."

From his sister and brothers he received scant thanks for his services. In later years his brother William rarely condescended to write a line to him, deputing the duty of communication to his sister, who, a copious correspondent with others, confined herself to hurried notes, briefly mentioning matters of business with the barest courtesies of family affection. They treated him rather as a mere business factotum, remembering his existence only when they needed money or advice, and then bitterly vilifying him for negligence or procrastination. Probably the breach between the two elder brothers began at the end of their schooldays, when the practical Richard escaped from their grandparents' home by diligent application to a profession, while William, who had been loudest in protest against his dependent condition and disagreeable surroundings, made no shift to secure an establishment in life. Possibly Richard taunted him with this, especially when he drew more heavily than his brothers upon the slender funds of his father's estate, and neither forgiveness nor forbearance belonged to Wordsworth's nature.

Any want of sympathy from Richard served to heighten Dorothy's loyal partiality for her brother William. She herself smarted under her uncle's hostility, from the querulous carpings of her grandfather and grandmother, "the former of whom never speaks to us but when he scolds." William and John were most nearly her own age, but John was younger than herself, besides being "not so bright." William's seniority, unlike Richard's, was too slight to remind her of her immaturity, yet sufficient to excite her admiration and hero-worship. Her heart swelled exultantly when he showed resentment to their oppressors, and overflowed with sympathy for his wounded pride when she saw him subdued in sullen humiliation. From the first she refused to admit any criticism of him; others might express disgust that he avowed no settled ambition, but she was quick to dress his excuses in a semblance of conviction. Not yet appreciative, or even aware, of the genius which ever provides excuse for eccentricities or inadequacies, she attributed his indecision to physical ailment. "He wishes very much to be a lawyer if his health will permit, but he is troubled with violent headaches and a pain in his side." She did not remark how the pain in his side failed to interfere with his long rambles over hill and dale, nor did she explain why his preparation for the legal profession, unlike Richard's, required the expense of a university education.

Wordsworth went up to St. John's College, Cambridge, in October 1787. "I had my Br. Wm with me for three weeks," wrote his sister; "I was very busy during his stay, preparing his cloaths for Cambridge." It was the last service she was to perform for him for nearly two years. Like Richard, he was escaping from the stuffy tyranny of the Penrith shop; his sister could be of no use to him in his Cambridge career, and Wordsworth never troubled about people who could be of no use to him.

"My spirit was up, my thoughts were full of hope," he wrote of his arrival at Cambridge. Like every eager freshman, to himself he seemed

> "*A man of business and expense, and went*
> *From shop to shop about my own affairs,*
> *To Tutor or to Tailor, as befell,*
> *From street to street with loose and careless mind.*"

But after the novelty of fledgling liberty had lost its charm, "from the first crude days of settling time," he had to admit

> "*A feeling that I was not for that hour,*
> *Nor for that place.*"

In *The Prelude* he wrote with such contemptuous condescension of Cambridge that commentators have been at pains to prove that the university was not a slough of degeneracy and sloth. Instead of sage teachers and profound thinkers, he professed to see only trivial butterflies and "chattering popinjays": his impatience of discipline revolted alike against compulsory chapels and prescribed lectures; he disliked "the timid course of our scholastic studies" and despised the examination system that weighed men "as in the balance." To preserve the continuity of the story of his apprenticeship to Nature's inspiration, he pretended that he sought refuge in a world of his own, lost in contemplation during country rambles; with a fine disdainful air, he pictured himself adorned with the grandeur of eccentric genius in the eyes of commonplace persons, who saw madness in his privileged sympathies with Nature. Affecting a jauntiness utterly foreign to his temperament, he confessed occasional descents from Olympian detachment "into the ordinary works of careless youth," airily declaring,

> "*Companionships,*
> *Friendships, acquaintances, were welcome all.*
> *We sauntered, played, or rioted; we talked*
> *Unprofitable talk at morning hours;*
> *Drifted about along the streets and walks,*
> *Read lazily in trivial books, went forth*
> *To gallop through the country in blind zeal*
> *Of senseless horsemanship, or on the breast*
> *Of Cam sailed boisterously, and let the stars*
> *Come forth, perhaps without one quiet thought.*"

A wealth of wistful regret lies hidden in these lines. Of all the books of *The Prelude*, "Residence at Cambridge," is most indicative of insincerity, most replete with rhetorical verbiage, most hesitant in thought and theme. In the throes of composition at Grasmere, with the requisite local colour outside his garden gate and Hawkshead itself only a day's excursion away, the recluse could readily sketch the scenes of his idealised boyhood. But the absence of specific reference to the rural beauties surrounding Cambridge is surely significant; alone " the pleasant Mill of Trompington " is identified as a resort of the solitary's communings with Nature, and its mention serves only to introduce a passage of theatrical apostrophes to " gentle " Chaucer, " sweet " Spenser, and " temperate " Milton. Wordsworth was hard beset to account to Coleridge for the stagnancy of his Cambridge years.

The few lines above quoted indicate the main source of his disappointment in university life. Among the Hawkshead bumpkins he had shone in brilliant relief; his " cleverness " was recognised in his family circle, though without due reference by his uncle and grandparents. At Cambridge he must have visualised himself at last basking in the sunshine of fitting appreciation; all would be eager for his acquaintance, to receive his recognising nod; the industriously sober would listen attentively to his pronouncements and seek discussion for enlightenment, while he would make choice of boon companions for his lighter leisure.

Instead he found himself ignored by those whose society he desired. His appearance and manner always militated against favourable first impressions. Even his sister had to confess that " his person is not in his favour," that he was " certainly rather plain." When Landor received Hazlitt at Florence and asked what Wordsworth looked like, Hazlitt replied, " Have you seen a horse, sir? Well then, you have seen Wordsworth, sir." Tall and angular, he had " something of a roll, a lounge, in his gait "; his voice was deep and guttural, and he spoke with a strong northern burr; his manner of address, even after time had mellowed the *gaucheries* of youth, was always stiff and ungracious. To the cream of Cambridge society, the latest products of Eton and Winchester, Harrow and Rugby, he was a rustic hobble-dehoy, a plebeian lout, unfit for association with the sons, legitimate or otherwise, of fathers more or less modelled on the image of the fourth Lord Chesterfield or the impeccable Sir Charles Grandison.

Nor could his attainments command admission to familiarity with the intelligentsia. He had read little, and lacked address to discuss entertainingly the little he knew; he never became a good talker. " You must be with him more than once," his sister warned Miss Pollard, " before he will be perfectly easy in conversation." In later life he evaded his conversational limitations by reading his poems aloud; but at Cambridge he had written no poems, and if he had, probably few would have listened to his reading of them—at least a second time. Lacking the means to purchase popularity by giving wine parties and breakfasts, he had to find companionship among social outcasts like himself—among those earnest, eager little men haunting obscure corners of every college, who beam their gratification when noticed, who busily pursue the appointed curriculum for the three or four years of their university career, and then vanish to curacies or some department of the civil or colonial service, unremembered even by those men of monumental memories, the college porters. This necessity irked his pride, and self-defence inspired the airs of aloofness remarked by all who met him; he made no advances from fear of rebuff, and his reserve, inspired by want of self-confidence in youth, ironically became arrogance in maturity, when he had learned to live without the warmth of friendship he would once have welcomed. The only friends he made at Cambridge were Robert Jones, who became a country parson, and William Mathews, son of a bookseller and brother of Charles Mathews, the actor.

Though dislike of mathematics was the reason he gave to his sister for not trying for a fellowship, he told his nephew and first biographer that he had learned at school so much Euclid and algebra that he " had a full twelve months' start of the freshmen of my year." Hence he " got into rather an idle way, reading nothing but classic authors according to my fancy, and Italian poetry ". But any taste he affected for Italian poetry must have been difficult of indulgence, for in the summer of 1791, lamenting his idleness on holiday in Wales, he remarked, " Were I furnished with a dictionary and a grammar, and other requisites, I might perhaps make an attack upon Italy." *The Prelude* admits that his years at Cambridge were saved from " utter waste " only by his introduction to social life!

Sick with disappointment after his first year at the university, he spent his first long vacation at Dame Tyson's cottage in the vale of Esthwaite, where his wounded self-love received healing balm from the admiration of the simple peasantry. It was another year before he proceeded to the solitary achievement of his Cambridge career in improving his intimacy with his sister. By that time she also had escaped from the mercer's shop at Penrith. Their grandfather died at the end of Wordsworth's first Cambridge term, and Dorothy recoiled from the prospect of continuing, a persecuted pensioner, under the roof of Uncle Kit and his bride, whom she described as " a mixture of ignorance, pride, affectation, self-conceit, and affected notability." Separated from her brothers, she lavished her devotion on her other uncle, the Rev. William Cookson, younger by fourteen years than Uncle Kit, and waiting, like his brother, for their father's death to enable him to marry. " He is a friend," she assured Miss Pollard, " to whom next to my aunt I owe the greatest obligations." He acted as her tutor, teaching her arithmetic, geography and French for two hours every morning; " every day gives me new proofs of his affection, and every day I like him better than I did before." He introduced her to his cousins, the Misses Cowper, to whom her visits afforded a welcome change from the fireside of her peevish grandmother; she was especially charmed with Miss Dorothy Cowper; " I wish my uncle and she would marry." They were married in October 1788, two months after Uncle Kit and Miss Cust, and Dorothy was one of the two witnesses to sign the register. Then her uncle was appointed rector of Forncett near Norwich, and proposed that his niece should join his household. " My happiness was very unexpected," Miss Pollard was told. " When my uncle told me, I was almost mad with joy. I cried and laughed alternately. It was in a walk with him that it was communicated to me."

As every day gave her fresh proofs of her uncle and aunt's goodness, she had now "nothing left to wish for on my own account"; she could now concentrate all her ardent hopes on the careers of her brothers.

On her way to Forncett she called at Cambridge and visited William, and he spent much of his second long vacation with her, visiting the dales of Derbyshire and the Yorkshire country-side around her old home at Halifax. For the first time he awakened to some appreciation of her worth—"she seemed a gift then first bestowed." His vanity fed on her eager admiration, but he also recognised the gift of quick perception on which he was to depend all his life. Now probably he first glimpsed the close communion with Nature which he describes in *The Prelude* as dating from boyhood. His imagination ever moved at pedestrian pace, never leaping with wild caprice or wanton fancy; he needed to nurse and brood over an impression before it developed an idea. But when he pointed out anything to her, her lively understanding expressed some observation which opened a trend of thought for him; she supplied the function of inspiration and stimulant. Her memory, too, was retentive; when he sought vainly to re-create an impression in imagination, she could recall it for him with fluent description. Later he used her journals as material for poetic composition; he used her mind as a photographic record, as is indicated by such entries as 30th January, 1798, "William called me into the garden to observe a singular appearance about the moon." Like a journalist he made copy of her conversation, as when he was writing his lines "To a Butterfly," and she told him how she had in childhood chased butterflies, but refrained from catching them, for fear of brushing the dust from their wings. In the years to come, she grew to recognise her function as a stimulant; she would walk backwards and forwards with him, working to ignite the flame of his inspiration, till she was tired—then "William kindled and began to write the poem."

Neither could yet foresee how much each was to mean to the other, but during this holiday with her he realised with surprise and pleasure a sympathy and understanding he had encountered in no other companion, while she, on her side, was delighted by his appreciation of her company. As yet she had no thought of devoting her life to him, nor even the longing to share his home, but after this holiday "my dear William" became definitely her favourite brother.

Her partiality was strengthened by strain on her loyalty. Richard and John were already settled in life, the one in law, the other in the merchant service; young Kit gave every promise at school of the successful opportunism which culminated in the Mastership of Trinity. William, by contrast, continued to endorse the opinion formed by his elders during his boyhood that he was the least satisfactory of his family. He had by now abandoned the notion of becoming a lawyer; he was to try for a college fellowship preparatory to taking orders, and his Uncle Cookson's influence would secure him church preferment.

At the end of his third year at Cambridge, he announced his intention of "giving up all thoughts" of a fellowship and went off with his friend Jones for a walking tour through France and the Alps. From Switzerland in September he wrote to his sister a long and perfunctory tourist's letter, probably intending to use it as memoranda for the material of the poem afterwards published as *Descriptive Sketches*, as he afterwards used her journals. Declaring himself "a perfect enthusiast in my admiration of nature in all her various forms," he told her—more sincerely, perhaps, than ever she suspected—how he never looked on each fresh vista of beauty without wishing that she was by his side. With the project of his poem in mind, he knew how her quicker perception would have "kindled" his ideas; she doubtless did not realise this, but was flattered by his desire for her companionship.

After his return to England, he spent six weeks "in the depths of winter" with his sister at Forncett. Every morning they walked for two hours, and at dusk they went into the country and paced backwards and forwards together for another two hours. "Unless you have accustomed yourself to this kind of walking," she told Miss Pollard, "you will have no idea that it can be pleasant; but I assure you it is most delightful." It was her first experience of the " kindling " process, indicating that the composition of *Descriptive Sketches* was begun.

From Forncett he went in January 1791 to Cambridge to take his B.A. degree, and thence to London. Again *The Prelude*, evading facts, affects unconvincing jauntiness:

> " *Free as a colt at pasture on the hill,*
> *I ranged at large, through London's wide domain,*
> *Month after month. Obscurely did I live,*
> *Not seeking frequent intercourse with men,*
> *By literature, or elegance or rank*
> *Distinguished. Securely was a year thus sent*
> *Ere I forsook the crowded solitude,*
> *With less regret for its luxurious pomp,*
> *And all the nicely guarded shows of art,*
> *Than for the humble book-stalls in the streets.*"

Not a year, but only three or four months he spent in London; he sought no intercourse with " distinguished " men, because he knew none. He says he was " undetermined to what course of life I should adhere," but he was supposed to be preparing himself to take orders. Before making his irrevocable vows to lifelong respectability he wanted to sate an adolescent craving for vice, to see for himself the " gorgeous ladies " of Vauxhall and Ranelagh, of whom he heard from envied bloods at Cambridge. Doubtless under the guidance of William Mathews or his brother Richard, he was shown the sights of London's night life; the theatre was his " dear delight," but though he saw Mrs. Siddons, his taste was not too fastidious to enjoy the antics of " clowns, conjurors, posture-masters, harlequins " at Sadler's Wells, then devoted entirely to pantomime and musical burlesque. He heard Burke speak in the House of Commons, but his applause of Burke's eloquence reflects the political thought of later years, and the more vivid memories of the hurly-burly of Bartholomew Fair were the result of a visit under Charles Lamb's guidance as late as the autumn of 1802.

"I filled an idler's place," he says, and still idling, he left
London in May to spend the summer at his friend Jones's home
in Denbighshire. Dorothy had no little trouble in defending
him from his uncle Cookson's displeasure. The habit of excusing
him was so strong that she wrote defensively to Miss Pollard:

> "William you may have heard lost the chance, indeed the
> certainty of a fellowship by not combating his inclinations,
> he gave way to his natural dislike of studies so dry as many
> parts of the mathematics, consequently could not succeed at
> Cambridge."

She mentioned for the first time his "great attachment to poetry,"
which, she regrets, "is not the most likely thing to produce his
advancement in the world." "His pleasures are chiefly of the
imagination, he is never so happy as when in a beautiful country."
Then, fearing that she has countenanced the charge against his
idling, she begs Miss Pollard not to think "from what I have
said that he reads not at all, for he does read a great deal." Unluckily Wordsworth himself discounted this assurance when
writing from Wales to William Mathews only six weeks later.
Replying to Mathews' request for his "observations on modern
literature," he said, "You might as well have solicited me to
send you an account of the tribes inhabiting the central regions
of the African continent." His "incursions into the fields of
modern literature," apart from *Tristram Shandy* and two or three
papers of *The Spectator*, were "absolutely nothing." He confided, "the truth of the matter is that in Town I did *little* and
since I came here I have done nothing." If he had remembered
to bring his Spanish grammar with him, "by peeping into it
occasionally I might perhaps have contrived to keep the little
Spanish or some part of it, that I was master of." His time was
more pleasantly employed in the society of Jones's three attractive sisters, who, since he was "without a rival" for their
attention, doubtless listened with sufficient sympathy to his
confidences about himself.

He remained idle in Wales till recalled in September by a

summons from the family patron, Mr. Robinson, "respecting my going in for orders, and taking a curacy at Harwich where his interest chiefly lies, which may be considered as introductory to the living." He thought it best "to pay my respects to him in person, to inform him that I was not of age." Apparently Mr. Robinson was unaware that Wordsworth had come of age in the previous April. The offer was too advantageous for refusal. Yet Wordsworth, still hankering after adventure, recoiled from the immediate prospect of permanent settlement in the shackles of clerical respectability; he therefore lied to his patron, and said nothing of the offer to any member of his family.

On 9th October his sister informed Miss Pollard that William was at Cambridge; she did not know when he was setting out for the north of England, but, on the advice of Uncle Cookson, he was to study "the Oriental languages." But on 23rd November he wrote to Mathews, not from the north, but Brighton, on his way to France. "I am doomed to be an idler through my whole life," he lamented; "I have read nothing this age, nor indeed did I ever." His uncle had suggested the study of oriental literature, as "the best field for a person to distinguish himself in, as a man of letters," and "to oblige him" he had agreed. "But," he asked, "what must I do amongst that immense wilderness, I who have no resolution, and who have not prepared myself for the enterprise by any sort of discipline amongst the Western languages? who know little of Latin and scarce anything of Greek." The excuse for his visit to France was communicated by his sister to Miss Pollard; he was there "to pass the winter for the purpose of learning the French language which will qualify him for the office of travelling companion to some young gentleman." It was flight to escape the advancing shadow of holy orders, which alone offered the necessary stable income; his university expenses having absorbed most of his patrimony, the need for earning money was urgent, and the hope of qualifying to bear-lead a rich boy round the continent was the last slender chance of salvation from the drab monotony of a country rectory.

3. A REVOLUTIONIST'S AMOUR

On his arrival in Paris, Wordsworth had twenty pounds, which he changed for six hundred and forty-three livres. His lodgings at Orleans cost him not more than thirty livres a month, with another fifty for board. He did not add to his expenses by employing a teacher to coach his French; instead he learned the language in the most effective and delightful manner—from the lips of a mistress.

At Orleans, Paul Vallon, the son of a surgeon at Blois, worked as a notary's clerk. An affable, amusing, witty young man, fond of gaiety and society, generous beyond his means, he probably made Wordsworth's acquaintance through some cavalry officers who were Wordsworth's fellow-lodgers. At this time his youngest sister Annette was staying with him. From her own supposed portrait and some probable resemblance to her small, paunchy brother, it is unlikely that she was pretty, but she had personality and charm. She shared her brother's impulsive generosity and inevitable amiability; her letters suggest a lively, if volatile, emotional if superficial temperament. Four years his senior at twenty-five she was sufficiently mature to seem an alluringly desirable woman of the world to one so raw and unused to society as Wordsworth. He was unlike any young man she was likely to have met; he was lonely, writing poetry, despondent about his future, undecided whether to be driven into the clerical profession by necessity and his family. His situation had obvious possibilities for sentiment, his letters to Mathews show no lack of aptitude for the heroics of self-pity, even his awkwardness might be an asset in engaging sympathy. Annette's generosity was not slow to bestow the fullest measure of consolation, for on 15th December 1792, the baptism was registered of "Anne Caroline Wordswodsth, daughter of William Wordswodsth, Anglois, and of Marie Anne Vallon."

Annette and her brother were royalists and remained so throughout the Revolution and the Empire. At this time

Wordsworth's political sentiments were as undefined as his ideas on anything else; he had read little, and at Cambridge his acquaintance had included none of much intellectual capacity. During his journey with Jones through France to Switzerland, he had caught the infection of exulting enthusiasm for the cause of liberty, but

> " *I looked upon these things*
> *As from a distance; heard, and saw, and felt,*
> *Was touched, but with no intimate concern.*"

When he arrived at Orleans, the Girondists were clamouring for war against the electorates sheltering emigrant aristocrats; there was a growing suspicion that counter-revolution was imminent; ministers in power like Lafayette were accused of favouring it; the Jacobins, with Danton and Robespierre at the head, were advocating purges to preserve the Revolution, and clouds were gathering for the storm which burst in the Reign of Terror. " I stood, 'mid these concussions, unconcerned," wrote Wordsworth;

> " *indifference this*
> *Which may seem strange: but I was unprepared*
> *With needful knowledge, had abruptly passed*
> *Into a theatre, whose stage was filled*
> *And busy with an action far advanced.*"

" Two or three officers of the Cavalry," he informed his brother Richard, were his fellow-lodgers; *The Prelude* records:

> " *A band of military officers,*
> *Then stationed in the city, were the chief*
> *Of my associates . . . .*
> *In age and temper differing, they had yet*
> *One spirit ruling in each heart; alike . . .*
> *Were bent upon undoing what was done:*
> *This was their rest and only hope; therewith*
> *No fear had they of bad becoming worse,*
> *For worst to them was come. . . .*"

Through these officers he probably met friendly, social Paul Vallon and his sister; they also introduced him to one or two debating clubs, which were doubtless as dull as most such provincial institutions, but seemed to the inexperienced Wordsworth " polished in arts, and in punctilio versed." Though, he says, they did not " disdain the wish to bring me over to their cause," the debates suffered from the necessity of discretion in expressing candid opinion; with the vigilant Robespierre daily declaiming against enemies of the Revolution, the reactionaries had to guard their tongues to save their skins. As " these restrictions soon proved tedious," Wordsworth " gradually withdrew into a noisier world, and thus ere long became a patriot."

This change from indifference to a decisive opinion occurred when he forsook the mainly royalist society of the cathedral city for the smaller town of Blois. Annette's stay with her brother came to an end; she returned to the home of her mother and step-father at Blois in the early spring, and Wordsworth followed her. Here he met Captain Michel Beaupuy, of whom his principal biographer has said, " no other man save Coleridge had so great an influence upon Wordsworth." *The Prelude* describes Beaupuy in terms of enthusiastic reverence. He was a younger son of an old and noble family, who in his youth had enjoyed his share of gallantries; at thirty-six, he had been for twenty years in the army, and doubtless owed his slow promotion to the unpopularity of his political opinions. For he alone of the officers at Blois was a devoted adherent of the Revolution—" a patriot, thence rejected by the rest "—a disciple of Rousseau, confident in the belief that the ideals of liberty, equality, and the brotherhood of man would emerge triumphant from the tide of political change. The failure of insults by his conventional brother-officers to disturb his gracious serenity impressed Wordsworth, contrasting such dignity of demeanour with his own sulky resentment of persecution at Penrith.

> " *Man he loved*
> *As man; and, to the mean and the obscure,*
> *And all the homely in their homely works,*

> *Transferred a courtesy which had no air*
> *Of condescension."*

Wordsworth was reminded that his happiest human contacts had been among the Hawkshead peasantry, that he had been spurned by fashionable Cambridge for his rustic ungainliness as Beaupuy by his brother-officers for his revolutionary opinions; hence enthusiasm for democracy burst upon him as an inspiration, as the means of salvation from his inferiority complex. Having found himself a misfit in his world, he now felt assured that the world, and not himself, was wrong. He was the malcontent in the market-place, but Beaupuy was more than the mob orator—he was an enthusiast contemptuous of the privilege bestowed by his own birth, a man of maturity and culture, whose opinions were the fruit of ripe experience and intellectual reasoning, and who yet welcomed the raw proselyte as the confidant of his hopes.

> " *Oft in solitude*
> *With him did I discourse about the end*
> *Of civil government, and its wisest forms;*
> *Of ancient loyalty, and chartered rights,*
> *Custom and habit, novelty and change;*
> *Of self-respect, and virtue in the few*
> *For patrimonial honour set apart,*
> *And ignorance in the labouring multitude."*

Under Beaupuy's guidance he read Rousseau and much propaganda besides; after his death there was found in his library a bundle of " French pamphlets and ephemera " testifying to his studies at Blois.

Till Beaupuy left for the Rhine with his regiment, Wordsworth divided his time at Blois between walks and talks with him and clandestine meetings with Annette. Divergence of political views could not disturb relations with Annette; there was no time for talk of politics at their furtive meetings. They had plans to make about the coming baby. The obvious and honourable course would have been for Wordsworth to marry his mistress. It may be argued that her family would hardly welcome the proposal of a penniless foreigner, but financial considerations would be set aside on the discovery of Annette's condition. Nor was the family approval necessary, since both Annette and Wordsworth were of age; there was nothing to prevent their marriage preceding its announcement to her relatives. Having married her and broken the news to her family, Wordsworth might have been expected to return immediately to England to procure a home and the means of keeping her.

By 17th May he must have received some intimation of her condition, yet on that date he wrote to Mathews that it was " at present " his intention " to take orders, in the approaching winter or spring." He still counted confidently on his uncle Cookson's good offices, though " had it been in my power, I certainly should have wished to defer the moment." Nevertheless, he assured Mathews, who advanced nebulous notions of founding a critical review, that his probable residence in a country parsonage need not hinder his participation " in any literary plan," and encouraged him to canvass booksellers on the prospects of establishing a magazine. Apparently he hoped to supplement his stipend as a curate by writing. Yet he must have recognised the probability of his uncle's reluctance to recommend for preferment the father of an illegitimate child. On the other hand, if he was married, with a wife and child to support, his uncle might have felt obliged, however disapproving, to do all in his power to assist him to a competence.

Why then did he not marry Annette? The only reason can have been his continued reluctance to take orders. However much he was charmed by the vivacious Annette, however intrigued by the prospect of paternity, however much he professed to yearn for the tranquillity of country life, he recoiled from the role of paterfamilias in a village parsonage. The prospect promised a settlement too permanent. With puppy eyes just opened to a glimpse of the limitless possibilities of social revolution, how could he hurry home to seek self-banishment from the world of affairs to a cloistered retreat?

He was not a man, even for a moment, to reckon the world well lost for love. Charles Lamb described him as " cold," and the record of his human relationships justifies the charge. But he had strong sensual instincts; sensuality is strongly marked in the mouth shown by both his portraits, by Hancock and Shuter, as a young man. *The Prelude* (iv. 317) speaks of " slight shocks of young love-liking " in his youth at Hawkshead, but it is unlikely that these inspired more than furtive philandering, some tumbling and tousing behind hayricks or in a barn's dark corners at a country hop. His middle-class respectability was too deeply rooted to risk the complications of a rustic amour near the homes of his relatives. It has been freely suggested that the Lucy of his poems was the idealisation of some early love—for if he disguised one amour in his poetry, why not half a dozen such?— but a recent biographer (Mr. Fausset) has more shrewdly supposed that Lucy was " an imagined being created out of his real feelings for Dorothy and Annette." More likely still, Lucy was an ideal creation of his fancy, such a mistress as he would have wished to have had if opportunity had offered, as he glimpsed in the flesh when he saw the " sweet Highland girl " by Loch Lomond in 1803. When he went to France, he was ripe for amorous experience; with the shadow of holy orders, and its doom to life-long continence looming over him, he possibly went with the settled intention of seeking a mistress. When he journeyed to Switzerland, the company of Jones prevented pursuit of women; at Orleans, for the first time in his life, he was among strangers, remote from relatives and acquaintances, free to explore the tantalising mystery of sex without risk of discomfiting gossip. Annette was the first to offer what he wanted; it was bad luck that she was not a woman of more experience.

It is fruitless to conjecture what tale he told to Annette, what excuses he made for dallying at her side month by month of her pregnancy, in what colours he painted the harshness of his uncles, the antipathy of his home environment. Doubtless he was as exercised to devise reasons for self-deception as for Annette's pacification, for he always liked to deduce a moral explanation of his conduct. Perhaps he told her, and convinced himself, that he could not tolerate the anxiety of separation

during her present condition; perhaps Annette was too proud
to point out that she would face her ordeal more serenely within
the bonds of wedlock. Anyhow, rather than return to England
to be ordained, he allowed Annette to sustain unassisted the
burden of their indiscretion—to disclose her condition to her
mother, to explain why he could not marry her, to advise the
best plans for her confinement. Her situation was less difficult
than it would have been in normal times, for all France was in
turmoil, conventions were discarded by necessity, and people
were too occupied in preserving their property and skins to have
time for tattle.

Nevertheless, when her condition could no longer be con-
cealed, she naturally preferred that her confinement should be
staged where she was less well known than at Blois. She chose
Orleans, because there she had friends but few acquaintants.
And back to Orleans Wordsworth followed her, having apprised
brother Richard on 3rd September of his imminent departure,
and requesting the remittance of another twenty pounds. Long
afterwards, when his memory could claim all too little reliance,
he declared that he was at Orleans when the September massacres
were committed, when Fournier, a soulless brute such as always
achieves military promotion at an epoch of violence, contrived
the assassination of the prisoners he was escorting from Orleans
to Versailles for trial. "The massacre of St. Bartholomew did
more injury to the cause of catholicism than would the blood of
a million catholics," sententiously wrote Lamartine at a comfortable distance of time; "the days of September 1792, were
the St. Bartholomew of liberty." It is not remarkable that *The
Prelude* mentions the massacres only casually, for Wordsworth,
schooled by Beaupuy, and not yet acquainted with Godwin's
doctrine of non-violence, recognised that, once bloodshed was
admitted, countless crimes could be committed in pretended
service of the cause before the desired objective was attained.
Unhappily, sundry English politicians, particularly Edmund
Burke, tempered their philosophy with less fortitude, and
allowed self-righteous sentimentalism to subvert reason so far
as to fasten the crimes of the Fourniers upon the entire French

nation and to regard such local atrocities as an excuse for the supreme atrocity of war.

4. IN DISGRACE

Wordsworth told Richard to expect him in London during October, but having proceeded as far as Paris, he lingered, fascinated by the rapid shiftings of the political scene. Encouraged to think that the " lamentable crimes " of September were " ephemeral monsters, to be seen but once," he hoped for the triumph of the moderate Girondists till the failure of Louvet's attempt to impeach Robespierre " the incorruptible." Enthusiasm so fired his spirit that he declared:

> " An insignificant stranger and obscure . . .
> Yet would I at this time with willing heart
> Have undertaken for a cause so great
> Service however dangerous."

Possibly he had some notion of seeking a job in Paris, perhaps at the suggestion of Annette, who argued that such a step would at once dispel the necessity of his taking orders and enable him to remain with her. But if his caution had not yet degenerated into the twittering timidity of his later years, his prudence denied the possibility of any dramatic gesture such as he suggested in *The Prelude*. During the summer Dorothy confessed to Jane Pollard that, hearing " daily accounts of insurrections and broils," she could not feel " quite easy " about him, " though I think he is wise enough to get out of the way of danger." He " withdrew unwillingly from France," according to *The Prelude,* " dragged by a chain of harsh necessity." But an English republican named Bailey, who subsequently shared Pichegru's imprisonment under Napoleon, long afterwards related that he knew Wordsworth in Paris, and " having warned him that his connection with the Mountain rendered his situation there at

that time perilous, the poet, he said, decamped with great precipitation."

"William is in London," wrote Dorothy on 22nd December; "he writes to me regularly, and is a most affectionate brother." He had good reason to prosecute an affectionate correspondence with his sister, for he intended her for the task of intercessor with their uncle on his behalf. But before he ventured to Forncett, he hurried through the press the poems he had completed during the summer at Blois, the *Descriptive Sketches,* dedicated to Jones and describing the scenes of their tour together, and *An Evening Walk,* probably begun during his first long vacation from Cambridge and flatteringly addressed to his sister. Both were published by Joseph Johnson early in February 1793, and bore such obvious traces of haste that Dorothy on 16th February expressed regret to Miss Pollard that "he did not submit the works to the inspection of some Friend before the Publication." Haste was obviously inspired by the hope that the publication would afford some argument against the inevitable charge of shiftlessly wasting his time, but unless he paid for the printing, the speed of their appearance suggests an influential introduction to the publisher. At that time Johnson ranked among the most eminent of his trade; an enlightened lover of literature and a progressive in politics, he employed Mary Wollstonecraft as reader, entertained hospitably a coterie of revolutionists, including Holcroft, Godwin, Horne Tooke, and Woodfall, publisher of the *Letters of Junius,* and like many other honest publishers, suffered a period of imprisonment during Pitt's subsequent repressive measures. Possibly Wordsworth received a recommendation to Johnson from Helen Maria Williams, a notorious revolutionist writer who had gone to live in Paris, to whom he left England with a letter of introduction from Charlotte Smith, whose poetry he admired and whose acquaintance he had been enabled to make through mutual connections in the East India Company. He was discreetly silent about his acquaintance with Miss Williams, whose staunch republicanism incurred a reputation too notorious for respectability, but he was friendly enough for her to send him a copy of her poems.

The two slim volumes of verse failed to propitiate Uncle Cookson. He was already seriously displeased by the discovery that Wordsworth had declined Mr. Robinson's offer of the Harwich curacy, and had lied that he was not of age to accept. He had, in fact, suffered personal inconvenience from Wordsworth's subterfuge, for he asked Dorothy in the previous spring to find out from brother Richard if Robinson had any design of placing Wordsworth at Harwich, "for if it would be any object for him to get ordained immediately he would keep his Title open for him, as he wishes to keep a Curate." He was in no mood for sympathy with such a confession as his nephew had now to make, and lacking the moral courage to face his uncle, Wordsworth deputed Dorothy to plead his case.

It has been argued that Dorothy would not be unduly shocked by her brother's paternity of an illegitimate child, as eighteenth-century manners were less morally critical than later became fashionable, and Dorothy herself afterwards proposed to superintend the education of a natural daughter of her cousin, Tom Myers. But the Wordsworths were middle-class, and the middle-class valued respectability in all ages, no less in Dr. Johnson's day than in the times of Samuel Pepys or Queen Victoria. The aristocracy still enjoyed privileges, for Leigh Hunt had not yet ventured to point in scorn and ridicule at the vices of the ageing Regent, nor had the Industrial Revolution promoted moneyed members of the middle class to competition with the hereditary peerage. Money, too, then as since, excused many sins; Dorothy was prepared to educate her cousin's bastard because Mr. Myers could afford to pay suitably for the service. Wordsworth had no money; he had disappointed his family by failure to secure a college fellowship; he had wasted his time instead of concentrating dutifully on settling to a career; common sense combined with morality to condemn his delinquency as incredible, criminal folly.

Dorothy was undoubtedly shocked, but her love and loyalty the more readily rallied to support his cause because she knew she would be its only supporter. She failed to conciliate their uncle, who indignantly refused to receive Wordsworth at his house, even to see his sister, but opposition intensified the warmth of her partisanship, and soon, just as she had adopted Wordsworth's own excuses for neglecting " the chance, indeed the certainty of a fellowship," so she now assimilated the terms of his apology for his conduct. She was " willing to allow that half the virtues with which I fancy him endowed are the creation of my love " ; she admitted that the subject was " an unpleasant one for a letter," but though she had to " confess that he has been somewhat to blame," yet she expected to convince Miss Pollard that " the excuse might have been found in his natural disposition."

> " In truth he was a strange and wayward wight,
> Fond of each gentle, and each dreadful scene:
> In darkness, and in storm, he found delight;
> Nor less, than when on ocean wave serene
> The southern sun diffus'd his dazzling shene.
> Even sad vicissitude amused his soul:
> And if a sigh would sometimes intervene,
> And down his cheek a tear of pity roll,
> A sigh, a tear, so sweet, he wish'd not to controul."

This verse by James Beattie " always reminds me of him," she declared; indeed the whole character of the hero of Beattie's *The Minstrel: or The Progress of Genius* " resembles much what William was when I first knew him after my leaving Halifax." Doubtless Wordsworth had not neglected to suggest to her this supposed resemblance; Beattie was one of the poets to whom he acknowledged indebtedness in the footnotes to *An Evening Walk.*

The shock to Dorothy's sense of moral fitness was also lessened by a feeling of disappointment amounting to dismay. The publication of his poems seemed to her vindication of her belief in her brother as complete as its refutation of her uncle's charges against him of idleness; in her eyes his genius was already established. Enraptured by his appreciation of herself, her

emotional imagination cherished the fond allusion in the last lines
of *An Evening Walk:*

> " *Thus Hope, first pouring from her blessed horn*
> *Her dawn, far lovelier than the Moon's own morn . . .*
> *Ev'n now she decks for me a distant scene,*
> *(For dark and broad the gulph of time between)*
> *Gilding that cottage with her fondest ray,*
> *(Sole bourn, sole wish, sole object of my way. . . .)*
> *Where we, my friend, to golden days shall rise,*
> *Till our small share of hardly-paining sighs*
> *(For sighs will ever trouble human breath)*
> *Creep hush'd into the tranquil breast of Death.*"

With whatever sentimental vision Wordsworth may have
dazzled her fancy in correspondence, this was enough to fire her
enthusiasm and—what was more to his immediate purpose—to
insure her devotion. Visualising a visit from her dear Jane
Pollard to her " little parsonage," her fertile imagination planned
a " particular scheme of happiness for each season."

" When I think of winter I hasten to furnish our little parlour,
I close the shutters, set out the Tea-table, brighten the Fire.
When our refreshment is ended I produce our work, and
William brings his book to our table and contributes at once
to our instruction and amusement, and at intervals we lay aside
the book and each hazard our observations upon what has
been read without the fear of ridicule or censure. We talk
over past days, we do not sigh for any pleasure beyond our
humble habitation ' the central point of all our joys '."

" With such romantic dreams," she confided, " I amuse my fancy
during many an hour which would otherwise pass heavily along."
Momentarily a chilling douche must have damped her glowing
fancy when she found that her idealised existence must be shared,
not merely by her dear Jane on a visit, but by the permanent
presence of the mother of her brother's child. But her hopes had

taken root too deeply to be thus easily stricken down. Not only did she agree to intercede with their uncle, but she immediately wrote in warm terms of sisterly affection to Annette. By 20th March Annette had received her consolations and responded with traditional gallic effusiveness.

Though war had been declared between England and France in January, Annette and Wordsworth were contriving to maintain frequent correspondence. When she received no letter for nine days, Annette suffered agony of mind lest he was ill. Her only letters to survive—one to Dorothy enclosed in one to Wordsworth at brother Richard's address—indicate plainly her expectation that, in spite of the war, Wordsworth would soon be returning to marry her. She speaks of herself as " ta femme," and describes how she tells her baby that, in a month, a fortnight, a week, she will be seeing " le plus chérit des hommes, le plus tendre des hommes." But " mon imagination ne ma donne que des inquiétudes sans jamais me donner un instant de plaisir," though she assures Dorothy that " si j'etois assez heureuse pour que mon cher William put faire le voyage de France pour venir me donne le titre de sa femme, je serois consolée." Her delight in her baby, in its likeness to its father, and in describing its habits and development, must have touched the hearts of men less doting in domestic affections than Wordsworth became. His presence for part of the summer at the Isle of Wight suggests that he might have been awaiting an opportunity to cross to France. It has even been suggested that he did brave the dangers of entering enemy territory in October, and that it was on this occasion that he received at Paris Bailey's warning and " decamped with great precipitation " without effecting the object of his visit. He told Carlyle, soon after Carlyle had published his history of the French Revolution, that he had witnessed the execution of Gorsas, and Gorsas was executed in October 1793.

But Wordsworth's reminiscences are always open to suspicion, and this one belongs to the period when, relating to a visitor his presence at Orleans at the time of the September massacres, he could remark unblushingly to his wife—of all people!—" I wonder how I came to stay there so long, and at a period so exciting."

Whether or not he was seriously seeking a means of reunion with Annette, he was still doing nothing about settling himself in life. Dorothy, whose daily intercourse with her uncle must have become strained from their difference about her brother, confessed despondingly to Miss Pollard in June: " I cannot foresee the day of my felicity, the day in which I am once more to find a home under the same roof with my brother: all is still obscure and dark, and there is so much ground to fear that my scheme may prove a shadow, a mere vision of happiness." She kept hope alive by bolstering up her confidence in her brother; " he is so amiable so good, so fond of his sister! " She recalled tenderly " the last time we were together "—at Forncett during the Christmas vacation of 1790—when " he won my affection to a degree which I cannot describe." As always, her emotional imagination decorated facts as she liked to think of them, and she believed that " there was no pleasure he would not have given up with joy for half an hour's conversation with me." He wrote to her bitterly of his uncle's attitude which prevented his seeing her, and sent her spirits soaring again to excited rapture with a proposal that she should arrange to meet him at Halifax by visiting her aunt, Mrs. Rawson, the former Miss Threlkeld, who had married a well-to-do merchant. But he showed no haste to avail himself of the joys of her conversation. Early in July she was begging Miss Pollard to " be upon your guard," excitedly admitting her, as a fellow conspirator, to the secret of the proposed meeting; nobody was to know that her brother designed to visit Halifax while she was there,—" after the meeting has taken place, I should by no means wish to conceal it from my uncle, yet I should be very averse to his knowing it beforehand, or even afterwards that my scheme was a *premeditated* one." She looked forward to meeting her brother in the autumn of 1793, but not till the following February did he find time to visit Halifax.

According to Dorothy, he was " looking out and wishing for the opportunity of engaging himself as tutor to some young gentleman, an office for which even friends less partial than I am, allow him to be particularly well-qualified." His uncle's refusal to receive him provided an excuse for finally abandoning the idea

of taking orders, and having remained in London probably as
long as brother Richard could be persuaded to make him small
advances, he joined an old schoolfellow, William Calvert, on
a visit to the Isle of Wight. Calvert's father was steward to the
Cumberland estates of the Duke of Norfolk, who represented
the local Whig interest against Lord Lonsdale's Toryism; apparently the Duke—the same who benevolently attempted to
reconcile Shelley's differences with his father—treated his dependents with more honesty and generosity than Lonsdale, for
William Calvert and his brother Raisley were young men of
fortune. Calvert paid the joint expenses of their lodging in the
Isle of Wight—Dorothy reported that, in return, he "only
requests the favour of William's company"—enabling
Wordsworth, inspired by the philosophy of Godwin's newly
published *Political Justice*, to parade his political views in an open
letter to the Bishop of Llandaff, and to loiter musing on the sea-
shore, within sight of the fleet at anchor in the Solent, hating the
war into which Pitt and the forces of reaction had plunged
England against revolutionary France and the symbol of liberty.

At the end of the summer, he was driven by Calvert as far as
Salisbury, where they parted, Wordsworth wandering on foot
over Salisbury Plain to Bath, thence to Bristol and through the
Wye valley, to find another free asylum with his friend Jones in
Denbighshire. There he apparently remained for some months
working on the poem published in the last decade of his life as
Guilt and Sorrow, till he went to Halifax in February 1794
to meet his sister. As residence at Halifax afforded daily meetings
with Miss Pollard—now engaged to rich Mr. Marshall of Leeds
—Dorothy wrote no record of her delight at reunion with her
brother. But after six weeks at Halifax, they set off together to
walk to Keswick, where Calvert owned a farmhouse called
Windy Brow, and there she wrote one of her usual effusive
epistles—"You cannot conceive anything more delightful than
the situation of this house. . . . I have never been more delighted
with the manners of any people than of the family under whose
roof I am at present." Calvert had set aside a parlour for their
private use, but they found their own food, which vied in

simplicity with Shelley's usual meal on half a loaf of bread. " Our breakfast and supper are of milk, and our dinner chiefly of potatoes, and we drink no tea." Significantly she remarks, " We please ourselves in calculating from our present expenses for how very small a sum we could live."

Fascinated by the vision of life with her brother in his parsonage, she had evidently determined not to return to Uncle Cookson's roof. Since her uncle's refusal of her pleadings on Wordsworth's behalf, relations between them must have lost their former frank affection, and she must have known that he would regard as deceit, as well as defiance of his wishes, her secret arrangements for meeting Wordsworth at Halifax. Expression of her elders' displeasure was deputed to Uncle Kit Crackanthorpe, as head of the family, whose wife wrote a protest against Dorothy's unlady-like conduct in wandering about the countryside in an un-protected condition. Dislike of the former Miss Cust tempered the pertness of her reply; in answer to the suggestion " that I may be supposed to be in an unprotected situation, I affirm that I consider the character and virtues of my brother as a sufficient protection "—an assertion which must have excited exclamations against Wordsworth's character as a sullen, moody boy grown into a singularly unsatisfactory young man, who had wasted his time at the university, lied to the family patron, and instead of settling to a career, had contracted shameful relations with a foreign woman, older than himself, who might be a common adventuress, and was anyhow an enemy alien.

Wordsworth merited censure, at least, in encouraging his sister in her independent attitude. Though not published till 1802, the lines beginning " Dear Child of Nature, let them rail," and addressed " To a Young Lady Who had been reproached for taking long walks in the country," were apparently inspired by this occasion. It was well enough to fall in with her fancy in playful speculation on how cheaply they might live together, but he showed scant consideration for her welfare by allowing her to prejudice her favour with her uncles without any prospect of providing for her as she desired. Not only had he no prospect, but he made no shift to bestir himself. Already he had dallied

c

uselessly for more than a year since he left Annette with her new-
born child, and Dorothy concluded her exposition of the delights
of Windy Brow with the complacent announcement: " Till my
brother gets some employment he will lodge here." It is difficult
to see how he expected to find employment in the remote
seclusion of a rural farmhouse.

To Mathews he excused himself from living in London on the
score of expense. His correspondence with Mathews represented
his only effort to find employment. Mathews still hankered after
the notion of establishing " a monthly Miscellany," and in May
1794 Wordsworth wrote from Whitehaven—whither he went
with Dorothy from Windy Brow to visit their uncle Richard
Wordsworth—to assure him " most heartily " of his wish " to
be engaged in something of that kind." " Besides essays on Morals
and Politics," he thought he " could communicate critical
remarks upon Poetry, &c, &c, upon the arts of Painting,
Gardening, and other subjects of amusement." Fortunately for
his convenience, his friend failed to find a publisher willing to
sponsor the proposed periodical, or he might have had difficulty
in excusing his inability to supply the promised contributions.
For never in his life did he reveal any facility of expression in
prose; he never sat down to write even a letter without an effort,
and he performed the distasteful task in a perfunctory, stilted style
which establishes his letters among the most tedious products of
a man of genius ever printed. But apparently he never seriously
contemplated the success of Mathews' plan, for when, in the
following November, Mathews ruefully announced the hope-
lessness of launching a periodical, he declared with a fine air of
superior foresight, that he was not " much surprised or mortified,"
as " the more nearly we approached the time fixed for action,
the more strongly was I persuaded that we should decline the
field."

From Whitehaven he returned to Keswick, while Dorothy
started on a tour of visits to relatives and friends. Before leaving
Whitehaven in June, he again declined Mathews' appeal to him to
come to town, and feeling impelled to offer a reason, garbled it
grandiloquently as usual. " I have a friend in the country who

has offered me a share of his income," he explained: " It would be using him very ill to run the risk of destroying my usefulness, by precipitating myself into distress and poverty, at the time when he is so ready to support me in a situation wherein I feel I can be of some little service to my fellowmen." The friend was William Calvert's brother Raisley, who was dying of consumption. Allowing for Wordsworth and his sister's invariable habit of disguising distasteful facts in fine phrases, it appears that Wordsworth, in return for board and lodging, acted as male nurse to the invalid. His taste for travel unabated, he sought to persuade William Calvert that a voyage to Lisbon might benefit his brother, but Raisley's condition was evidently too desperate for such exertion. He confided to the invalid the sad story of his family's victimisation by Lord Lonsdale, and Raisley instructed his London lawyers to inquire into the details with a view to leaving Wordsworth a legacy of six hundred pounds if affairs stood as he said. The lawyer's report presumably proved satisfactory. As evidently, Wordsworth excelled in bedside eloquence. Late in December he was " much engaged with my sick friend," who "worsens daily," and a few days after Raisley's funeral on 12th January 1795, Dorothy informed brother Richard that William's " poor friend," by a second late alteration of his will, had increased his legacy to nine hundred pounds. In November Wordsworth was already planning on his prospects; he wrote to Mathews that, if " you say a newspaper would be glad of me, do you think you could insure me employment in that way on terms similar to your own? " In spite of the nostalgic craving for rural seclusion he confided to Dorothy he had not yet lost taste for the pleasures of the town if his pockets were lined. " Cataracts and mountains are good occasional society," he told Mathews, expressing a sentiment unmentioned in *The Prelude,* " but they will not do for constant companions." And having followed his benefactor's body to the churchyard, he set off to London to purchase an annuity with the proceeds of his profitable six months' attendance on a sick bed.

5. "GUILT AND SORROW"

Though it was not in Wordsworth to allow fidelity to principle
to interfere with personal comfort, and the story of the two years
since his separation from Annette—indeed, the story of his whole
life—shows uninterrupted preoccupation with self-interest, he
probably spent the first months of 1795 looking for some
journalistic employment in London which might enable him to
contribute to the cause of liberty. It has been sometimes suggested
that he hurried home in December 1792 on account of alarm at
the imminence of war, but such suggestions imply ignorance of
historical fact. Wars are always the result of secret scheming—
or want of scheming—among statesmen; the general public is
uninformed of the real state of affairs and presented only with a
garbled version when it is necessary to secure its acquiescence in
the crime. While Wordsworth was in France, Englishmen were
popular with the French people, who regarded England, in spite
of the recent American revolution, as the European champions
of liberal government and likely to sympathise with their revolt
against despotism. Wordsworth returned to England absorbed
in his private affairs, and Pitt's declaration of war came as

> *" No shock*
> *Given to my moral nature had I known*
> *Down to that very moment."*

He felt " pity and shame " that his native country should have
joined forces with the enemies of France—with, therefore, the
enemies of liberty. He was not a convinced pacifist, like Godwin
and Coleridge, for he had never thought sufficiently deeply even
to contemplate the right or wrong of war as an ethical matter.
Beaupuy, too, was a soldier, and Beaupuy so far supplied his
paramount intellectual influence. But Beaupuy was in France,
and Wordsworth's puppy understanding, its eyes so newly
opened to the light, wanted the support of some such moral

force as convinced pacifism to sustain his instinctive revulsion from the lies of political propaganda. Hitherto he had been, he said, like a light and pliant harebell, wantoning carelessly in the easy breeze; now he found himself " torn and tossed about in whirlwind."

> " Not in my single self alone I found,
> But in the minds of all ingenuous youth,
> Change and subversion from that hour."

Unable to uproot in a moment every foundation of his waking intellect, he felt himself desolate in a war-shocked world of fear fermenting hate; like Shelley, he knew that " everybody saying a thing does not make it right," but he lacked both Shelley's equipped intellect and purity of purpose to achieve the vaguest shadow of his serenity.

So he took refuge, as in boyhood's rebellion against unjust authority, in sullen brooding. Wars in those days were fought by the professional services, supplemented by recruits cajoled by bribery or drunkenness; there was no conscription of a country's man-power, since war was not yet " total war." In a later age Wordsworth would have been a conscientious objector, and since he based his objection, not on religious, but political and senti-mental grounds, he would have been sent to prison. Perhaps he might even, before he could face a conscientious objectors' tribunal, have been persecuted and imprisoned as a " fifth-columnist," for in his bitter resentment of the war he confessed that he

> " Exulted, in the triumph of my soul,
> When Englishmen by thousands were o'erthrown."

Yet, wanting the fortitude of philosophical or religious con-viction, he resented the necessity of infidelity to the shibboleth of patriotism, exclaiming,

> " Oh! much have they to account for, who could tear,
> By violence, at one decisive rent,
> From the best youth in England their dear pride,
> Their joy, in England."

This outburst, in which is more of spleen than honest indignation, is some of the writing on the wall to give warning of his subsequent career. Wordsworth at his best was a rebel *malgré lui;* fate for a time cast him among the persecuted and free-thinking minority, but he always wanted to be on the side of self-righteous convention. The story of his career finds a parallel in that of Mrs. Catherick in Wilkie Collins's *Woman in White,* the woman who stoically remained in her native town, stonily defying scandalous gossip, till long years of negative rectitude eroded memory of her former character and her title to respectability was recognised by the parson's lifting his hat to her.

For the present, circumstances conspired with Beaupuy's doctrine to cast his lot with the rebel minority. The month of February 1793, in which war was declared, in which *Descriptive Sketches* and *An Evening Walk* were published, also witnessed the publication of William Godwin's *Inquiry concerning Political Justice.* " No work in our time gave such a blow to the philosophical mind of the country," wrote Hazlitt thirty years later. Appearing at a time when the king's speech at the opening of Parliament had expressed " serious uneasiness " at the tendency of the French Revolution " to excite disturbance in other countries," and when the deputy leader of the Tories declared that " great alarm was really felt " by " every man who venerated the institutions of his country, had property to lose, or a true English aversion to anarchy and bloodshed," Godwin's book might have become the Bible of an English revolution as the *Contrat Social* was of the French. But English liberal leaders seem fated ever to be faint of heart, fickle of purpose, and easily jockeyed into a false position by their opponents. The most prodigal exponent of verbosity in his day, Edmund Burke, who had irritated ministers to nervous fevers by his perorations in praise of liberty during the American revolution, decided that there were discreet limits to legitimate demonstration of popular indignation; pitching chests of tea from Boston quay into the waters of the Atlantic was not comparable with flinging aristocratic human heads from the Paris guillotine into a sea of blood. When the execution of Louis XVI provided the Tories with a pretext for exciting popular alarm, Burke lost his logical balance, not only resigning his reformist hopes by siding with reaction, but electing to avenge atrocities affecting hundreds by plunging millions into the miseries of an exhausting war.

His apostasy procured such a breach in the Whig party as Ramsay MacDonald and Philip Snowden caused in the Labour party of 1931. Like MacDonald and Snowden, he had few followers, the majority of the party remaining loyal to the leadership of Charles James Fox, but his attitude provided the Tories with an apt platform for propaganda to discredit the opposition. Like MacDonald, he lived only a few years with his strange bedfellows, who rewarded him with no office but fittingly with the traditional pay of turncoats—a pension.

Godwin, an obscure working journalist, was not accepted even by the unpopular Whigs, for his book was a sincere statement of a philosophical system, untainted by any opportunist intentions. Two articles alone of his advocacy sufficed to alienate conventional sympathies. He denied the right to make war except to repel invasion, stating the maxim that " nothing can be a sufficient object of war, that is not a sufficient cause for beginning it "; he attacked the principles of property, and advocated the abolition of the marriage system as " the worst of monopolies." Even so, as Hazlitt remarked, " Tom Paine was considered for the time as a Tom Fool to him, Paley an old woman, Edmund Burke a flashy sophist," and intellectual youth for two generations felt Godwin's influence.

Wordsworth was among his earliest converts. Already prepared by Rousseau and Beaupuy for sympathy with Godwin's ideas, he discovered strengthening support for his own convictions that purposes of restraint and reformation of a system of government provided unjustifiable excuses for making war, and that revolutions, though " necessarily attended with many circumstances worthy of our disapprobation " and " by no means essential to the political improvement of mankind," have " often been coeval with important changes of the social system." Professor Harper and others have sufficiently shown that *Guilt and Sorrow*—which, as Wordsworth stated in the " advertisement "

to the poem in 1842, was written with the conviction that
the war, just begun, "would be of long continuance, and
productive of distress and misery beyond all possible calculation"
—bears unmistakable traces of Godwin's influence, but the heat
of his enthusiasm for Godwin found immediate expression in
*A Letter to the Bishop of Llandaff on the Extraordinary Avowal of
his Political Opinions. . . . By a Republican.*

Bishop Watson had been distinguished among ecclesiasts for
the liberalism of his opinions, but like Burke, he had allowed his
reason to be subverted by tales of atrocities, and, true to the
axiom that none is so fanatical as the newest convert, worked
himself into a fever of hysterical militancy. Wordsworth cut
straight at the root of such apostasy as Burke's by disdaining
sentimental indignation at the execution of Louis XVI as " irrational and weak." Paraphrasing both Beaupuy and Godwin, he
argued that, however " she deplored such stern necessity,"
Liberty has been " obliged to borrow the very arms of Despotism
to overthrow " the despot, and, harassed by reaction, " in order
to reign in peace, must establish herself by violence." De-
nouncing the effect of government propaganda on the public
mind, he asked if, without it, the people would have condoned the
persecution of reformers like Priestley, if, " deprived almost of
the necessaries of existence by the burden of their taxes, they
would cry out, as with one voice, for a war from which not a
single ray of consolation can visit them to compensate for the
additional keenness with which they are about to smart under the
scourge of labour, of cold and of hunger? " Echoing Godwin's
attacks on privilege and property, he asserted that " the extremes
of poverty and riches have a necessary tendency to corrupt the
human heart," and called for reforms to balance " that inequality
among mankind which proceeds from the present *fixed* disproportion of their possessions."

For the modern reader the *Letter* contains no unfamiliar or
original ideas; it might have been written by a member of the
Fabian Society in the eighteen-nineties, by Ramsay MacDonald
in his nonage, or by Mr. Herbert Morrison during the war of
1914–1918. But it shows Wordsworth as an extremist among

contemporary reformers, a disciple of Rousseau, Tom Paine, and Godwin, a deponent of opinions for which men were then enduring imprisonment and transportation. Hitherto a shiftless, unsatisfactory idler, of no serious opinions or ambitions, he appears now for the first time as a young man of emphatic, even passionate, convictions. Truly his situation among the unconventional minority suited his character as an outcast from his family and a victim of circumstance in love, but the sincerity of his convictions cannot be doubted. Nor was his zeal abated after a year's endurance of the bleak loneliness afflicting minds maintaining a sense of reason, decency, humanity and honesty in time of war, when mob hysteria—in his words, " the mighty class of selfish alarmists "—will persecute as a traitor or " fifth columnist " the humanitarian who declines to degrade himself with barbarous emotions of hate and blood-lust. To Mathews he announced in June 1794:

" I disapprove of monarchical and aristocratical governments, however modified. Hereditary distinctions, and privileged orders of every species, I think must necessarily counteract the progress of human improvement: hence it follows that I am not amongst the admirers of the British Constitution."

With Godwin, he deplores " the bare idea of a Revolution," but " would give every additional energy in my power " to further the cause of democracy.

Again he expresses disdain of government propaganda—" I severely condemn all inflammatory addresses to the passions of men, even when it is intended to direct those passions to a good purpose. I know that the multitude walk in darkness." But in another letter, in which he indicated to Mathews the assistance he could offer to their proposed magazine, he declared:

" I solemnly affirm that in no writings of mine will I ever admit of any sentiment which can have the least tendency to induce my readers to suppose that the doctrines which are now enforced by banishment, imprisonment, etc., etc., are other than pregnant with every species of misery. You know perhaps already that I am of that odious class of men called democrats, and of that class I shall for ever continue."

A fine declaration of integrity, worthy of such courageous idealism as Landor's or Shelley's, but alas! to be read with shame and sadness in the light of Wordsworth's subsequent career.

Justly Professor Harper has described the *Letter* to Bishop Watson, " in its buoyant eloquence, its fearless logic, its trust in the supremacy of goodness," as " splendidly youthful." Such qualities are associated with youth, innocent yet of the circumlocution, sophistry, and cynicism required by the humbug of pharisaic society; they may even be praised in youth with the condescending tolerance of age. But few possess the fortitude and courage to persevere with their idealism beyond the excusable confines of youth, and those who persevere as unrelenting rebels, refusing to compromise with conscience at convention's bidding, like Landor and Trelawny, are stigmatised as eccentrics, not quite respectable, and not to be taken seriously.

Fortitude and courage were not among Wordsworth's virtues. Apart from the extract called *The Female Vagrant, Guilt and Sorrow* was not published till 1842 and then in a version doubtless much emasculated; the *Letter* to Bishop Watson was never published during Wordsworth's life, and in view of his later aspirations to respectability, it is remarkable that he allowed the manuscript to survive among his papers. Evidently he never attempted to publish it, for the manuscript ends in the middle of a sentence. His reason is indicated in a letter from his brother Richard, urging him to " be cautious in writing or expressing your political opinions. By the suspension of the Habeas Corpus Act the Ministers have great powers." Richard himself was refraining from pressing their claim against Lord Lonsdale " because his Lordship has so many spies in every part of the country." Already Wordsworth was beginning his lifelong habit of leaving tiresome correspondence to his womenfolk, and Dorothy replied to Richard on 28th May 1794: " I think I can answer for William's caution about expressing his political opinions. He is very cautious and seems well aware of the dangers of a contrary conduct."

Here was the writing on the wall. At twenty-four the revolutionary, the rebel, the reformer, was "very cautious"; increasing with years, caution was to grow a blight on his character, till a morbid, old-maidish fear of life fastened like a fungus to strangle his genius.

Lack of opportunity probably conspired with caution to keep Wordsworth out of controversial journalism when he went up to London after Raisley Calvert's funeral in January 1795. Though the *Letter* to the Bishop, warmed by the heat of conviction, is livelier than his usual, heavy, frigid dogmatic style in prose, he had neither the fertility of intellect nor facility of expression which made Coleridge an ever-welcome contributor to periodicals, nor had he any influential acquaintance in London journalism. Presumably he sought the acquaintance of the admired Godwin, but though biographers assume that they met in 1795, Wordsworth's name does not appear in Godwin's diary before 1798. But at least he became acquainted with two of Godwin's close associates, William Nicholson and the Rev. Joseph Fawcett.

Nicholson was at some time continental agent to Wedgwoods, the famous potters; he "translated from the French with great facility," collaborated with Holcroft, and edited a paper called *The Philosophical Journal*. At this time he lived over the family shop, a haberdasher's, in Cateaton Street, where Wordsworth, according to his unreliable reminiscences dictated to Miss Fenwick, used to dine with him sometimes on Sundays. With him Wordsworth attended the dissenting meeting-house in Old Jewry, where Fawcett preached to "the largest and most genteel London audiences that ever assembled in a dissenting place of worship."

An enthusiast for the French Revolution and for the doctrines of Rousseau, Fawcett was also a fervent pacifist. In a sermon on "Christianity vindicated in not particularly inculcating Friendship and Patriotism," he declared, "Social virtue consists not in the love of this or the other individual or body of individuals, but in the love of man." Through Wordsworth's publisher, Johnson, he published in 1795 a poem called *The Art of War,* later reprinted under the ironic title, *Civilised War.* Journalists then had either an even greater capacity for hypocrisy in unctuous discussion of religious sincerity, or a greater integrity in declining to be degraded into wartime hysteria, for an authority so respectable as the *Gentleman's Magazine,* refusing to praise Fawcett's poetic talent, considered that he " deserves commendation for awakening the milder feelings, and his expression will be pardoned for his sentiments." Wordsworth himself thought the poem " had a good deal of merit, and made me think more about him than I should otherwise have done." He thought so much of Fawcett that he used his recollections of him for the character of the Solitary in *The Excursion,* and was indebted for his lines, " I met Louisa in the shade," to a poem of Fawcett's called *Louisa: A Song.*

Reminiscing in old age, Wordsworth's respectability required an attitude of moral condescension to a revolutionary like Fawcett, whose character he deliberately maligned. " Poor Fawcett," he told Miss Fenwick, became " pretty much such a person " as his Solitary; " Like many others in those times of like showy talents, he had not strength of character to withstand the effects of the French Revolution, and of the wild and lax opinions which had done so much towards producing it "—he " early disappeared from the stage, having fallen into habits of intemperance, which I have heard . . . hastened his death." Professor Harper has remarked that " the aged poet's reminiscences should never be accepted without scrutiny, except in regard to his own emotional life," and " the gossip about him (Fawcett) which Wordsworth heard is only an instance of the way in which men's reputations were assailed by those who took for granted that heterodox opinions must of necessity spring from a wicked heart and end in an evil life." Clearly Wordsworth himself became one of these gossipping moralisers at the expense of possessors of heterodox opinions, for there is no evidence of any source for this malicious gossip beyond his own imagination. On the contrary, he might be expected to have been acquainted with Hazlitt's reverent tribute to Fawcett in the *Life of Holcroft*, published in 1816, only twelve years after Fawcett's death.

"The late Rev. Joseph Fawcett, author of *The Art of War*, . . . delivered the Sunday evening lectures at the Old Jewry, which were so popular about twenty years ago. He afterwards retired to Hedgegrove in Hertfordshire. It was here that I first became acquainted with him, and passed some of the pleasantest days of my life . . . the conversations I had with him on subjects of taste and philosophy (for his taste was as refined as his powers of reasoning were profound and subtle) gave me a delight, such as I can never feel again. . . . Of all the persons I have ever known, he was the most perfectly free from every taint of jealousy or narrowness. Never did a mean or sinister motive come near his heart. He was one of the most enthusiastic admirers of the French Revolution, and I believe that the disappointment of the hopes he had cherished of the freedom and happiness of mankind, preyed upon his mind, and hastened his death."

Fawcett was one of the "four principal oral instructors" (Holcroft and Coleridge were two of the others) to whom Godwin felt his mind "indebted for improvement," and he took Fawcett as the model for Mr. Clare, the only highly moral character in his novel *Caleb Williams*.

With Fawcett or Nicholson, Wordsworth met two young revolutionary sympathisers, Basil Montagu and Francis Wrangham, who were temporarily earning a precarious living by taking pupils at Cobham in Surrey. With Wrangham he may have had already a slight acquaintance, since they were exact contemporaries at Cambridge. Wrangham knew Coleridge, was in frequent correspondence with him, and had just published a volume of poems containing two contributions by Coleridge. From him Wordsworth doubtless first heard how, a few months before, Coleridge had sacrificed a brilliant career at Cambridge to join with an Oxford undergraduate named Southey, also a poet, in a plan to establish an ideal society in America.

Montagu, also a Cambridge contemporary, was Lord Sandwich's illegitimate son by Martha Ray, an actress celebrated for her beauty, who was murdered by a disappointed lover outside Covent Garden Theatre, and whose name Wordsworth gave to the heroine of *The Thorn*. He had already married, and had a small son, whose care and education were becoming a problem since he and Wrangham had decided to abandon their tutorial experiment, he to enter the law and Wrangham the Church. Apparently Wordsworth referred to his former plan of " engaging himself as tutor to some young gentleman," and confided his sister's desire to set up housekeeping with him. Montagu saw an admirable opportunity for getting his child off his hands; the boy was of an age to require feminine attention as well as education, and he would receive both by living with Wordsworth and his sister.

Wordsworth was easily persuaded to renounce his hopes of aiding the cause of liberty by journalism in London. After the flight of Priestley and Tom Paine to America, the transportation of Muir, Palmer, and Joseph Gerrald, and the trial for treason of Horne Tooke, Hardy, Holcroft, and Thelwall, many reformers, like Fawcett and Thelwall, felt it advisable for safety's sake to retire into the country. It happened that two boys named Pinney, sons of a wealthy Bristol merchant, were among the pupils of Montagu and Wrangham; their father had a house in Dorset used only for occasional holidays, and with Montagu's recommendation, it might be available for Wordsworth. At Bristol, too, besides creating a favourable impression on Mr. Pinney, he could meet Coleridge and Southey, whose poetical theories, as well as political opinions, accorded with his own.

6. RETREAT

So Wordsworth took leave of William Mathews and his journalistic hopes, and went to Bristol. Mr. Pinney was well content to have his country house looked after and kept aired for his family's occasional visits, and on 2nd September, with her usual portentousness, Dorothy announced to Jane Marshall: " I am going now to tell you what is for your own eyes and ears alone; I need say no more than this, I am sure, to insure your most careful secrecy. Know then that I am going to live in Dorsetshire." Then " methodically " she confided " the whole plan." William was to receive from Montagu fifty pounds a year for looking after his boy, and Dorothy herself was offered the care of " a natural daughter " of her cousin Tom Myers; " with these two children and the produce of Raisley Calvert's legacy " they would have an income of " at least £170 or £180 per annum," while " a very rich merchant of Bristol " had presented William with " a ready furnished house rent free " at Racedown, near Crewkerne in Dorset.

Wordsworth was then staying with the Pinneys, and while he was there he made the acquaintance of Coleridge and Southey in the lodgings they had shared in Bristol for the past eight months. He " saw but little " of Coleridge; " I wished indeed to have seen more," he told Mathews—" his talent appears to me very great." Southey's manners pleased him " exceedingly " and he had " every reason to think very highly of his powers of mind."

Tom Myers's natural daughter did not materialise, but Dorothy arrived at Bristol in due course and stayed a night with the Pinneys before travelling with the boy Basil in a chaise to Racedown. Wordsworth wrote his news to Mathews and Wrangham during the two following months. He quoted some lines he had written in imitation of Juvenal, the " two best verses " of which were presented to him by Southey.

" *Heavens! who sees majesty in George's face?*
Or looks at Norfolk, and can dream of grace? "

He asked Wrangham if he had " any interest with the book-sellers," as he had a poem " to dispose of "—he recollected having read the first draft of it to Wrangham in London. This was evidently *Guilt and Sorrow,* and it has been suggested that

Dorothy referred to this poem also when telling her Jane in September that Wordsworth had " had the offer of ten guineas for a work which has not taken him much time."

The education of little Basil was conveniently devised to avoid encroachments on Wordsworth's time. They did not believe in forcing knowledge on the child, but allowed him to develop his own mind by asking questions, which they professed to answer with scrupulous consideration for exactitude and candour. Apparently Wordsworth's tutorial energies were thus limited to casual conversation at meal-times, and the care and entertainment of the boy devolved on Dorothy. " Our present life is utterly barren of such events as merit even the short-lived chronicle of an accidental letter," he told Mathews after six months at Racedown: " We plant cabbages; and if retirement, in its full perfection, be as powerful in working transformations as one of Ovid's gods, you may perhaps suspect that into cabbages we shall be transformed."

In the new year of 1796, Southey sent him a copy of his epic, *Joan of Arc,* through his Bristol publisher, Joseph Cottle. Unless Wrangham had presented him with a copy of his poems, this was the first presentation copy Wordsworth had ever received from an author, and he might have been forgiven for fulsome praise. But his comment was typical of a critical attitude to contemporaries which became notoriously habitual. Southey's preface proved him " certainly a coxcomb," he informed Mathews: " This preface is indeed a very conceited performance, and the poem, though in some passages of first-rate excellence, is on the whole of very inferior execution."

But in thanking Cottle for the book, he asked him to give his " best compliments to Coleridge and say I wish much to hear from him." Perhaps he did hear, as Coleridge was then busily collecting subscribers for his periodical, the *Watchman.* Soon afterwards, the Pinneys came on a visit, and when they left early in March, they carried back to Bristol the manuscript of *Guilt and Sorrow.* Immediately Dorothy wrote to Jane: " William is going to publish a poem. The Pinneys have taken it to the booksellers." Wordsworth himself asked Wrangham if he would

WORDSWORTH IN 1798

(*from the portrait by Robert Hancock in the National Portrait Gallery.*)

be able to dispose of "a dozen copies or more" among his friends. But instead of giving express orders to his printer, Cottle only handed the manuscript to Coleridge to read.

By contrast with Wordsworth, Coleridge was ever ready with enthusiastic encouragement for contemporary poets. He had contributed to Wrangham's volume, and helped Southey to re-write his epic and even presented him with a long passage of his own composition; he was continually correcting Charles Lamb's verse by correspondence, and included the work of Lamb and Charles Lloyd in the second edition of his own poems. Eagerly he read *Guilt and Sorrow* and interleaved it with his suggestions and emendations, promising Cottle that he would return the manuscript to Wordsworth. But he kept it more than two months, and hearing that Wordsworth was going to London at the end of May, he sent the manuscript to Charles Lamb to give to him, thinking thus to make the two acquainted. Lamb read the poem, and had it conveyed to Wordsworth, being too ill to see him himself.

So Wordsworth returned to Racedown with *Guilt and Sorrow* in his pocket. During the following months he tinkered a little with the poem according to Coleridge's suggestion, but his and Dorothy's faith now shifted from *Guilt and Sorrow* to a tragedy he was writing called *The Borderers*. His visit to London was probably mainly to go to theatres and study stage conditions; he asked Mathews to send him news of the theatre, and occasionally read some of the latest plays—he read Holcroft's new comedy and thought little of it. His satire in imitation of Juvenal, to be written in collaboration with Wrangham, was shelved and never published, probably because Wrangham's attention was concentrated on his clerical career, in which he succeeded, thanks largely to a wealthy marriage, in becoming an archdeacon.

His reading was as limited as ever, though he had unlimited time at his disposal. Mr. Pinney's library contained a run of the *Gentleman's Magazine*, and these volumes seem to have constituted his staple intellectual food. On his walks with Dorothy, he developed his faculty for observation of nature, but otherwise he was stagnating, and he must have known it. His continual bouts of depression originated mainly from prickings of conscience, from the consciousness of futility, of the best years of his youth passing without achievement. Dorothy, too, must have known it, but loyalty, becoming in time force of habit, impelled her to explain his depression as due to over-work and fastidious worrying over the perfection of his composition.

From Annette he received a letter soon after arrival at Racedown, in which she mentioned having written half a dozen others which he never received. The bogey of his obligations to her continued to loom over him, but the war had now settled to the prolonged monotony of a toothache with no evident prospect of ending for years. Suspense of his ultimate settlement with her was a source of anxiety ever present at the back of his mind, but too remote for present depression. His sense of horror at the war was also dulled by time and the monotony of peaceful retirement, and further lulled by Dorothy's lack of interest in politics. Her concern and conversation centred on his work, and his failure to gratify her hopes by tangible achievement, his fear of failure ever to justify her belief in his powers, fretted his conscience and damped his spirits in despondency.

He continued to invite Coleridge's correspondence. His literary acquaintances were few, and as in Wrangham's case he made the most of them. But his few meetings with Coleridge had shown him a man of genius far beyond any he had ever met, of dazzling potentialities to which he could himself never aspire. Coleridge was easily accessible, readily appreciative, and possessed of influential connections—a useful man to know. And when, after reading *Guilt and Sorrow,* Coleridge sent him a volume of his poems, he recognised in his poetry gifts of originality greater than anything else in contemporary poetry, he saw in *Religious Musings* an ambitious effort in metaphysical poetry such as he would have liked himself to attempt, and he realised that the poetic aims, like the political sentiments, were akin to his own. He was also pleased with the puff—the first he had ever received—which Coleridge made in a note acknowledging his debt to *An Evening Walk* for a phrase in "Lines Written at Shurton Bars."

So, in March 1797, when Mary Hutchinson was paying them a protracted visit, he took the opportunity to visit Bristol, ostensibly to see the Pinneys and perhaps the publisher Cottle, but principally to improve his acquaintance with Coleridge. Three months before, Coleridge had removed, with his wife and baby, from Bristol to a cottage at Nether Stowey, where in spite of the poverty of accommodation and his pocket, he offered warm hospitality to his friends. There Wordsworth went on his homeward journey from Bristol. Coleridge's conversation confirmed his opinion of his exceptional genius, and when he left, he carried a promise that Coleridge would soon visit him at Racedown.

On 5th June, as Dorothy's friend Mary Hutchinson left for London in the morning, Coleridge arrived from Taunton in the evening. Dorothy was fascinated; in the limited circle of her acquaintance, in which her brother had stood apart as the only person who conceived matters of imagination and fancy to be more important than the drab details of daily routine, she had never met anybody like Coleridge. " You had a great loss in not seeing Coleridge," she wrote to Mary. " He is a wonderful man. His conversation teems with soul, mind, and spirit. Then he is so benevolent, so good-tempered and cheerful, and, like William, interests himself so much about every little trifle. At first I thought him very plain, that is, for about three minutes: he is pale and thin, has a wide mouth, thick lips, and not very good teeth, longish loose-growing half-curling rough black hair. But if you hear him speak for five minutes you think no more of them. His eye is large and full, not dark but grey; such an eye as would receive from a heavy soul the dullest expression; but it speaks every emotion of his animated mind; it has more of the ' poet's eye in a fine frenzy rolling ' than I ever witnessed. He has fine dark eyebrows, and an overhanging forehead."

Two months later Dorothy wrote again to Mary—from " a large mansion, in a large park, with seventy head of deer round us." Though they were so little remote from poverty that Dorothy asked her brother Richard to " take care of your old cloaths," as they would " be of great use at Racedown," the Wordsworths had sacrificed their privilege of living rent-free

to move to Alfoxden House in the Quantocks. The move had
other advantages, but " our principal inducement," said Dorothy,
" was Coleridge's society." A few months short of his twenty-
fifth year, Coleridge was living at Nether Stowey. To those who
knew him, the revolution he so swiftly effected in the
Wordsworths' lives was not remarkable, for meeting him for the
first time marked an epoch in the lives of many contemporaries.

PART TWO

COLERIDGE'S PRELUDE

I. THE INSPIRED CHARITY-BOY

" I COULD inform the dullest author how he might write an interesting book," wrote Coleridge to his friend Tom Poole in 1797. "Let him relate the events of his own life with honesty, not disguising the feelings that accompanied them." He began his autobiography in a series of letters to Poole, but after five letters, it became one of his countless uncompleted projects. If he had carried out only a quarter of the works he conceived he would have filled a handsome library and needed to live three ordinary lifetimes; his inexhaustible imagination leapt ahead of any human power of execution, even by his methodical and tirelessly diligent friend Southey. And he was never diligent in execution. To his wife he said of De Quincey that he was "as great a *to-morrow* to the full as your poor husband." Physical suffering and addiction to drugs enhanced his natural tendency to procrastination till he became a derelict adrift on the waters of life; shame on his conscience prevented his writing to his family or friends; he failed to support his children—failed even to support himself—and accepted the charity of friends, whom he repeatedly disappointed by omitting to fulfil promised undertakings. Yet he still contrived to leave a name famed among the greatest poets, to write some of the shrewdest criticism in the language, and to build the foundations of a philosophy that influenced the religious and political thought of a century. Moreover, through all his sorrows, trials, troubles, disappointments and divagations, he never lost the fascination that cast its spell on all who knew him. To the last his conversation still enthralled his listeners; even in the days of his greatest degradation and despair, "his face when he repeats his verses hath its ancient glory," said Charles Lamb, "an Arch-angel a little damaged."

Odd that such a man—who, possessing genius equal to any in literary history, so squandered his gifts as to be accounted a complete failure according to worldly measurement of material success—should have sprung from such a stock. Coleridges prodigally abound in the reference books—Sir John Taylor Coleridge, privy councillor and judge, whose brother was a prebendary of Exeter, begot a lord chief justice of England, thereby acquiring a peerage and so reserving for his eldest male descendants a permanent place in *Who's Who*. These Coleridges waxed from strength to strength, ever impeccably respectable, ever increasing wealth and reputation, through the golden Victorian era of machinery and money, a race as truly representative of prosperity by private enterprise as Galsworthy's Forsytes. And as the Forsytes sprang from little "Superior Dosset," the aspiring jerry-builder, so all the Coleridges in the reference books, the successful lawyers and clerics as well as the incongruously unsuccessful poet, shared a common ancestor no more exalted than a country schoolmaster.

The Rev. John Coleridge might have been more surprised at producing a succession of successful lawyers than at fathering a great writer, for "in learning, good heartedness, absentness of mind, and excessive ignorance of the world, he was a perfect Parson Adams." He published a Latin grammar intended to simplify the study for beginners and including such simplifications as renaming the ablative the "quale-quare-quidditive" case; as his son said, "my father made the world his confidant with respect to his learning and ingenuity, and the world seems to have kept the secret very faithfully." The son of a Crediton woollen-draper, he probably had a hard time in his young days; he was a schoolmaster and a married man when he matriculated at Sidney Sussex, Cambridge, in 1747. He left without a degree on being offered an appointment too good to be missed, the mastership of the grammar school at South Molton with the curacy of Mariansleigh. His first wife having died after bearing three daughters, he married for his second Anne Bowden, and in 1760, aged forty-one, he became, by the patronage of the Buller family, vicar of Ottery St. Mary, near Exeter (the Clavering St. Mary of Thackeray's *Pendennis*) and master of its free grammar school. At Ottery, on 21st October 1772, the tenth and last child of this second marriage, Samuel Taylor Coleridge, was born.

As the youngest of a large family, with the eldest already dispersing about the world to make their livings, little Sam was the spoiled child of his middle-aged parents. His mother's spoiling excited the jealousy of his immediate senior, Frank, and his nurse, who lavished affection on her favourite, reserving for him all the sweetest tit-bits while Sam received scoldings and slappings. Complaints to his mother evoked reprisals from both brother and nurse, so that he became timid and fretful. The handsomest of a handsome family, Frank was a hearty, healthy boy, popular, good at games, and careless of his books; when Sam arrived at school age, he suffered from him the same torments as those De Quincey suffered from his elder brother. He was habitually bullied and, when momentarily in favour, laughed at with contemptuous condescension.

Unlike De Quincey, he did not always submit without showing resentment. Once he flew in ungovernable rage at his tormentor, and on being struck in the face, seized a knife. His mother disarmed him, and he ran away to nurse his distress in one of his secret retreats near the river. As darkness came, he fell asleep. It was late October and a stormy night; he awoke so wet, stiff, and cold, that he could not move. He was found in the early morning by Sir Stafford Northcote, one of a search party which had been out all night, and carried home, where his parents were too overcome with joy and relief at his safety to think of punishing him for his escapade. "I hope you'll whip him, Mrs. Coleridge," exclaimed one officious young woman among the searchers, and twenty years later the poet remarked, "Neither philosophy or religion have been able to conquer the antipathy which I *feel* towards her whenever I see her." He seemed none the worse for the night of exposure after a day or two, but it is significant, in view of his later rheumatic affection, that he " was weakly and subject to the ague for many years after."

Apart from this adventure, his reactions to persecution were the same as De Quincey's; shrinking from other boys, he sought refuge from the miseries of this world in one of his imagination. At an "everything" shop kept by an aunt at Crediton, he obtained books of fairy stories, and after reading them in peaceful retreat, he ran up and down in the long grass of the lonely churchyard, acting the scenes he had been reading about. When, at six, he read the *Arabian Nights*, his imagination recreated horrors so vividly that he grew afraid of the dark. He became " a *dreamer*," with " an indisposition to all bodily activity "; he flatly refused to join in games, and as his manner was defensive, aggressive and resentful, he was the more bullied and baited by other boys. But instead of seeing himself, like De Quincey, in self-pity as a pariah, he conceived a fine contempt for his assailants. He read everything that came in his way " without distinction," and a lively understanding, deriving from his vivid imagination, combined with amazingly retentive memory to impress everybody with his precocity. He was " flattered and wondered at by all the old women," and grew consequently vain of his own cleverness and contemptuous of his less brilliant contemporaries. So, as he said, before he was eight years old, he was reckoned " a *character*," and a character he remained all his life to most of his friends. He was never to be measured by ordinary standards, and while this attitude assured due homage to his genius, it banished him beyond range of the sympathy readily bestowed on lesser men, which he would have prized more than praise in the long, desolate, distressful years of his middle age.

When he was nine, he was relieved from the oppression of the ebullient Frank, who departed to be a midshipman. But he enjoyed only for a brief space the opportunity to indulge his solitary habits unmolested, for his father, on his return from taking Frank to Plymouth, fell suddenly ill and died. Such was the extent of contemporary medical knowledge that the cause was diagnosed as " gout in the heart "; Coleridge more acutely

thought " probably it was a fit of apoplexy." For a few months
he continued at home under the tutorship of his father's successor,
Mr. Smerdon (probably William Gifford's benefactor of that
name), whose son's early death was commemorated in the
" Lines on a Friend Who died of a Frenzy Fever." Then the
local potentate, Judge Buller, procured for him a presentation to
Christ's Hospital, and he went to London to stay with his uncle
John Bowden, " a tobacconist and (at the same time) clerk to
an underwriter," who received him " with great affection " and
showed great pride in his unusual nephew, taking him the round
of his favourite taverns and coffee houses, where he " drank and
talked and disputed " as if he was a man, and was appraised by
his hearers as a prodigy.

After several weeks of petting by his uncle's family and
friends, he donned the charity boy's uniform of blue coat and
yellow stockings, and was sent in July 1782 to Hertford, where
the youngest boys were prepared for entry into the main school.
At Hertford he was " very happy, on the whole," having " plenty
to eat and drink, and pudding and vegetables almost every day."
But after only eight weeks, he was drafted to the main school
in London, where the diet was " very scanty "; " appetites were
damped, never satisfied "; breakfasts consisted of dry bread and
" bad small beer "; there was meat only three times a week and
no vegetables. The boys were " under excessive subordination
to each other" ; older boys, as monitors, were responsible for
discipline; as markers, they heard the lessons of their juniors.
Obviously the system offered scope for bullying and victimisation. Leigh Hunt, Coleridge's junior by twelve years, remembered a monitor " who had a trick of entertaining himself
by pelting lesser boys' heads with a hard ball." There was no
recognised fagging, but monitors sometimes terrorised juniors
into fagging for them, and if, like Hunt, they refused to be
intimidated, they were liable to systematic bullying in reprisal.
Coleridge suffered the agonies of a lonely small boy suddenly
plunged into this rough-and-tumble world from the gentle care
of his mother and the jocular affection of his uncle. Vivid
memories of his feelings he recorded some fifteen years later in

Frost at Midnight, describing how he lay at night in misery, staring into the darkness to conjure up the scenes of his Ottery home.

> " *So gazed I, till the soothing things, I dreamt,*
>   *Lulled me to sleep, and sleep prolonged my dreams!* "

These lines, enlivened probably by Coleridge's verbal confidences, inspired Charles Lamb to write in his Elia essay on " Christ's Hospital Five-and-Thirty Years Ago," of " How I would wake weeping, and in the anguish of my heart exclaim upon sweet Calne in Wiltshire! "

In *Frost at Midnight* he tells how he day-dreamed in class of home,

> " *Awed by the stern preceptor's face, mine eye*
>   *Fixed with mock study on my swimming book:*
>   *Save if the door half opened, and I snatched*
>   *A hasty glance, and still my heart leaped up,*
>   *For still I hoped to see the* stranger's *face,*
>   *Townsman, or aunt, or sister more beloved.*"

In occasionally receiving visitors he was more fortunate than his loneliest schoolfellows; after two years at school he wrote to his mother, " were it not for my kind friends I should be as destitute of many little necessaries as some of my school-fellows are." At first his Bowden uncle, aunt, and cousins were probably his only visitors—he had dinner with them every Saturday—but in 1785 his brother George became an assistant master at Newcome's Academy, Hackney, where he remained till he received in 1794 his father's old appointment as master of the grammar school at Ottery. Sixth of the family of ten, George was eight years older than Coleridge, who came to regard him as head of the family; " he is father, brother, and everything to me," Coleridge told their mother, and George, solid and reliable, if occasionally heavy in admonition, kept tender paternal watch over his youngest brother for several years.

The upper and lower grammar schools sat in one huge room, the former under the Rev. James Boyer at one end, the latter under the Rev. Matthew Field at the other. Field was a good-looking dandy, reputed to be a ladies' man, who came late to school and left early, languidly carrying his cane like a lily—" a good easy man, that did not care to ruffle his own peace, nor perhaps, set any great consideration upon the value of juvenile time," better suited perhaps to the leisured gentility of a fashionable parish. Boyer, by contrast, is described by Leigh Hunt with the vividness of painful memory as

" a short, stout man, inclining to paunchiness, with large face and hands, an aquiline nose, long upper lip, and a sharp mouth. His eye was close and cruel. The spectacles threw a balm over it . . . his clothes were cut short; his hands hung out of the sleeves, with tight wristbands, as if ready for execution; and as he generally wore grey worsted stockings, very tight, with a little balustrade leg, his whole appearance presented something formidably succinct, hard and mechanical. In fact, his weak side, and undoubtedly his natural destination, lay in carpentry; and he accordingly carried in a side-pocket made on purpose a carpenter's rule. The merits of Boyer consisted in his being a good verbal scholar, and conscientiously acting up to the letter of time and attention. I have seen him nod at the close of the long summer school-hours, wearied out; and I should have pitied him if he had taught us to do anything but fear. Though a clergyman, very orthodox, and of rigid morals, he indulged himself in an oath, which was ' God's—my—life! ' When you were out in your lesson, he turned upon you a round, staring eye like a fish; and he had a trick of pinching you under the chin, and by the lobes of the ears, till he would make the blood come. . . . He was, indeed, a proper tyrant, passionate and capricious."

Under such contrasting rulers the character of the upper and lower school was " as different as that of the inhabitants on the two sides of the Pyrenees." Field's pupils could read *Peter Wilkins* while supposed to be concentrating on the fables of Phaedrus, or beguile their time in making paper sundials or in playing the military game of "French and English." Boyer's thunders "rolled innocuous" over their heads, and seeing something of his disciplinary methods, many, like Lamb, were not anxious to change their present pleasant situation by seeking promotion to the upper school.

According to the system of the charity school, backward or idle boys were turned out at fourteen or fifteen to be found places as clerks or trade apprentices. The more promising boys were retained to be trained for the professions, the select few to become " Grecians," or classical scholars receiving Boyer's special coaching, intended for scholarships and exhibitions to the universities, mostly to Cambridge. If Coleridge, like Lamb, had rested content with untroubled idleness in Field's class, he too might have received a clerkship in the " South Sea " office—a reflection arousing curious speculations on what might have been. But he knew that he must work to avoid such lasting disgrace in his family and to achieve a university career like his brothers George and Ned, or at least entrance to the medical profession like his brother Luke. With his amazing memory and ability to absorb any sort of knowledge, no very arduous application was necessary to insure his speedy advancement.

Accustomed to the monotony of drumming against thick skulls with as little result as a pigeon pecking concrete, Boyer eagerly made the most of an apt pupil. Hunt's sharp portrait of the master is spiced with the lasting smart of resentment under intimidation, and Lamb sketched him with the detached irony of glad escape, but Coleridge, looking back across the combe of years, gratefully recognised his debt of scholarship to Boyer's early guidance. " Severe " but " sensible," Boyer taught him to prefer Homer, Theocritus, and Demosthenes to Virgil and Cicero, and Virgil to Ovid, to recognise the superiority of Lucretius, Terence and Catullus over the later Roman poets, and with a grounding in Shakespeare and Milton, to realise the fastidious choice of words in great writers—that " there is a reason assignable, not only for every word, but for the position of every word." He derided fine writing and fancy metaphors— " Harp? Harp? Lyre? Pen and ink, boy, you mean! Muse, boy,

Muse? Your nurse's daughter, you mean! Pierian spring? Oh, aye! the cloister-pump, I suppose!" Boyer sent Coleridge to Cambridge a classical scholar far superior to either Southey or Wordsworth, superior probably to all contemporary writers save Landor, and he also encouraged his literary genius. Several of Coleridge's early verses were preserved in Boyer's *Liber Aureus*, in which were copied compositions selected by the master as of special merit. After nearly thirty years Coleridge paid his " tribute of recollection to a man, whose severities, even now, not seldom furnish the dreams, by which the blind fancy would fain interpret to the mind the painful sensations of distempered sleep; but neither lessen nor dim the deep sense of my moral and intellectual obligations."

Twice at least he felt the physical pain of Boyer's displeasure. Aged about fifteen, he was apparently tempted to sacrifice ambition and escape from Boyer's dominion into trade; having made friends with a cobbler, he exerted his unfailing charm to persuade the man to apply personally to Boyer for Coleridge to become his apprentice. The irate Boyer drove the unfortunate cobbler with violence from his house, and doubtless did not omit due chastisement of his pupil. Rather later, after reading Voltaire's *Philosophical Dictionary*, he " sported infidel." Boyer wasted no words on theological discussion, and administered a severe flogging. Coleridge declared with truth that " my infidel vanity never touched my heart." From the time of his flogging till his last year at Cambridge, he lived in " a kind of *religious twilight*" between the Evangelists and deistic philosophers; " my heart . . . forced me to *love* the Jesus, whom my reason (or perhaps my reasonings) would not permit me to worship."

To this stage of his development belongs the famous reminiscence of him in Elia's essay:

"Come back into memory, like as thou wert in the day-spring of thy fancies, with hope like a fiery column before thee—the dark pillar not yet turned—Samuel Taylor Coleridge—Logician, Metaphysician, Bard!—How have I seen the casual passer through the Cloister stand still, entranced with admiration (while he weighed the disproportion between *speech* and the *garb* of the young Mirandula), to hear thee unfold in thy deep and sweet intonations, the mysteries of Jamblichus, or Plotinus (for even in those years thou waxest not pale at such philosophic draughts), or reciting Homer in his Greek, or Pindar—while the walls of the old Grey Friars re-echoed to the accents of the *inspired charity-boy*!"

This is the earliest glimpse of the greatest talker of his time, whose deep, sweet voice cast a spell on all listeners for nearly half a century. Already he was like the Vandyke portrait painted in his twenty-third year—above medium height, slenderness lending a semblance of tallness; flowing black curls, parted in the middle, flung back carelessly from the broad noble brow; thick black eyebrows above the great luminous eyes which conspired with his voice to fascinate. "I have the brow of an angel, and the mouth of a beast," he said once; "I cannot breathe through my nose, so my mouth, with sensual thick lips, is almost always open." He and Wordsworth both probably suffered from undiagnosed adenoids—the mouth is loose, but the thick sensual lips now show a sensitive, girlish curl, without the coarseness and drawn sadness of the ravaged face that North-cote saw in 1804. He was described as "striking" in adolescence, and commanding "much deference" from his schoolfellows.

His brother Luke, the next junior to George, came to London to walk the hospitals, and fired him with ambition to become a surgeon. So for some time his Saturdays were spent at the hospital, where he swelled with eager importance when "permitted to hold the plaisters or attend the dressings." He read all the medical books he could lay hands on, and acquired a rough working knowledge of medicine which in later years embellished lengthy expatiations on his body ailments. The phase quickly passed; the dream of becoming a surgeon "gradually blending with, gradually gave way to, a rage for metaphysics occasioned by the essays on Liberty and Necessity in Cato's *Letters*." Such swiftly changing crazes are the common whim of intelligent youth, but they continued characteristic of Coleridge

all his life. His intellectual career was an odyssey among fresh
lands for exploration, and so he had no sooner planned a work of
exhaustive magnitude, which was to be the supreme authority
on its subject, than it was abandoned for a no less ambitious work
on something else.

Metaphysics and theology were alike cast aside when the
senior Grecian of the school, Thomas Fanshawe Middleton, who
had been Coleridge's patron and protector, went up to Cambridge
and presented him, as a parting gift, with a copy of Bowles's
sonnets. Bowles is little remembered as a poet, apart from his
influence on Coleridge, and hence upon Wordsworth, Southey
and the later romantics. With Thomas Warton he was an
early revivalist of the Italian or Miltonic sonnet, which became
Wordsworth's favourite medium for expressing a single impression or idea.

Nearly thirty years later, in *Biographia Literaria*, recording his
regard for " the obligations of interest among the most sacred
of the claims of gratitude," Coleridge related the effects of his
first reading of Bowles. Though he was already " above par in
English versification " and had impressed Boyer with the poems
preserved in the school book, he despised imaginative literature,
including poetry and novels, as " insipid," concentrating his
inquiring mind on metaphysics and theology. Reading Bowles
revolutionised this taste. While he had appreciated the beauties
of Shakespeare and Milton, these were writers of a remote age,
to be accepted submissively as classics; but the work of a contemporary assumed a present reality, reminding him that beauty
still existed, could be aspired to, and demanded interpretation.
To Bowles therefore he owed emancipation from controversial
speculations, which threatened to stifle his creative gift.

" Well would it have been for me, perhaps, had I never
relapsed into the same mental disease," he said; " if I had continued to pluck the flower and reap the harvest from the cultivated
surface, instead of delving in the unwholesome quicksilver
mines of metaphysic lore."

Well it would have been, but in due time he " sought a
refuge from bodily pain and mismanaged sensibility in abstruse

researches which exercised the strength and subtilty of the understanding without awakening the feelings of the heart." Before
that time of stress and sadness, there was to be "a long and
blessed interval" of ten years, "during which my natural
faculties were allowed to expand, and my original tendencies
to develop themselves; my fancy, and the love of nature, and the
sense of beauty in forms and sounds."

Bowles also led him to revolt against the fashion of artificial
poetry which had prevailed since Pope. Almost at the same
time Landor was learning the same lesson from the Wartons;
later Coleridge himself was inspired by reading Akenside to
form his opinions on the functions of imagination and fancy.
But Bowles first showed him that mere metrical translation of
prose thoughts does not make true poetry, and that " whatever
lines can be translated into other words of the same language,
without diminution of their significance, either in sense of
association, or in any worthy feeling, are so far vicious in their
diction." Thus, still a schoolboy, he began speculation on the
theory of expression eventually stated by Wordsworth in the
preface to the *Lyrical Ballads* of 1800.

He found a source of poetic inspiration in Mary Evans, sister
of a small schoolfellow whom he befriended and protected
as Middleton had befriended and protected him. He and his
earliest intimate friend, Bob Allen, became the regular squires
of Mary and her two sisters—" and oh! from sixteen to nineteen
what hours of paradise had Allen and I in escorting the Miss
Evanses home on a Saturday, who were then at a milliner's . . .
and we used to carry thither, of a summer morning, the pillage
of the flower-gardens within six miles of town, with sonnet or
love-rhyme wrapped round the nosegay." During this "era of
poetry and love " he recalled at the age of fifty, that "to be
feminine, kind, and genteelly (what I should now call neatly)
dressed, these were the only things to which my head, heart,
or imagination had any polarity, and what I was then I still am."
Aside from physical sex, his relations with Mary Evans formed
the pattern of what he desired in women—a sympathetic
and encouraging audience, tender consideration, affectionate

companionship, a sense of beauty and humour. In return he gave reverence, sentimental and tender regard with moods of romantic ecstasy, sensitive understanding, and the sundry thoughtful attentions moving grateful affection. To the girls he was "dear brother Coly" (to none outside his family was he ever "Sam" or "Samuel"), while their widowed mother taught him "what it was to have a mother," and he loved her as such. An intimate in the family circle, he recited his verses and expounded his latest opinions, exciting laughter by the excesses of his enthusiasm and delighting them with the rich warmth of his personality.

One of the best-known love lyrics ever written by a poet under twenty, "Genevieve," was inspired, not by Mary Evans, but the daughter of the school nurse. Though careless of games, he was a good swimmer, and one day he swam across the "new river" in his clothes and let them dry on him, with the result that "full half his time from seventeen to eighteen was passed in the sick-ward" with jaundice and rheumatic fever. Latent weakness from the ague bouts following his childhood exploits was aggravated by this serious illness, which left him permanently a rheumatic subject, susceptible to acute attacks of pain from contact with damp. Opium was then the drug prescribed to relieve pain, and during this illness Coleridge first learned the fatal relief afforded by laudanum.

At the early age of sixteen he became a Grecian and duly fulfilled Boyer's hopes of him when the Almoners of Christ's Hospital appointed him to a school exhibition at Jesus College, Cambridge, in January 1791. Leaving school in the following summer, he spent his holidays at Ottery. It was only his second visit since he left the home of his childhood in his tenth year, and he found himself a stranger among his own family. Only two of the brothers older than George, the sixth in order, now survived—James and Edward. "The wit of the family," Edward, took orders, became a schoolmaster at Salisbury, and after marrying a woman old enough to be his mother, who soon conveniently died, he settled at Ottery as a bachelor uncle to his brothers' children and as a disappointed man. Apparently, in a

D

style of heavy condescension common in disillusioned school-
masters, he exercised his wit at the expense of the enthusiastic
adolescent, who was irritated into passages of dialectic arms.
Coleridge decided that "Edward never thought, that all his
finer feelings were the children of accident, and that even these
capricious sensibilities were too often swallowed in the vanity
of appearing great to little people."

Having entered the army at sixteen, James retired with the
rank of captain on marrying a lady of fortune, and returned to
settle at Ottery, as his youngest brother remarked, "a respectable
man." Respectability was his ambition, in which he admirably
succeeded, becoming himself a justice of the peace and begetting
both a prebendary and a justice of the Queen's Bench. He died
full of years in the year before Victoria ascended the throne,
on the threshold of the age to which he was spiritually suited.
Feeling acutely his importance as head of the family, he expected
due deference from the brother thirteen years his junior, and
assumed an attitude of chilly disapproval when he was disappointed. Apologising to brother George for his failure to
satisfy James, Coleridge provided an early example of that
unerring shrewdness in assessment of his fellows which contrasts
so strikingly with his mismanagement of his own life. "In my
brother James I recognised a man of reflection and *therefore*
of virtue. But as the object of that reflection was from his
peculiar situation necessarily himself, I saw or thought I saw, an
interested somewhat, a too great attention to external appear-
ances, a warmth in his own concerns, a coldness in those that
related to others, which seemed to render him unapt to be
beloved."

His only sister, on hearing of whose approaching death he
wrote a sonnet of tender pathos, had died in the previous spring.
Luke, the brother he loved next best to George, died on the
threshold of a promising career in 1790; the midshipman, Francis,
was to follow in 1792. Only George remained to link Coleridge
with his family. Their mother was apparently unable to reconcile
the oddly striking young man with the beloved child bereft
from her nine years before. Doubtless she inclined towards the

elder sons who shared her narrow interests at Ottery; with her
youngest son she was unable to establish any close sympathy.
When writing to Ottery, Coleridge always asked that his
"duty" should be presented to her, but to other women he
looked for glimmers of the mother love he had so early lost.

2. THE PRODIGAL AT CAMBRIDGE

Public schoolboys enter the universities with a social advantage over those who come from small schools and have to
find a footing by making new acquaintances. On his arrival at
Cambridge in October 1791, Coleridge immediately sought out
his schoolfellow Middleton, who, though he had "not the least
acquaintance with any of Jesus except a very blackguardly fellow
whose physiog. I did not like," conducted him to Jesus College,
and introduced him to his own friends at Pembroke. But,
without this advantage, he would not have remained long lonely,
like Wordsworth, whose awkward manner and halting speech
rebuffed tentative advances. Coleridge's arresting appearance,
ready loquacity, and engaging charm, always gained him friends
readily. He was a good mixer, and when he travelled on a
coach, tongue-tied rustic and self-important dignitary were
equally surprised to find themselves drawn into conversation.
During his first year he worked hard and established his
reputation as a classical scholar by winning a gold medal for a
Greek ode on the Slave Trade, the theme supporting the nineteen
years' crusade for abolition of slavery begun by Wilberforce,
Clarkson, and the Quakers in 1788. He found Cambridge "a
damp place—the very palace of the winds," and he repeatedly
suffered from bouts of rheumatism. After being "nailed to my
bed" by such a bout during his first term, he complained of
"a disagreeable *tearing* pain" in his head, and remarked significantly, "Opium never used to have any disagreeable effects on
me." Spending part of the Christmas vacation at Mrs. Evans's
house in London, he reported an improvement in his health,

from her maternal care; at the same time, he fell in love with Mary Evans, and letters to his " dear sister " indicate that he habitually hid his feelings from her in exchanges of playful badinage.

Middleton, his closest friend and the chief influence on his mind, was an enthusiast, like all young intellectuals of the day, for the principles of the French Revolution. The notoriety of his views so displeased the college authorities that, when he went down from the university in the summer of 1792, the fellowship he had fairly earned was " withheld as a punishment for his ' republicanism '." Though the uncompromising Boyer had probably checked expression of revolutionary fervour in his pupils, Coleridge was already a convert at school, having celebrated in an ode the destruction of the Bastille in 1789. The last stanza, beginning " Shall France alone a Despot spurn ? " and ending

> " And still, as erst, let favour'd Britain be
> First ever of the first and freest of the free! '

shows that he imbibed the views of those who wished to see the principles of Liberty, Equality and Fraternity applied in England, where Pitt's reactionary government was feverishly devising measures to repress free expression of such opinions. After Middleton had left the university, Coleridge, with the second-year man's zest of feeling his feet firmly planted on manhood's estate, became prominent among republican undergraduates; nightly his rooms were thronged to hear his expositions on the latest political pamphlets. His schoolfellow, Charles Le Grice, whom Lamb remembered as the most brilliant foil at school to Coleridge's eloquence, was among his Cambridge disciples; there was no need, he said, for them to have with them the book under discussion, as Coleridge had read it in the morning, and in the evening repeated whole pages verbatim.

According to Le Grice, Coleridge's reading was " desultory and capricious," and he always welcomed interruptions by visitors to his rooms, coming for the entertainment of his conversation. He nevertheless worked hard enough at classics to be

selected in his third year—by the celebrated scholar, Richard
Porson—as one of the four final contestants out of an original
entry of about eighteen for the Craven Scholarship. The other
three were Bethel, afterwards a member of Parliament, John
Keate, who became headmaster of Eton, and Samuel Butler,
later a bishop and grandfather of the author of *Erewhon*, who
had rivalled Landor for scholastic supremacy at Rugby. The
Vice-Chancellor decided that among the four, who stood out
markedly superior to all the other candidates, there was nothing
to choose, and therefore awarded the scholarship to Butler, as
the youngest. Coleridge confessed himself " perfectly satisfied "
with the result, but the Master of Jesus, Dr. Pearce, complained
that, if the examination had included Greek prose and verse and
original English composition, Coleridge " would have beat them
hollow," and presented him with a consolation prize of the
appointment as college librarian and chapel clerk, worth something over thirty pounds a year.

When war with France broke out in the new year of 1793,
Coleridge was a pacifist, because he believed that, as the war
could have been averted by negotiation, it was unnecessary and
therefore unjust. With reason he argued, along with all left-
wing liberals, that fear of democracy on the doorstep, following
so soon on the successful American rebellion against imperialist
reaction, inspired Pitt's government to go to war, in the belief
that it was better to attack France while she was diplomatically
friendless and domestically unsettled, rather than to await her
access of strength by the stabilising of her government and the
spreading of her democratising doctrine to neighbouring
countries. Government apologists refuted these arguments by
saying that, firstly, " we could not honourably negotiate with
men so stained with atrocious guilt, so avowedly the enemies of
religion, as the popular leaders in France "; secondly, they
disclaimed all intervention in French internal affairs. But, as
Coleridge noted, the government quickly disclosed its deceit
in the latter assurance: " not six months passed, ere with matchless
insincerity the restitution of monarchy became its avowed aim."
Though all parties united in prosecuting the second war of

1803-1815 against Napoleon, Pitt's government sought vainly—
even by undermining constitutional liberties with repressive acts
of panic legislation—to silence the protests of all honest thinkers
against the first war of 1793-1802, which was a war promoted
by fear of the propertied class for the encroaching popularity of
progressive ideas. Even if justification is allowed for the second
war as necessary to curb the aggressive ambitions of a military
dictator, France might never have been driven by military
necessity into acceptance of such a dictatorship if the revolutionaries had been allowed peacefully to develop their socialist
system. Pitt's policy of aggressive reaction plunged Europe
into more than twenty years of unprecedented bloodshed, followed by another forty years of poverty and revolution, and put
back the clock of progress even to our own time.

Foremost among extreme opponents of the war at Cambridge
was William Frend, a fellow of Coleridge's own college, already
notorious from having resigned four years before his church
living from conscientious motives. When he published a pamphlet on *Peace and Union Recommended to the Associated Bodies of
Republicans and Anti-Republicans*, his theology was condemned
as derogatory to church doctrines and his politics as socially
subversive. The fellows of Jesus excluded him from residence,
and in May 1793 he was tried before the Vice-Chancellor's court
for offending against university statutes and banished from
Cambridge. Coleridge and John Copley (who became years
later Lord-Chancellor as Lord Lyndhurst) were leading demon-
strators on Frend's behalf, and at the trial Coleridge was con-
spicuous by clapping loudly in applause. The Proctor responsible
for order happened to feel sympathy with Frend, and accused of
the clapping a one-handed undergraduate, who had only to show
the stump of his arm to be exonerated. The story goes that
Coleridge went afterwards to the Proctor and confessed to the
clapping, whereon the Proctor replied that he knew who it was,
and purposely picked on one who could not have committed
the offence.

Popularity as a brilliant talker on current politics incurred
expenditure beyond his means; refreshment and other amenities

had to be provided for the listeners who thronged his rooms. He had a taste for conviviality, which censors of his habits afterwards chose to interpret as a weakness for alcohol, but he drank then, as always, only in company, with zest in good fellowship and the loosening of tongues that enlivened controversial conversation. In telling George of his stay at Salisbury with their brother Edward on his way to Ottery in the summer of 1793, he shows characteristic undergraduate swagger in posing as the man of the world who can carry his wine. With Edward and a friend he " sat from four till ten drinking! and then arose as cool as three undressed cucumbers. Edward and I (O! the wonders of this life) disputed with great coolness and forbearance . . . we neither of us were *convinced* though now and then Ned was *convicted*."

During this stay at Ottery his thoughts were not too absorbed in Mary Evans to omit admiration of a Miss Fanny Nesbitt, " a very pretty girl " with whom he travelled in the diligence from Exeter to Tiverton. She inspired some verses sent to brother George as " Cupid turn'd Chymist," afterwards published as " Kisses," and adapted to suit other ladies at different times by simply changing " Nesbitt's lovely lips " to " Mary's," " Brunton's," and finally " Sara's." After a pleasant excursion with " a party of young ladies " to the cave by the Otter called the Pixies' Parlour, he was moved to write the charming irregular ode, " Songs of the Pixies," which compares in spontaneous grace and feeling with the fanciful lyrists of the seventeenth century.

His poetic gift was fast developing, and he thought of using it to relieve his accumulating debts. In the previous spring he had begun translations of " the best lyric poems from the Greek, and the modern Latin writers," to be published in a volume by subscription, but this was the first of manifold plans to be abandoned. But when his return to Cambridge in the autumn brought oppressive reminder of his debts, he sent some verses " To Fortune —On buying a Ticket in the Irish Lottery " to the *Morning Chronicle*, with a covering note ending, " I am, with more respect and gratitude than I ordinarily feel for Editors of Papers, your obliged &c." It was published, and he received a guinea—the first payment earned by his pen.

During this term he apparently sought forgetfulness of his debts by reckless social activities. The circumspect Christopher Wordsworth, just come up to Trinity, spotted the popular Coleridge as a desirably useful acquaintance and joined him in forming a literary society. In his journal—for, as a dutifully earnest young man, he kept a record of his daily doings for the benefit of future generations—Christopher noted a discussion of his brother's poetry with Coleridge, who "spouted out of Bowles." At another meeting Coleridge recited to the society his "Lines on an Autumnal Evening"; again, in Christopher's rooms, having neglected to prepare the paper he was to have read, he repeated more of his own poetry.

Already he had confided to brother George that he was in arrears with his tutor's bills, having spent in extravagance the money set aside for their payments. Still a young man, with his own Oxford days only eight or nine years behind him, George had undertaken to lay the matter before the unsympathetic James and Edward, and persuaded them to join with him in advancing money to meet the bills. But Coleridge had feared to inform George of all his debts, and on returning to Cambridge, he distributed his brothers' money among the most pressing tradesmen. "So small a sum remained, that I could not mock my Tutor with it," so this he spent on present pleasures. His was not a winning ticket in the Irish lottery; his literary earnings were limited to a solitary guinea; as the term drew towards its close, the perspiration of horror damped his neck at thought of the pained expression of his trusting brother, the chill displeasure of James, and the sneers of Edward, when he confessed his deception of them. One Sunday night, in an agony of despair, he "packed up a few things, went off in the mail, staid about a week in a strange way" in London, probably seeking forgetfulness by drinking and talking in alehouses, and "looking forward with a kind of recklessness to the *dernier ressort* of misery." From suicide he was deterred by "an accident of a very singular kind," which caused him to enlist as a trooper in the Light

Dragoons. Some four years later, hearing Coleridge's sermon
against the wickedness of war, Hazlitt was struck by a contrast
between "the simple shepherd boy, driving his team afield,"
and "the same poor country-lad, crimped, kidnapped, brought
into town, made drunk at an alehouse, turned into a wretched
drummer-boy." Coleridge was neither crimped nor kidnapped,
but almost certainly drunk, his wits befuddled by despair exaggerated, instead of drowned, by drink, when he enlisted on 2nd
December 1793 under the name of Silas Tomkyn Comberbacke.

3. THE PENITENT DRAGOON

"Comberbacke" was a name given on the spur of the moment,
and "Silas Tomkyn" were probably the first names occurring
to him other than his own that preserved his initials. "Being
at a loss when suddenly asked my name, I answered *Cumberback*,
and verily my habits were so little equestrian, that my horse,
I doubt not, was of that opinion." He never acquired any
proficiency in riding; a few years later he regularly walked to
Bridgwater from Stowey when he might have had a mount for
the asking. Equally inept at grooming his horse and cleaning
accoutrements, he was an unsatisfactory recruit, but as always the
charm of his personality won everybody's affection and he
became popular by his talent for telling stories and writing love-
letters for illiterate comrades.

Stationed at Reading, he was for nearly two months lost to
friends and relatives. Then, "under the most solemn imposition
of secrecy," he wrote to friends at Christ's Hospital—Samuel
Favell or Le Grice's younger brother, who as juniors had been
his devoted followers—asking probably that they should bear a
word from him to Mary Evans or her mother. But the secret
was too exciting for schoolboys to keep; they confided it to one
of Coleridge's Cambridge friends, Tuckett, who immediately
informed George Coleridge. On 6th February 1794 Coleridge
wrote, reproaching Tuckett for this betrayal, from Henley

Workhouse, where he had gone generously to nurse a comrade "sickened of the confluent small-pox." On the 8th he made his first apology to brother George: "My more than brother! What shall I say? . . . I have been a fool even to madness. . . . My mind is illegible to myself. . . . One wish only can I read distinctly in my heart, that it were possible for me to be forgotten as though I had never been! . . . The anguish of him who protected me from my childhood upwards, the sore travail of her who bore me! . . . Oh that without guilt I might ask of my Maker annihilation! . . . pray for me, comfort me, my brother! I am very wretched. . . ."

Read in cold-blooded detachment, his contrite letters seem like theatrical gallery-playing, intended to impress with a sense of the distraction he was suffering in the hope that his brothers might be so impressed and rescue him. But such interpretation ignores both Coleridge's emotional temperament and the gift of unerring sympathetic insight—ever fatal alike to his resolution and peace of mind—that enabled him vividly to imagine the effect of his conduct on others. In his mind's eye he saw the troubled expression on his brother's face, saw the shock and heard the sharp exclamation of his mother on hearing the news; and seeing them, he felt them, and in feeling, attributed to them deeper capacity for emotion than they actually possessed, by assuming them to be endowed with his own sensitiveness. In susceptibility to impression he had at least one skin less than the average human—a liability to be remembered in examining all his relationships, especially with the Wordsworths.

His mental wretchedness was enhanced by the squalor of his situation. For eight days and nights he did not remove his clothes; his assiduous nursing saved his comrade's life. Much donnish fun has been made of his reference to the sympathy of "a beautiful girl." Truly he may have exaggerated her attractions, for the plainest might seem angelic who brought an element of feminine tenderness into the filth and stench of such sanitary conditions as prevailed in a workhouse infirmary of 1794. And what woman would have withheld sympathy from the striking young man, with the luminous eyes and beautiful voice, haggard from want of sleep and "fatiguing struggles with his delirious comrade-in-arms," who must have seemed as incongruous in that place as a richly-dressed woman at a welfare centre.

George promptly responded with comfort, and asked whether Coleridge proposed to return to Cambridge if his discharge was secured. On the night of 11th February Coleridge replied, " I am indeed oppressed, oppressed with the greatness of your love! . . . Undoubtedly, my brother, I could wish to return to College: I know what I *must suffer* there, but deeply do I feel what I *ought* to suffer. . . . What my future life may produce I dare not anticipate . . . Mr. Boyer! indeed, indeed, my heart thanks him; how often in the petulance of satire, how ungratefully have I injured that man!" The much maligned Boyer, on hearing of his former pupil's escapade, acted as promptly and practically as in the case of the unlucky cobbler; spending his days with dull mediocrity, he was not prepared to see, if he could help it, a career of brilliant promise shipwrecked by a crazy escapade. He took up Coleridge's case with the college authorities, persuaded them to insist on no report to the Christ's Hospital almoners likely to cause cancellation of his scholarship, and himself assumed the onus of suppressing mention of the matter to the almoners.

Having heard from his eldest brother, Captain James Coleridge, on 20th February, he replied, giving his colonel's name, so that the captain could negotiate for his discharge. But six more weeks of wretchedness passed before his discharge was secured. He was moved from Henley to High Wycombe and thence back again to Reading, where a friend from Devon, a brother-in-law of Lord Teignmouth, was so touched by his misery under "all the drudgery of a dragoon recruit," that "he has never been from my thoughts since," and persuaded him to accept a guinea from him. The report of this kind friend may have expedited arrangements and inspired influence to alleviate his condition, for he spent the last three days before receiving his discharge on 7th April at Bray, near Maidenhead, as the guest of one of those friends he never failed to make wherever he went. He was able " in some measure to repay his kindness by the revisal of a performance he is about to publish, and by writing him a dedication and preface." With this friend, apparently, he met the musician Charles Claggett, who set four songs of his " most divinely, for two violins and a pianoforte," and wanted him to write an opera libretto.

On 9th April he travelled from Reading to London and thence to Cambridge " on the outside of the Mail," which exposure brought on a bout of rheumatic pains. On the 12th he was convened before the fellows of the college. Dr. Pearce " behaved with great asperity," which was mitigated by his tutor Plampin's " exceeding and most delicate kindness." After a formal reprimand, he was sentenced to a month's confinement to college and to translate the works of Demetrius Phalareus into English. Thanks to Boyer, he suffered no financial penalty by loss of his scholarship.

His tutor considered the returning prodigal's demeanour " extremely proper," and in a fervour of contrition and gratitude, Coleridge began to rise at five in the morning, dropped all his frivolous acquaintances, and announced his intention of competing for all the prizes. His plan of translating modern Latin writers, begun in the previous year, progressed as far as advertising during June in the *Cambridge Intelligencer* " proposals for publishing by subscription *Imitations from the Modern Latin Poets, with a Critical and Biographical Essay on the Restoration of Literature, by S. T. Coleridge, of Jesus College, Cambridge.*" He proposed to " aim at correctness and perspicuity, not *genius*," as his last ode was " so *sublime* that nobody could understand it." But, harnessed to academic correctness, his muse refused to move, and a few of the imitations only survive from having been printed later in newspapers. His genius sought expression in original composition, and at this time the first draft of *Lewti, or the Circassian's Love-Chant*, was written, though the lover roves, not to banish unkind Lewti from his mind, but

> " *In hopes fond fancy would be kind*
> *And steal my Mary from my mind.*"

Lytton Strachey lamented that critics and biographers of poets are usually "highly respectable old gentlemen," since poets are apt to be young and not highly respectable. So while they recognise the charm and the infallible ear for melody and rhythm inevitable in Coleridge's verse, academic critics deprecate the emotions of poems like *Lewti* as excessive and their sentiment as silly. Even if in youth they could have experienced such emotions as Coleridge felt, self-conscious respectability would compel repression of feelings that they would never have dreamed of expressing in words; so, when they read an outburst of enraptured desire like *Lewti*, they feel uncomfortable, as if confronted with a breach of good form. Coleridge idealised women, and while he was ready to endow with his ideals every personable woman he met, he craved in the monastic seclusion of Cambridge the presence of his idealised woman. Because she was the most attractive and sympathetic woman he knew, he idealised Mary Evans, and though whenever he met her, he still took refuge in brotherly jocularity, he had no sooner left her than he was again working himself into a fever of desire for her and the essential womanliness her image embodied in his mind.

Term ended sooner at Cambridge than Oxford that year, and having arranged to spend the weeks of the summer vacation on a walking tour in Wales with a friend named Hucks, Coleridge decided to call at Oxford and see his friend Bob Allen, who had gone up three years before to Oriel, with a Christ's Hospital exhibition. Though he was studying medicine, Allen had literary aspirations—Coleridge had written for him a paper " on the comparative good and evil of novels," and blushed to tell brother George what credit Allen had got for it—and among his literary friends was a Balliol undergraduate named Robert Southey. Coleridge left Cambridge on 9th June, intending to stay three or four days at Oxford, but he prolonged his stay to about three weeks.

PART THREE

THE YOUTH OF SOUTHEY

I. A CLEVER YOUNG PRIG

NEARLY two years younger than Coleridge, Robert Southey was in his second year at Oxford when they met. He was born at Bristol on 12th August, 1774, the son of an unsuccessful draper, whose wife came from a family of small country squires in superior social and financial circumstances. Coleridge and Wordsworth both lost their fathers in childhood, and though Southey's father survived till his son's university matriculation, Southey received no more paternal influence than his fellow-poets.

The Southeys were Somerset stock, and Southey's grandfather was a farmer at Lydiard St. Laurence, at the foot of the Quantocks. Of his two sons, John, the elder, became an attorney at Taunton, and flourished, but Robert showed no talent for anything but country sports. "The fields should have been his station, instead of the shop," said his son, but he was placed at Britton's, in Wine Street, Bristol, then the best draper's shop in the West of England. Among his friends was Edward Tyler, an easy-going young man employed at a Bristol warehouse and living with his twice-widowed mother, Mrs. Hill, at Bedminster. At Mrs. Hill's he became " a regular Sabbath guest," and in 1772, when he was twenty-seven, he married her twenty-year-old daughter, Margaret Hill.

Mrs. Hill came from a Herefordshire county family named Bradford. By her first husband, Tyler, also of Herefordshire, she had four children, Elizabeth, John, William, and Edward; by her second, Edward Hill of Bedminster, she had a son, Herbert, and Margaret Southey. Elizabeth Tyler was brought up by her uncle Bradford, a clergyman of considerable fortune, who provided the means for sending his nephew, Herbert Hill, to Oxford. Even as a girl, she showed personality, managing her uncle's parish as well as his house; " she had influence enough to introduce inoculation there," an achievement as remarkable in those days as the enlightenment that inspired it. On her uncle's death, she inherited the bulk of his fortune, and having developed fashionable tastes outside the suburban ken of her mother's home, made a habit of travelling to watering places. In the course of a continental trip, she settled her half-brother Herbert, who had just taken orders, as chaplain to the English factory at Lisbon, and returning to England, took a house on the outskirts of Bath. She was then thirty-four, and " remarkably beautiful, as far as any face can be called beautiful in which the indications of a violent temper are strongly marked."

To her house, at the age of two, came Robert Southey, her eldest nephew (the Southeys' first child died in infancy), in time to avoid the domestic complications of his mother's third confinement. Apparently his aunt did not formally adopt him; she received him to live with her, as her uncle had received her, paying all expenses and assuming responsibility. His parents were well content with the arrangement, his father being always financially embarrassed and his mother bearing or burying babies.

Miss Tyler's imperious caprice as a courted beauty degenerated in middle age to a spinster's eccentricities. She spent prodigally on her house furnishings, but kept only two servants, a maid and an old man, who used to feed the crickets every night. She insisted on her little nephew's sleeping with her, so that he was first put into the maid's bed, lest he burnt himself or his aunt's bed with the warming-pan, and transferred when his aunt retired, thus being regularly wakened from sound sleep; in the mornings he had to lie awake till his aunt's late hour of rising, fearing to move lest he disturbed her. She had him inoculated in defiance of his mother, who fancied that the treatment injured his constitution, since from being a plump infant, he became " the lean, lank, greyhound-like creature " he afterwards remained. Though he was tall for his age, she refused to allow him to be breeched till he was six, compelling him to the shame of wearing a girlish fringed tunic. He had no playmates, little exercise, and was never allowed to do anything to dirty himself, so that he never afterwards cared for outdoor games. On the other hand, he remained ever grateful to her for teaching him " never to spoil nor injure anything." Among the wide circle of acquaintance attracted by her beauty and talents was the London bookseller Newbery, who presented the child with a complete set of his children's books, encouraging him early to learn to read and care for books.

She hoarded everything except money, and possessed a collection of play-bills, which the child was allowed to " illuminate " by pricking out with a pin. She was considered an amateur and patroness of the stage, knew the dramatists Sheridan, Colman, Cumberland and Holcroft, and when other children of his age were long asleep, young Southey was often sitting beside his aunt in the best seats of the theatre. Before he was eight, he had read Shakespeare and Beaumont and Fletcher, and begun to write a play about Scipio. He informed an old spinster crony of his aunt's—who would exclaim, " Lord, Miss Tyler, what do you think this child has been saying! "—that it was " the easiest thing in the world to write a play . . . you have only to think what you would say if you were in the place of the characters, and to make them say it." At school, as he says in his unfinished autobiography, it seemed to him " very odd " that other boys " should not be able to write plays as well as to do their lessons." Soon, reading Ariosto, Spenser, and Pope's Homer diverted his muse from the drama to epics about Arcadia, the Trojan Brutus, and Richard III, and by his thirteenth birthday he had written three heroic epistles in rhyme, besides translations from Ovid, Virgil, and Horace.

When he began school at six, he returned to his parents' home, going as a day-boy to a school " then esteemed the best in Bristol," kept by an old Baptist minister named Foot. Southey's memories of tyranny and bullying during his year at this school were probably coloured by the contrast with peaceful seclusion at his aunt's; he was terrorised into forgetting his lessons, and received from old Foot the only caning of his schooldays. Foot died, and was succeeded by the Rev. John Prior Estlin, afterwards Coleridge's friend, but Southey was removed to a school at Corston, nine miles from Bristol, where he boarded. Here the master was a man of parts, impatient of the fate which condemned him to the drudgery of teaching, which he mostly delegated to his son, called Charley by the boys, " whose consequence you may appreciate accordingly." Father and son frequently saved themselves trouble by setting brighter boys to coach the others, and Southey learned more Latin by helping boys older than himself than from his own lessons.

Miss Tyler gave up her house at Bath, but he continued to spend most of his holidays with her at Weymouth and other such resorts, where her companions were inevitably maiden ladies of mature years. But on her mother's death she temporarily took possession of the latter's house at Bedminster. Here her dominion was leavened by the society of her two bachelor brothers, William and Edward Tyler, who both had the inevitable charm of ineffectual men. Of his uncle William, Southey left affectionate sketches in his autobiography, and as William Dove in *The Doctor*. He was a harmless uncertifiable mental deficient, of the same temper as Mr. Dick in *David Copperfield*. He could never be taught to read, though he could tell his letters individually, without combining them into words: he could write to the extent of copying, but only letter by letter, without understanding a word. Though not responsible for his actions, he had " an excellent memory, and observing eye and a sort of *half-saved* shrewdness which would have qualified him, had he been born two centuries earlier, to have worn motley, and figured with a cap and bells and a bauble in some baron's hall "—the more so as he possessed an inexhaustible store of old saws and anecdotes. He was what country folk, with unintentional irony, used to call a " natural "—one who, unable to learn the artifices of civilisation, retained unimpaired his native simplicity. Besides incessantly chewing tobacco and swilling beer, his only occupation was watching neighbours from the window, acquiring intimate knowledge of their concerns. He delighted to lure his nephew into a game of marbles, and in the evening played cards with him and Miss Tyler.

His uncle Edward was devoted to the garden and taught Southey love of flowers and the study of insect life. But when Miss Tyler sold their mother's house and took one of her own in Bristol, while the useless William remained with her, poor Edward had to go to work as a clerk. Here, for the first time, Southey acquired a companion of his own age, Shadrach Weeks, brother of his aunt's maid, who was employed as house-boy. From Shad he learned carpentry and made a puppet theatre; with him he roamed the rocks and woods of the Avon valley, learning the love of nature as Wordsworth was learning in the hills above Windermere.

After leaving Corston, he spent four or five years as a day-boarder at another Bristol school. Though he was there taught better than by "Charley," when his uncle Herbert Hill proposed to send him to Westminster in the hope of his winning a Christ Church scholarship, he was so backward that he had to go for twelve months to a clergyman "crammer" to be prepared for entrance to a public school. He was still short of his fourteenth year, when, early in 1788, he entered Westminster School.

At this point in his life his autobiography, written between 1820 and 1825, ceased. He was not an outstanding figure at school, like Coleridge and Landor. He had neither the social charm of the one, nor the independent arrogance of the other, which, allied with individual brilliance, attracted popular admiration. Precocity and lack of holiday playmates engendered a social awkwardness which he never overcame. "I am indifferent to society," he wrote at twenty, "yet I feel my private attachment, growing more and more powerful." Casual acquaintances felt liking but inability to penetrate his stiff formality of manners though he was fervent in family affection and fidelity to his few close friends; his Westminster school fellows, Grosvenor Bedford and Williams Wynn, remained friends for life.

An aloof attitude of critical detachment rebuffed general cordiality. Most likely at Westminster, as later at Oxford, he belonged to a small circle of select friends, which, content in its own company, was ignored by the majority. Of his three hundred contemporaries at school there were " few upon whose countenance Nature had set her best testimonials "; on the other hand there were not many more who " bore the stamp of reprobation."

" The great majority were of a kind to be whatever circumstances might make them; clay in the potter's hand, more or less fine; and as it is fitting that such subjects should be conformed to the world's fashion and the world's uses, a public school was best for them. But where there is a tendency to low pursuits and low vices, such schools are fatal. They are nurseries also for tyranny and brutality. Yet, on the other hand, good is to be acquired there, which can be attained in no other course of education."

His school career might have followed conventional lines but for his sensitive pride, which resented dictatorial discipline and especially the indignity of corporal punishment. His aunt's domineering strictness, the blight on his childhood, had inspired a jealous regard for individual liberty, which was stimulated by the democratic doctrines of the French Revolution into a tendency to rebellion against authority. As a senior boy, he and his friends, inspired by a desire to set the world straight according to the latest libertarian ideas, founded a magazine called *The Flagellant* in the spring of 1792. Each number contained an essay in the manner of Addison's *Spectator*, and for the fifth Southey took floggings as his subject. He treated it in " a strange whimsical and ironical sort of manner," which he fancied an imitation of Voltaire, and being " full of Gibbon at the time," he argued that, since it formed part of heathen religious ceremonies and the Fathers had held the heathen gods to be devils, flogging was an invention of the devil, and therefore unfit to be practised in Christian schools. Incredible as it seems, the headmaster of Westminster, Dr. Vincent, immediately instituted libel proceedings against the printer of the magazine, and when Southey owned himself the writer of the anonymous essay, expelled him from the school.

It seems likely that Southey was already unpopular with the headmaster. A letter years later states that he had some share in a school rebellion, and Dr. Vincent was obviously the sort of schoolmaster to inspire rebellions. Expulsion in itself was no considerable deprivation, since he was normally due to leave in the summer, and fear that it might interfere with his chance of a Christ Church scholarship was dispelled by the headmaster's promise that he would not mention the matter to the college authorities. In gratitude for this forbearance, he was persuaded—probably by Miss Tyler, to whose Bristol house he returned till his going to Oxford—to write a letter to Dr. Vincent, " expressing contrition I did not feel, and apologising for an action which I thought needed no apology." Bitterly he regretted this concession when, true to his type, the headmaster went back on his word and made representations which convinced the Dean of Christ Church that a rebel so irrepressible might embarrass college discipline. As late as September 1792 he was expecting to go into residence at Christ Church for the October term; within a fortnight of the beginning of term, he was informed that the college had rejected him.

Such shabby treatment naturally induced a sense of victimisation. Mentally he was " in a perilous state—a heart full of feeling and poetry, a head full of Rousseau and *Wert(h)er*," and " religious principles shaken by Gibbon." Still eager to express himself in print, he proposed to Grosvenor Bedford the publication of a miscellany, to be called " The Medley," " The Hodge Podge," or " Monastic Lucubrations," and ironically suggested its dedication to "Envy, Hatred, and Malice, and all Uncharitableness." " Many circumstances tended to give me a wrong bias," he wrote in reminiscence, " none to lead me right, except adversity." His father's " affairs " (about which he and his biographers were decently nebulous) added to his troubles. Apparently Robert Southey Senior, having failed in business, was in danger of arrest for debt. Courageously Southey travelled to Taunton to request his father's brother, the successful lawyer, " to assist my father to recover that situation into which the treachery of his relations and injustice of his friends had thrown him." The rich uncle was out; Southey left a letter, and two days later received a curt answer containing a refusal of help. The fact that Miss Tyler generously came to the rescue, and paid her brother-in-law's debts, did not mitigate the impression upon youth of this pretty specimen of generosity in human nature—a bachelor, possessed of property valued at a hundred thousand pounds, who could refuse a loan to save his only brother from a debtor's prison. Broken in health and spirits by his misfortunes, Southey's father died towards the close of the year.

Under the burden of these troubles, sufficiently oppressive on a boy of eighteen, "an instinctive modesty, rather than any purer cause," said Southey, "preserved me for a time from all vice." This self-confessed priggishness combined with circumstances to reject temptation; living under the severity of his aunt's eye, in a provincial town where unconventional conduct would be speedily reported, and with limited pocket-money, he had small scope for self-indulgence. According to himself, he reinforced his natural repugnance to vice with the philosophy of Epictetus, "for many months literally my manual." But he needed an audience—a feminine audience—more sympathetic and satisfying than his aunt and harassed mother. This he found in Edith Fricker, who—like Coleridge's Mary Evans—worked with her elder sisters as a milliner to assist in supporting a widowed mother. She was his own age, pretty, gentle, quiet, a little commonplace, but very ready to listen in admiring silence while he declaimed his poetry or political opinions; even if his "instinctive modesty" had not deterred him, her impregnable middle-class respectability would have repudiated all but honourable advances. Her social inferiority appealed to his chivalry; his attachment stifled the already faint invitations to vice. He anchored his affections to her, because the determination to marry her as soon as possible afforded an incentive to duty.

Thus long before Jowett's time, Balliol College apparently valued personality and brains above correct deportment, and accepted the rejected of Christ Church in November 1792. At the same time a letter from his uncle at Lisbon wisely refrained from recriminations on his expulsion, inspiring gratitude to "one who has been to me more than a parent" as an additional stimulant to duty.

2. STOIC AND REPUBLICAN

He went up to Balliol in January 1793—the month when war broke out between England and France—" a Stoic and a Republican." But his stoicism was a refuge, his republicanism a passionate belief. Expecting to encounter at Oxford " pedantry, prejudice, and aristocracy," he felt none of the normal freshman's exultation on finding himself a free individual with a foot on the threshold of life's adventure ; on the contrary, he thought it " rather disgraceful, at the moment when Europe is on fire with freedom . . . to sit and study Euclid or Hugo Grotius."

He expressed his republicanism in one of youth's flamboyant gestures by declining the services of the college barber and wearing his hair unpowdered, a mark of rebellion against prevailing aristocratic fashion. Next door at Trinity, Walter Savage Landor, a freshman the same term, did the same, but Landor was " notorious as a mad Jacobin," and Southey's prudence deterred him from such an inflammatory acquaintance. Always he was seeking to curb his instincts in an effort to conform with his conception of duty. " Four years hence I am to be called into orders," he wrote, " and during that time (short for the attainment of the requisite knowledge) how much have I to learn! I must learn to break a rebellious spirit, which neither authority nor oppression could ever bow; it would be easier to break my neck. I must learn to work a problem instead of writing an ode. I must learn to pay respect to men remarkable only for great wigs and little wisdom."

As at Westminster, he made no attempt to mix, but withdrew himself into a small circle of friends. Edmund Seward, whose early death doubtless caused Southey to magnify his virtues in retrospect, was his closest friend; Southey declared that Seward confirmed in him all that was good. If he still credited himself with tendencies to vice, these he may have been confirmed by Seward's influence in quelling, but his correspondence and conduct indicates scant confirmation in anything else. His attitude to life was based on the shifting sands of continual conflict between inclination and duty; in a fog of self-questioning, he tried to feel his way.

To his schoolfellow Bedford, now in a government office, he expounded Seward's virtues. Seward converted him to early rising; he allowed himself only six hours' sleep. Two years before, Seward had drunk wine and eaten butter and sugar; now water was his only drink, dry bread his only breakfast. So Southey went to no wine parties, refusing to drink " more wine than suited my inclination and my principles." Once when reading Hutchinson's *Moral Philosophy* in Latin with Seward, Southey asked if he did not find his attention flagging, remarking that, if their studies were made interesting, they would pursue them with pleasure. " Certainly we should," replied Seward, " but I feel a pleasure in studying them because I know it is my duty." This remark—worthy of the hero of a novel by Miss Charlotte M. Yonge—Southey hailed delightedly as " true philosophy, of that species which tends to make mankind happy, because it makes them good." Unconscious of self-accusation, he described " morose austerity and stern enthusiasm " as " characteristics of superstition "; asking " what is in reality more cheerful or happy than Religion," he declared that a philosopher should be " shunned like pestilence, who, because Christianity has to him no allurement, seeks to deprive the miserable of their only remaining consolation." Thus he fobbed off the metaphysicians who tantalised Coleridge, and convinced for the moment that he had achieved reconciliation between duty and inclination, he sedulously kept a diary, " as an account of time which I ought to be strict in."

His political opinions were more difficult of conformity with peace of mind. When Louis XVI was deposed, he admitted that the French had accepted a worse tyranny, but denied that French errors detracted from " sanguine dreams of romantic liberty." He saw in the French Revolution " a structure raised by the hand of wisdom, and defended by the sword of liberty, undermined by innovation, hurled from its basis by faction, and insulted by the proud abuse of despotism," but, he asked,

"Is it less respectable for its misfortunes?" Retaining his faith in the ideals of the Revolution, he condemned the French for betraying them. Their "horrid barbarities" rendered him "totally indifferent to the fate of France," and in the manner of Lord Vansittart's *Black Record* against the Germans, he compiled a list of crimes—the St. Bartholomew massacre, the torturing of Jean Calas, the bestial execution of the would-be regicide Damiens, their "enormities" in America—as evidence of "national ferocity." When war came, he sneered at his anti-democratic friends. "The state of French affairs pleases *you* I hope," and exclaiming that "Peace! Peace! is all I wish for," he avoided argument by saying, "Time may alter my opinions: I do not much think it will."

"I read and write till my eyes ache," he said, and he was always writing poetry. He translated parts of Horace and Juvenal, and frequently wrote letters in verse to the father of a schoolfellow. He had not come across Bowles, but felt the influence of the Wartons, Mason, and Sayers, the last leading him to experiment with irregular verse, which he afterwards used to advantage in *Thalaba*. Spending several weeks with his friend Bedford during the summer vacation, he wrote the first draft of *Joan of Arc*, an epic celebrating the theme of liberty "in a republican spirit, such as may easily be accounted for in a youth whose notions of liberty were taken from the Greek and Roman writers, and"—as he wrote forty years later—"who was ignorant enough of history and of human nature to believe, that a happier order of things had commenced with the independence of the United States, and would be accelerated by the French Revolution."

For a reason unrevealed—possibly the death of his uncle William Tyler—he did not return to residence at Oxford for the Michaelmas term of 1793, but remained with his aunt at Bristol. Deprived of Seward's proximity, he found the armour of his stoicism uncomfortably vulnerable. After Marie Antoinette's execution on 16th October, Bedford, having joined the herd infected by the patriotic fever of government propaganda, wrote jeeringly of this latest atrocity by the European champions of liberty. Southey replied with heat and bitterness: " To suppose that I felt otherwise than grieved and indignant at the fate of the unfortunate queen of France was supposing me a brute, and to request an avowal of what I felt implied a suspicion that I did not feel. You seemed glad, when arguments against the system of republicanism had failed, to grasp at the crimes of wretches who call themselves republicans, and stir up my feelings against my judgment." Ironically the Stoic was as indignant at being accused of want of feeling, as the republican by the traditional device of reactionaries in construing the errors of progressives as premises arguable against progress.

When, a fortnight later, the guillotining of Brissot and other Girondists followed the Queen's, the news kept Southey " a whole night sleepless." To Bedford he confessed: " The murder of Brissot has completely harrowed up my faculties, and I begin to believe that virtue can only aspire to content in obscurity; for happiness is out of the question. I look round the world, and everywhere find the same mournful spectacle—the strong tyrannising over the weak, man and beast; the same depravity pervades the whole creation; oppression is triumphant everywhere, and the only difference is, that it acts in Turkey through the anger of a grand seignior (? vizier), in France of a revolutionary tribunal, and in England of a prime minister." Hopeless of improvement, disgusted alike with Tory England's aggressive war against democracy and with republican France's betrayal of liberty by accepting tyrannies and perpetrating atrocities, he went for comfort, like Wordsworth, to Godwin.

He took *Political Justice*, some nine months after its publication, from Bristol public library on 25th November, and kept it a fortnight. As Coleridge—ever discerning in appraisement of others as disastrous in direction of his own life—remarked years later to Godwin, systems of philosophy were never Southey's taste or forte: " he just looked enough into your books to believe you taught republicanism and stoicism; ergo, that he was of your opinion and you of his, and that was all." He found a momentary sedative for the shock of French atrocities in Godwin's assurance that " no important revolution was ever bloodless ";

he was satisfied that pain might be "contemned and defied by the energies of intellectual revolution"; both his individualism and his democratic ideals approved that the province of political justice lay in "removing as much as possible arbitrary distinctions, and leaving to talents and virtue the field of exertion unimpaired," while affording "to all the same opportunities and the same encouragement." But it is conceivable that he was most impressed by Godwin's definition of duty as "that mode of action on the part of the individual which constitutes the best possible application of his capacity to the general benefit."

Was Seward wrong after all in finding pleasure in reading boring books because he conceived it his duty to do so? Might he not be deceived in his conception of duty? Godwin said that "self-deception is of all things the most easy." Southey saw that he had deceived himself in conceiving his duty to lie in obeying his uncle's wish, against his own inclinations, that he should take orders. His life was his own, not his uncle's. His inclination and his talents lay with literature; he would best apply his capacity to the general benefit in writing.

Godwin, moreover, exposed the futility and unfairness of tests and oaths. Oaths lightly undertaken as mere legal formalities were meaningless, but if conceived literally as imposing real obligation, honest men could not take oaths of subservience to any institution, since they condemned themselves "to think no more for the rest of their lives." As he agreed with Godwin that "sincerity is not less essential, than equality, to the well-being of mankind," Southey saw that he could not in conscience comply with the Test Act, requiring acceptance by clergymen of all the forms of the Church of England.

So within a week of returning *Political Justice* to the library, he exclaimed, "What is to become of me at ordination heaven only knows! After keeping in the straight path so long the Test Act will be a stumbling-block to honesty." He was glad of an excuse to abandon the Church; he afterwards derided in *Letters of Espriella* the custom of clerical preferment by which men wasted their prime in waiting for deaths of their seniors to afford succession to college benefits. During the months at Bristol continual contact with Edith Fricker rendered unendurable the prospect of long years of waiting till he could afford to marry—" Let me have 200 l. a year and the comforts of domestic life," he declared, " and my ambition aspires not further."

The idea of emigration came to him at this time. Godwin argued that, if a majority of a community was agreed upon reform, it might attain its end without violence. But, so far from seeing possibility of any such agreement by a majority in England, Southey saw the massed forces of property entrenched behind Pitt's government, resisting all reform, passing repressive legislation and promoting devices of social victimisation against reformers, not scrupling to plunge half the civilised world into ruinous war so that a movement menacing their personal privileges might be stifled in its infancy. " If this world," he said, " did but contain ten thousand people of both sexes, visionary as myself, how delightfully would we repeople Greece, and turn out the Moslem." So thought Byron's supporters thirty years later. But Byron's appeal fell upon the ears of a generation bred in the shadows of war, fresh from recognition of its criminal futility, and infuriated by the present suffering of starvation, poverty and disease left in its wake. Southey felt the helplessness of a rational mind among emotions whipped to frenzy by the ruthless propaganda of warmongers. He saw a tediously grim prospect of a long and exhausting war, with people each year more hysterically unreasonable under the accumulating burden of misery and privations. " The more I see of this strange world," he wrote, " the more I am convinced that society requires desperate remedies." For the madness of war, once inflamed, there is no remedy but the disillusion incidental equally upon victory or defeat. He and his like might rush into the street, call on the maddened mob to halt and hear reason, and be trodden into the mud of ignominy by the stamp of patriotic feet. Or, like Godwin, they might scatter seeds of wisdom on the roadside, and stand aside, hoping that some seeds might grow to flower for future generations. But it is hard for youth to stand aside, and so Southey found it.

Without hope of Europe, he naturally looked across the Atlantic to the land which had lately with success asserted its independence of imperial misrule, hacked off the shackles of exploitation, declared itself the home of democratic liberty, and welcomed as valued recruits to its republic such distinguished refugees from repression as Lafayette, the first popular idol of Paris revolutionaries, Tom Paine, the outlawed author of *The Rights of Man*, and the learned Dr. Priestley, whose home was wrecked by a patriotic mob for his refutation of Edmund Burke's *Reflections on the French Revolution.* " It was the favourite intention of Cowley to retire with books to a cottage in America, and seek that happiness in solitude which he could not find in society," he wrote to an Oxford friend. " My asylum there would be sought for different reasons (and no prospect in life gives me half the pleasure this visionary one affords); I should be pleased to reside in a country where men's abilities would ensure respect; where society was upon a proper footing, and man was considered as more valuable than money; and where I could till the earth, and provide by honest industry the meat which my wife would dress with pleasing care." This last vision of himself as husbandman was conjured up while thinking of Miss Fricker after hewing wood in company with his old playmate Shad, who was still in his aunt's service.

When he returned to Oxford in January 1794, he definitely discarded the idea of taking orders—"innumerable and insuperable objections appeared to divinity," he told Bedford—and decided to read medicine, appeasing the prickings of conscience with the reflection that this alternative afforded " at least as many opportunities of benefiting mankind." Dutifully he attended lectures on anatomy, but nausea in the dissecting-room decided him that he could never become a surgeon. Continually recurred the vision of himself as an American pioneer—on " ground uncultivated since the creation . . . wielding the axe, now to cut down the tree, and now the snakes that nestled in it "—though he would not " leave rhyming or philosophising," and so would " realise the romance of Cowley, and even outdo the seclusion of Rousseau." He daily repined over " the education that taught me to handle a lexicon instead of a hammer." No longer Seward's example of taking pleasure in duty afforded any consolation, and he "execrated" the work demanded by his tutor; he longed for "emancipation from these useless forms, this useless life, these haunts of intolerance, vice, and folly!"

Above all else he wanted Miss Fricker. "My views in life are surely very humble," he wrote in self-pity; "I ask but honest independence." And again—"had I a sufficiency in independence, I have every reason to expect happiness. The most pleasing visions of domestic life would be realised. . . ." He sought short cuts to the desired state of independence. First, he asked Bedford to inquire at Doctor's Commons about the possibility of selling the reversion of what he thought he might inherit from his Taunton uncle; then he inquired about the chances of an ap-pointment in the same office as Bedford. In case of obtaining such a post, he would "joyfully bid adieu to Oxford, settle myself in some economical way of life, and, when I know my situation, unite myself to a woman whom I have long esteemed as a sister, and for whom I now indulge a warmer sentiment."

But his hopes were dashed by Bedford's reminder that application for an official appointment would be attended by inquiries at Oxford concerning his character and conduct, and his well-known republican views would obviate any chance of a government job. Bedford counselled him to reconsider taking orders. So "the only ray that enlivens the scene beams on America."

In this state of mind Coleridge found Southey when they met at Oxford in June 1794.

PART FOUR

PARTNERS IN PANTISOCRACY

I. THE EMIGRANTS COLLECT

WITHIN two days of their meeting the stiff and aloof Southey was a conquest of Coleridge's charm. Allen's "friend from Cambridge, Coleridge, whose poems you will oblige me by subscribing to," he wrote to Bedford, "is of most uncommon merit,—of the strongest genius, the clearest judgment, the best heart. My friend he already is, and must hereafter be yours." According to Southey, the scheme of "Pantisocracy" was first broached by Coleridge. But there is no evidence that the notion of emigration had previously occurred to Coleridge, while we know that it was uppermost in Southey's thoughts.

Their first bond of union was poetry. Southey must have been impressed when Coleridge "spouted out of Bowles" and then, with his great eyes lighting to every cadence of his melodious voice, talked interminably of Pope's weakness in seeking subjects in an artificial state of society while Bowles treated the simple realities of nature, of the inferiority of Dr. Johnson's taste to Thomas Warton's, of his own preference for Collins's odes to Gray's, of the habit of translating prose thoughts into poetic language induced by the malpractice of writing Latin verse. Southey's associates had been hitherto mediocrities, admiring his superior powers and accepting his ideas as inspirations of genius. But all his supposed innovations were commonplaces in this man's conversation, which itself, in its limitless variety and spate of words, was unlike any he had ever heard. It may have been later that Coleridge first expounded his deductions from Akenside's *Pleasures of Imagination,* arguing that imagination is the faculty by which man perceives and reveals virtue, truth, and beauty, as they exist only in nature. It may have been that Southey first drew Coleridge's attention to Akenside's poem, which influenced the work of both during the next few years. In either case, when Southey succeeded in interrupting the flow of Coleridge's monologue, he mentioned his *Joan of Arc,* and how its moral lay in Joan's deriving her power from being natural and, hence, sincere and honest. The antithesis of Wordsworth in his attitude to the work of others, Coleridge never stinted praise for merit; most likely he won Southey's heart by reading aloud passages of *Joan* with interjections of appreciation and applause.

The ice of his reserve thus thawed, Southey spoke freely of himself, his ambitions and his present problems. The bond between them strengthened on discovering their kinship in politics, and Southey's quotation of Cowley's desire to retire with books to America fired Coleridge's romantic imagination. While Southey saw himself alone, returning after a day's hard work with his hands to a domestic hearth graced by his Edith and then settling to write by candlelight, Coleridge pictured a community of congenial souls enjoying this attractive existence, escaping from Europe and England where the ideal of liberty was being crucified by war, where the few advocates of truth were ostracised and persecuted, where the means to live depended on moral prostitution and lip-service to convention.[1] He had devoted friends who would follow him; Southey had the faithful Shad and could persuade the Fricker family by joining his influence with that of Robert Lovell, a young Quaker who had lately married Edith's eldest sister Mary. Why should they not follow Dr. Priestley's example in emigrating to the new world and founding a model state which would in time convert the old world by its example?

[1]Apparently D. H. Lawrence was unaware that Coleridge had been inspired by the same idea and emotions a hundred and twenty years before, when, in 1915, he wrote: "I want to gather together about twenty souls and sail away from this world of war and squalor and found a little colony where there shall be no money but a sort of communism as far as necessaries of life go, and some real decency. It is to be a colony built up on the real decency which is in each member of the community. A community which is established upon the assumption of goodness in the members, instead of the assumption of badness."—*Letters of D. H. Lawrence,* edited by Aldous Huxley, London, 1932, p. 215.

Thus the scheme was introduced by Coleridge, but only after Southey had suggested it by confiding his own inclination to emigration. "The scheme was talked of," said Southey, "but not by any means determined on." Allen agreed to be an emigrant; so did George Burnett, one of Southey's closest Balliol friends. But Southey could not definitely commit himself till he had made sure that his Edith would consent to the project. Coleridge immediately supplied the name of the scheme— pantisocracy. All kinds, in every way, were to be equally strong, as opposed to aristocracy, the creed of individualism, by which the best governed inferiors, and democracy, by which the people elected representatives whom they believed to be the best.

Coleridge remained at Oxford till the end of term. He then proceeded on his walk to Wales with Hucks, while Southey and Burnett went together to Bath. From Gloucester, "a nothing-to-be-said-about town," Coleridge wrote his first letter to Southey, full of enthusiasm for their project. But in this letter appeared the first germ of dissension. While he and Hucks, at the end of a day's walk, were dining on lamb, green peas, and salad, "a little girl with a half-famished sickly baby in her arms" looked in at the open window and begged a bit of bread and meat. Coleridge was affected with pity, and with anger at the system which permitted such poverty, but he was diverted from these reflections by Hucks's reaction. Hucks was annoyed at an impertinent intrusion; no doubt it was bad that such things could be, but he had paid for his dinner, and a gentleman ought to be free to eat in peace. Hucks, said Coleridge, was "a man of cultivated, though not vigorous understanding," with feelings "all on the side of humanity," but he was occasionally capable of such want of feeling owing to "the lingering remains of aristocracy." Under the system of pantisocracy, Hucks's feelings and the child's poverty would be alike impossible, for—Coleridge coined another word—they would "aspheterize" (from ά, non, and σφέτερος, proprius—not their own), everything being vested in common ownership.

Coleridge told Southey that his reply "made me melancholy." He rebuked Southey for "mock-humility" in saying that Hucks

E

had "my understanding." But Southey was not pretending to modesty; he was hinting that he felt sympathy with Hucks in resenting the child's intrusion on genteel privacy. At this stage he was not prepared to say so, but he had no feeling for "aspheterism." On the contrary, he had an exclusive sense of property. "My views in life are surely very humble," he had written; he wanted "a sufficiency in independence," and he was aggrieved against the society which denied him such independence without apprenticeship to a distasteful calling. He was, in fact, like so many democrats, an individualist, resentful of the privilege that afforded to inferior minds opportunities denied to his own, but prepared jealously to cherish the privilege to which his accomplishments were entitled.

But so far Coleridge did not doubt Southey's idealism. He thought he was only momentarily depressed by the antagonism of home influences. He warned him against such despondency as had driven himself into his army escapade, begging him, "Be you wise by my experience," and exhorted him to be strong in his resolution not to take orders. He sent him the "Lines Written at the King's Arms, Ross," celebrating the memory of "the Man of Ross," who had formerly occupied the inn,—one of the "wild flowers of poesy" which he plucked as he walked, and wrote down in "a little blank book" he had bought at Gloucester.

From Ross he and Hucks proceeded to Hereford and Leominster, and thence by Llanfyllin and Llangollen to Wrexham. There, on Sunday morning 15th July, he saw a face which recalled "'Thoughts full of bitterness and images' too dearly loved! now past and but 'Remembered like sweet sounds of yesterday!'" It was Eliza Evans, Mary's sister, who lived with her grandmother at Wrexham. He "retreated with all possible speed" to the inn, and escaped being seen. But worse followed; as he stood at the window, he saw Eliza pass down the street with Mary herself, who was on a visit to her grandmother from London. He "turned sick and all but fainted away." He was unable either to eat or sleep till he moved next day to Ruthin and resumed his letter to Southey.

The cause of his consternation is easily surmised. Since his enlistment in December he had not seen Mary. Before going from Reading to Cambridge, he had had no opportunity, and after humbling himself to his brothers and the college dons, he had hesitated before the greater humiliation of excusing his conduct to her. At Cambridge, expressing hunger for his idealised woman in the first draft of *Lewti*, he had dressed his ideal in Mary's image. He was not explicitly in love with her, but he passionately adored the ideal she represented in his mind. The sight of her smote him with aching desire, yet he panicked at the prospect of explaining his long silence at a chance encounter, when his presence on a pleasure trip would discount his excuse of having lacked an opportunity to visit her.

To Southey he wrote that " her image " remained " in the sanctuary of my heart "—that, though he knew she loved him, he had never dared " even in a whisper " to avow his passion, since he had no immediate prospects and feared to " make her miserable." He told Southey that there were few men of whose delicacy he thought so highly as to confide " all this," but while all his life he could never resist the self-relief of disemburdening his emotions to his friends, this present confidence at once witnessed the friendship he already felt for Southey and the sincerity of his feelings towards Mary Evans. He consoled himself that " love is a local anguish "; already he felt " not half so miserable " by being at Ruthin sixteen miles distant from Mary, and looked forward to forgetfulness " amid the terrible graces of the wild wood scenery."

While Coleridge walked in Wales with Hucks—who wrote an account of the tour, but unluckily in commonplace guide-book style—Southey was engaged with practical arrangement of his personal affairs. He confided the scheme to Robert Lovell, who agreed to join the party and introduced him to Joseph Cottle, a young Bristol publisher, whose publication of *Joan of Arc* Southey hoped might pay his passage and purchase " some few acres, a spade and a plough." He had arranged to meet Coleridge in Wales, and take him to meet Edmund Seward, whom he hoped to interest in the scheme. But he could not venture upon revealing his plans to Miss Tyler, who, he knew, would be even more outraged by his proposed misalliance with a milliner than by his emigrant design.

So he delayed at Bristol till Coleridge, having completed his tour, joined him there. " Then it was that we resolved on going to America," and after confirming the decision with Lovell, Coleridge and Southey set off to convey news of their final decision to Burnett at his father's farm near Bridgwater. Burnett himself was enthusiastic for the plan. Talented, highly-strung, fervent in his belief in the principles of the French Revolution, he suffered vexation from the disapproval of orthodox country neighbours, and asked nothing better than to shake from his shoes the soil of an England engaged in a hypocritical war to reinstate the Bourbons in France. His father was sympathetic, but probably offered the practical advice that, as they proposed to live by agriculture, they would do well to include among their number a practical farmer. So George Burnett proposed that they should invite his friend Tom Poole of Nether Stowey.

Poole was a man of rare worth such as occasionally occurs in the lives of men of genius but never figures in the world of success. Now aged twenty-nine—seven years older than Coleridge and nearly nine than Southey—he was born and he died in the small, unprepossessing town of Nether Stowey, where he inherited his father's tannery business, his early apprenticeship to which denied him the education that his love of books eagerly craved. The wrongs of the people excited his sympathy with the French Revolution, and after reading Paine's *Rights of Man*, he became " a kind of political Ishmaelite " among the local farmers and small gentry, who voted Tory on the principle that what was good enough for their grandfathers was good enough for them, and provided the readiest dupes for newspaper propaganda. To encourage education he founded a lending library at Stowey, and was thereupon suspected of distributing seditious pamphlets among the common people. He believed that " if the French are conquered, Europe is enslaved," and George Burnett may have heard him declare, as he wrote to another friend, that " America seems the only asylum of peace and liberty—the only place where the dearest feelings of man are not insulted."

His highly respectable cousins were much concerned about his reputation, many of the locals declaring that he " ought to be denounced as a public enemy." With family loyalty they defended him, but wished " he would cease to torment us with his democratick sentiments; but he is never happy until the subject of politicks is introduced, and, as we all differ so much from him, we wish to have no conversation about it." One of these cousins, John Poole, had just secured an Oriel fellowship and was about to take orders. So far from being a reactionary, he had advocated at Oxford " abolition of the slavish duties affix'd to the office of servitors, Bible-clerks, etc.," and in an age when country parsons cared mainly for field sports and the pleasures of the table, he took pains to preach in the simplest language as best suited to his congregations' understanding. But when his cousin Tom introduced him, on 18th August 1794, to two strangers, one " an undergraduate of Oxford, the other of Cambridge," he felt " extremely indignant " at their " odious and detestable ill-feeling," since both were " shamefully hot with Democratic rage as regards politics, and both Infidel as to religion."

Inevitably Coleridge impressed Tom Poole, and though he and Southey passed only part of a day at Stowey, he contrived in so short a space to leave a familiar knowledge of his history and personality. Poole, who spelt his name " Coldridge " in the old Devon way and took him for " about five and twenty," described him as possessing " splendid abilities—he is, I understand, a shining scholar, gained the prize for the Greek verses the first or second year he entered the University, and is now engaged in publishing a selection of the best modern Latin poems with a poetical translation. He speaks with much elegance and energy, and with uncommon facility, but he, as it generally happens to men of his class, feels the justice of Providence in the want of those inferior abilities which are necessary to the rational discharge of the common duties of life. His aberrations from prudence, to use his own expression, have been great; but he now promises to be as sober and rational as his most sober friends could wish. In religion he is a Unitarian, if not a Deist; in politicks a Democrat, to the utmost extent of the word."

With the less expansive Southey, Poole was not so impressed; he was "a younger man, without the splendid abilities of Coldridge, though possessing much information, particularly metaphysical," and " more violent in his principles than Coldridge himself. In Religion, shocking to say in a mere Boy as he is, I fear he wavers between Deism and Atheism." It seems that Southey, feeling himself outshone, sought to impress with vehemence whenever he contrived to interrupt his companion's loquacity.

According to the plan expounded to Poole, " twelve gentlemen of good education and liberal principles " were to leave for America the following April with " twelve ladies." In the meantime they intended to see as much as possible of each other, to become intimately acquainted and to settle details of their procedure on arrival at the Susquehanna river, which had been lately publicised as a frontier settlement of supreme natural beauty. From Adam Smith's remark in *The Wealth of Nations*—recently borrowed by Southey from Bristol library—that there is not more than one productive man in twenty, they argued that, if each man worked two or three hours a day, their produce—which would be " aspheterised " for the common use—would suffice to support the colony. With the aid of a large common library, their remaining time would be spent in " study, liberal discussions, and the education of their children." While the women would be concerned with the care of children " and other occupations suited to their strength," great attention would be paid to cultivating their minds. Each would be free " to enjoy his own religious and political opinions," but—significantly— Coleridge and Southey had not yet agreed " whether the marriage contract shall be dissolved if agreeable to one or both parties."

Poole allowed that, if the scheme succeeded, " they would, indeed, realise the age of reason." But he doubted if human nature was " yet perfect enough " for its success, especially as its exponents were handicapped by education in " a society in a high degree civilised and corrupted." He liked the idea of settling in America and of accompanying them to watch the outcome of their scheme, but he thought " a man would do well first to see the country and his future hopes, before he removed his connections or any large portion of his property there." He was not prepared to pull up his roots for a hazard. The tannery business depended on his management; his father, who died the following year, was old and ailing; if his father died, he could not leave his mother.

Coleridge and Southey thus returned to Bristol without Poole's promise to participate, but fortified by the qualified approval of a practical man of affairs. Coleridge, as always, was intoxicated in elaboration of an idea, and stimulated by the need for repeatedly producing arguments to combat protests from intended converts. Southey, once committed definitely to the project, devoted all his energies to the single purpose of achieving the plan; he had shocked Poole by his vehemence into supposing him an atheist, and he used the same vehemence to persuade George Burnett to his own objections against taking orders, as a means of reconciling him to emigration. He decided that each emigrant would require an initial capital of £125. Burnett's father would supply his share, Coleridge intended that his " Latin Poems " should provide his, and Southey, while cherishing hopes of something from his aunt, staked faith in his *Joan of Arc*. He and Lovell also proposed to publish their occasional verse in a joint volume, and to swell the common fund, he, Lovell, and Coleridge collaborated in a poetic drama, *The Fall of Robespierre*, each engaging to write an act in twenty-four hours—Coleridge the first, Southey the second, and Lovell the third. Characteristically Coleridge failed to complete his contribution in the allotted time, though his share alone contains passages of merit; Lovell's act failed to conform with the design, so Southey re-wrote it, and by the time he had supplied the second and third acts, Coleridge had completed the first.

To all their activities and declamations the Fricker girls, their mother, and Southey's mother formed an admiring audience. With Lovell married to the eldest sister and Southey partnered by his Edith, Coleridge and Burnett were thrown much into the company of Sarah (whose name Coleridge always wrote "Sara") and Martha Fricker. Coleridge's fatal fascination captivated the plump, pretty, rather fluffy Sara, and encouraged by her evident admiration and the excitement of prospective comradeship in a great adventure, a less sentimentally romantic young man than Coleridge would have been tempted to tender by-play in the intervals of declamatory eloquence—a handclasp, graceful compliments, caressing glances. According to Southey, "Coleridge made his engagement with Miss Fricker . . . not a little to my astonishment, for he had talked of being deeply in love with a certain *Mary Evans.*"

Remembering the emotional avowal of Coleridge's letter from Wrexham written only six weeks before, Southey might have been expected to feel more than astonishment; he might have felt indignant suspicion that Coleridge was trifling with the affections of his prospective sister-in-law. That he expressed neither indignation nor suspicion suggests that Coleridge made no definite engagement with Sara Fricker, and that the impression of its existence was created by Southey himself. Intent on the success of the pantisocratic plan, he was determined that his colleagues should be as closely wedded to the scheme as he himself would be when he announced his decision to discontinue residence at Oxford, and how could Coleridge's participation be more certainly assured than by his being engaged to marry one of the Frickers? For the same purpose he persuaded Burnett to decide against taking orders, and possibly persuaded him to propose marriage to Martha Fricker. Burnett did propose, but he was a pedestrian campfollower in the project of which Coleridge was the nobly-mounted inspiration, and Martha rejected him.

To suspect Southey of implementing the engagement is not to accuse him of cold-blooded design. The Frickers, pretty and penniless, needed husbands, and seeing that Sara was attracted, Mary and Edith, themselves in love with Lovell and Southey, cannot have been wanting in devices to leave her much in Coleridge's company and in playful innuendoes exciting Sara's blushes and so flattering Coleridge's vanity. Southey was puritanical in his attitude to women. During youth and early manhood he never cast a glance at another besides his Edith; he could feel no tolerance for Coleridge's tendency to sentimentalise in the company of every pretty woman he met. Certainly he used all his powers of persuasion to make Coleridge commit himself. Begging him not to allow " any *individual* feelings " to interfere with his allegiance to the pantisocratic plan, he declared vehemently that a fanciful apostle of the system " must comparatively disregard his father and mother and wife and children and brethren and sisters, yea and his own life also, or he could not be our disciple." We are the creatures of circumstance, he argued, and our emotions must conform with our motives. How then could Coleridge embrace uncertainty in lingering loyalty to Mary Evans, when he could accept the certainty of Sara Fricker as his partner in pantisocracy?

So, fortified in his axiom that " love is a local anguish," Coleridge accepted the situation. After spending August between Bristol and Bath (where Southey's mother lived after his father's death), he left for London, feeling, in the flush of pantisocratic enthusiasm, that he might go far and fare worse in finding an emigrant partner.

2. COMPLICATIONS IN LOVE AND POLITICS

Aware of its hurried origin, Joseph Cottle, the Bristol bookseller, declined to publish *The Fall of Robespierre,* and on his arrival in town, Coleridge lost no time in seeking a publisher. A fellow Cantab and Christ's Hospitaller named Franklin introduced him to George Dyer, also an old boy of Christ's Hospital, though seventeen years Coleridge's senior. Amiable, sensitive, simple-minded, a devoted friend and fervent in his enthusiasms, Dyer was a hack journalist. He hung, said Hazlitt, " like a film and cobweb upon letters, or like the dust on the outside of knowledge, which should not too rudely be brushed aside." A democrat, he had lately published by subscription *Complaints of the Poor People of England*; when Coleridge expounded

pantisocracy, "he was enraptured—pronounced it impregnable."
Himself a Unitarian, he knew Dr. Priestley, who, he was sure,
would join the pantisocrats on their arrival in America. He
liked "hugely" Coleridge's first act of *Robespierre;* it was a
"nail that would drive," and he offered to approach his own
bookseller, Robinson. As "Rob. was in the country," he took
the manuscript to Johnson, the publisher of Wordsworth's first
poems. He also obtained "a few guineas" from the *Morning
Chronicle* for some of Coleridge's verses, including the "Elegy
imitated from Akenside."

Coleridge called on Southey's friend Bedford, but was frigidly
received. Bedford was "sorry, very sorry" about the decision
to emigrate, and assured that Southey would "leave *all* his
friends behind him." Coleridge felt malicious delight in shocking
Bedford's propriety by giving his address as the Angel Inn,
off Newgate Street, where he had gone to be near Christ's
Hospital. Bedford "did not stare, and I thought highly of his
civility—So you see, Southey, your new Cambridge friend has
not done you much Honor."

Nightly he went to "an Alehouse, by courtesy called a Coffee
house," the Salutation and Cat in Newgate Street, where he and
his friends drank porter and punch round the fire in a private
room. Here he met an old schoolfellow just returned from five
years in America, who came every evening, as he said, to "benefit
by conversation." According to his information, land was
cheaper in America than in England. Twelve men could "*easily*
clear *three hundred* Acres in 4 or 5 months," and "for six hundred
Dollars a thousand Acres might be cleared and houses built on
them." "He never saw a Byson in his life"; besides "its
excessive beauty," the Susquehanna had the advantage of
"security from hostile Indians"; "the Mosquitoes are not so
bad as our Gnats"; the women's teeth there being bad was
probably due to neglect and diet rather than climate. All this
he punctually reported to Southey, with remembrances to
everybody; "to Lovell and Mrs. Lovell my *fraternal* love—To
Miss F. *more*" and "do not forget to give my respects to Shad."

After a fortnight in London, he returned to Cambridge and

reflected in his room at Jesus on how much had happened since he left it. "America! Southey! Miss Fricker!" "Yes," he told Southey, "you are right. Even Love is the creature of strong motive. I certainly love her. I *think* of her incessantly and with unspeakable tenderness." With pantisocracy " my head, my heart, are all alive," and in democratic ecstasy he wrote in capital letters, "SHAD GOES WITH US. HE IS MY BROTHER!"

Having reached Cambridge on 17th September, he wrote thus ecstatically to Southey on the 18th. But next morning came a letter from Southey upbraiding him for not writing to Sara. Immediately he wrote again, saying that from the moment of his arrival at Cambridge, he had been writing letters to Southey, his mother, and Lovell, "to complete a parcel." He had not written to Sara, because "Miss F. did not authorise me to direct immediately to her," apparently the arrangement being that news of him should be conveyed to her through Southey. Evidently Sara had not then the same conception of her engagement's finality as Southey. From London he had written twice to Southey; he had not written more because he intended "daily to go to Cambridge." But he had been "taken ill, very ill," and "Recollect, Southey, that when you mean to go to a place to-morrow, and to-morrow, and to-morrow, the time that intervenes is lost." Though mercifully he could not recognise this remark as prophetic of his future fatal procrastination, he was characteristically always conscious of his weakness. Years later he was to tell Sara that De Quincey was "as great a *to-morrower* to the full as your poor husband."

Southey's reproaches were clearly undeserved. Coleridge had written weekly, which was frequent for those days of expensive postage, and kept Southey fully apprised of his doings. Johnson had declined *The Fall of Robespierre*, but Coleridge quickly persuaded the Cambridge Bookseller, Benjamine Flower, to take it, and it was published within a month. If he could show little success in securing converts to pantisocracy, it was not for lack of eloquent persuasion. Samuel Favell and the younger Le Grice, who each had still another year at Christ's Hospital, had asked to be allowed to join the colony in America when they had completed their residence at Cambridge. But George Caldwell, Coleridge's friend and contemporary at Jesus, evaded argument, laughingly fearing for his own sanity in the presence of "a madman of genius." He shrewdly remarked that the strength of Coleridge's imagination had intoxicated his reason, while the acuteness of his reason had given a directing influence to his imagination.

The sceptical Caldwell further cooled enthusiasm already chilled by Southey's impetuously outspoken distrust. Coleridge argued against Southey's "precipitance." He confessed that he had been himself "the slave of impulse," but his own "inconsistencies" had inspired "reluctance to think ill of any one"; Southey, on the other hand, "having never erred," felt "more *indignation* at error than *pity* for it." With truth he said that there was "*phlogiston*" in Southey's heart. Within a week he had evidence that Southey considered nobody's feelings in pursuit of his ends, for a letter came from young Favell saying that Southey had written to him, expressing indignation at Coleridge's neglecting to write to Sara. Coleridge practised his principle of forbearance; he was "beyond measure distressed and agitated" by Southey's letter to Favell, but instead of expressing annoyance at such disloyalty, he exclaimed, "My God, My God! what a deal of pain you must have suffered before you wrote that letter to Favell."

But he misjudged Southey in attributing to him his own emotional sensibility. Southey was hotly intent only on keeping Coleridge up to scratch. He lacked the sensibility to appreciate that the surest way of keeping him was by appealing to his better feelings and encouraging his enthusiasm—that the attempt to drive him by distrusting reproach only plunged him into a whirlpool of unhappy introspection and self-distrust, in which, floundering helplessly, he caught at straws for safety. As Coleridge wrote to his brother two months later, when pleading guilty to the constitutional vice of indolence, "anxieties that stimulate others infuse an additional narcotic into my mind." Southey had not returned to Oxford, and having thus abandoned his uncle's wish that he should take orders, satisfied his puritanical self-righteousness by renouncing his uncle's financial assistance. He had burnt his boats, and wanted Coleridge to burn his likewise; Coleridge's return to Cambridge seemed to him a compromise suggestive of keeping open an avenue of retreat. He did not reflect how far his conduct was influenced by the inclination to remain near his Edith, and that Coleridge lacked the same attraction at Bristol to keep him from Cambridge.

His failure to return to Oxford and his association with the Frickers at last compelled a confession of his plans to his aunt. Miss Tyler did not bother to consider the possible advantages of pantisocracy; she concentrated all her anger on her nephew's proposed misalliance with a penniless milliner. She abused " poor Lovell most unmercifully," attributing to him " the whole scheme " on account of his relationship to the obnoxious Frickers, and finally ordered her nephew out of her house, saying she would never see his face again and, if he wrote, she would return his letters unopened. Southey went to his mother's house at Bath, and next morning wrote theatrically to Sara Fricker (significantly to Coleridge's Sara—not to Edith, her mother, or Mary Lovell): " Amid the pelting of the pitiless storm did I, Robert Southey, the Apostle of Pantisocracy, depart from the city of Bristol, my natal place—at the hour of five in a wet windy evening on the 17th of October, 1794, wrapped up in my father's old greatcoat and my own cogitations." What admiration was such heroic nonchalance calculated to excite in the fluttered bosoms of the little milliners!

To his younger brother Tom, who had lately joined the navy as a midshipman, he wrote jauntily: " Here's a row! here's a kick-up! here's a pretty commence! we have had a revolution in the College Green, and I have been turned out of doors in a wet night." He described how he left his aunt's; how " poor Shadrach " saw him depart with astonishment—" Why, Sir, you be'nt going to Bath at this time of night, and in this weather!" —and asked to be sent for when the emigration party was ready; how he went to Lovell's, clapt on his father's old greatcoat, "swallowed a glass of brandy, and set off." But they had all been unhappy "till this grand scheme of Pantisocracy flashed upon our minds, and now all is perfectly delightful." He is full of enthusiasm, determined to leave for America in March, and ends in Henley's "captain of my soul" style—"I am fully possessed by the great cause to which I have devoted myself, my conduct has been open, sincere, and just; and though the world were to scorn and neglect me, I should bear their contempt with calmness." In the whole length of a long letter he made no reference to Coleridge. Defending Lovell from his aunt's attributing to him the "whole scheme" of pantisocracy, he told his brother, "you know it was concerted between Burnett and me."

To Coleridge he wrote theatrically, but not jauntily. He emphasised the sacrifice he had already made for their scheme, and proceeded to practical details. He could not approve of Coleridge's idea of treating poor Shadrach as his brother: Shad's children would be educated as theirs and in such a manner as to render them incapable of blushing at want of education in their parents, but while Shad and his wife should dine at the same table and "be treated with as much equality as they would wish," they would be expected to "perform their part of labour for which their education has fitted them."

Coleridge meanwhile had made the disconcerting discovery that, while the thought of Mary Evans in absence awakened the ache of desire, he could endure without emotion the absence of Sara Fricker. To Cambridge at this time came a theatrical troupe including a Miss Brunton, one of the six beautiful daughters of John Brunton of Norwich, the eldest of whom had married Robert Merry, the Della Cruscan poet. Coleridge, in his friend Caldwell's company, deliberately paid court to the young actress in the hope that "her exquisite beauty and uncommon accomplishments might have cured one passion by another." He presented her with a copy of *The Fall of Robespierre* together with some verses in manuscript, which he gave to another Cambridge friend, Francis Wrangham, for inclusion in a book of verse about to be published. Like Middleton, Wrangham was denied an expected fellowship on account of his political views, and on a final visit to Cambridge before settling at Cobham, in Surrey, to take pupils, he joined Coleridge and Caldwell in their attentions to Miss Brunton. Coleridge told Wrangham that Caldwell was " the rather a favourite " with Miss Brunton, but she confided to Caldwell her admiration of Coleridge's " *courtly* and polished manners " and " *gentlemanly* address," and when the party left Cambridge, her father and mother warmly invited him to visit them at Norwich in the Christmas vacation. He looked forward the more to visiting Norwich as Middleton was living there, and he proposed to stay with Wrangham before going.

But pleasant thoughts of Miss Brunton, Norwich, and Cobham were dispelled by the reception of Southey's letter, along with one from brother George and another from Mary Evans. It has been suggested that Coleridge invented the letter from Mary for Southey's benefit, and it may be that, the better to dramatise the pathos of his position, he ascribed to her passages from George's letter, which he described as " all remonstrance and anguish, and suggestions that I am in danger! " On the other hand, George Coleridge may have asked her to unite her influence with his in dissuasion from the pantisocratic scheme, or she may have written on her own initiative after hearing of the scheme from Favell or other Christ's Hospital friends. Anyhow, on 21st October Coleridge wrote the sonnet " On a Discovery Made Too Late," and on the same day began his letter to Southey, " To you alone, Southey, I write the first part of this letter," meaning that it was not for Sara to read. He then quoted from Mary's letter arguments which might have been equally well submitted by Caldwell, his brother George, or even Miss Brunton.

Though " you have already suffered too much from self-accusation," she begged him " to consider long and deeply " before entering into any rash schemes. " There is an eagerness in your Nature, which is ever hurrying you in the sad Extreme." She had heard that he meant to leave England " on a Plan so absurd and extravagant " that, if she could suppose it true, she would be obliged " to listen with a more patient Ear " to suggestions which she had " rejected a thousand times with scorn and anger." She then appealed (as brother George undoubtedly did) to his love of country and his religion—" You have too much sensibility to be an Infidel "—and finished, " I shall always feel that I have been your *Sister*."

" I loved her, Southey, almost to madness," he declared, adding with more sober truth, " Her image was never absent from me . . . for *more* than three years." He assured Southey that his resolution had not faltered, " but I want a comforter," and asked him to appreciate how, with such feelings, he found it " no easy task " to write to Sara. Replying to Southey's revised idea of their scheme he said: " I will most assuredly go with you to America, on this plan, but remember, Southey, this is *not our plan*, nor can I defend it." The " leading idea of pantisocracy " was " to make men *necessarily* virtuous by removing all motives to evil," which was impossible without complete equality to exclude competition, jealousy, and envy. Southey should have said to his dependents, Shad and his wife, " Be my slaves, and ye shall be my equals," and to his wife and sister, " Resign the *name* of Ladyship and ye shall retain the *thing*." Sarcastically he asked, " Is every family to possess one of these unequal equals, these Helot Egalités? " If so, the inference was that " the scheme of pantisocracy is impracticable." He doubted too if the hearts of the women were " *all* with us," and whether they fully recognised their part in the scheme, though he thought Edith and Sara were exceptions.

Finally he talked of his proposed book on pantisocracy, which would comprise " all that is good in Godwin." On Southey's recommendation he had been reading *Political Justice* " with the greatest attention," but " I think not so highly of him as you do."

A few days later, he wrote again, after spending an evening with Dr. Edwards, " the great Grecian of Cambridge and heterodox divine," and a democrat named Lushington, with whom he discussed pantisocracy for six hours, at the end of which both " declared the system impregnable, supposing the assigned quantum of virtue and genius in the first individuals." This provision prompted a renewal of his expostulations on equality and on the need for "strengthening the minds of the women," while reminding him that they had not originally intended to welcome children in the party. "These children—the little Frickers, for instance, and your brothers—are they not already deeply tinged with the prejudices and errors of society? Have they not learned from their schoolfellows *Fear* and *Selfishness*, of which the necessary offsprings are Deceit and desultory Hatred? How are we to prevent them from infecting the minds of *our* children?" He repeats that he will accompany Southey "on an imperfect system," but asks, "must our system be thus necessarily imperfect?"

Again, in the first week of November, he reverted to these protests, interrupting his letter by reading *The Robbers* of Schiller, which excited him to address a sonnet to Schiller and exclaim, "My God, Southey, who is this Schiller, this convulser of the heart?" Besides the menace of inequality to the system he could not see its practical advantage. Since the men were to contribute equal shares of labour, Shad could give them no service and as to Shad's wife, was she to be denied domestic concerns of her own? He wished that "the two mothers were *not* to go, and that the children stayed with them." He hoped Southey would not think him wanting in feeling, but "*That* Mrs. Fricker! We shall have her teaching the infants *Christianity*—I mean, that mongrel whelp that goes under its name,—teaching them by stealth in some ague fit of superstition."

He reassured Southey on the score that his family might attempt to prevent his emigration. "*Advice* offered with *respect* from a brother; *affected coldness*, an assumed *alienation* mixed with involuntary bursts of *anguish* and disappointed *affection*; questions concerning the mode in which I would have it mentioned to my aged mother—these are the daggers which are plunged into *my* peace." But he was more disturbed mentally than he confided to Southey. To suggest that he trumped up objections to Southey's plan in the hope of evading participation is not only to ignore the facts, but to be cynical at the expense of psychology. He said plainly that he would go to America on Southey's plan, but he was genuinely distressed by Southey's practical compromise threatening the integrity of the pantisocratic idea. Older men whose opinion commanded respect, from Tom Poole to Lushington and Dr. Edwards, had emphasised the necessity in the pioneers of virtue untainted by worldly vices, and Coleridge saw that, while he and his colleagues might mould their young wives' minds, they could not hope to alter commonplace women of middle age, like Mrs. Southey and Mrs. Fricker, with characters unstirrably stagnant in suburbanism.

Nevertheless there was nothing to tempt him to emigration except his disgust with the war-stricken world that preferred outworn abuses to every argument of humanity or reason. On 6th November he wrote soberly to his brother George in defence of his views. Hysterical patriots accused him of sedition in putting pro-French sentiments into the mouths of French politicians in the play, and making them utter the usual politicians' rhetorical platitude that their country's spirit of liberty could not be subdued by its enemies. Suppose it was his opinion that France could not be subdued by force, was it " an anti-pacific one? " Because he was against the war, he was labelled a democrat, but he knew " many violent anti-reformists . . . as violent against the *war* on the ground that it may introduce that reform which they (perhaps not unwisely) imagine would chant the dirge of our constitution." But he denied that he was a democrat. He saw plainly that " the present is *not* the highest state of society of which we are *capable*," and after studying Locke, Hartley, and other philosophers, he thought he could see " the point of possible perfection " at which the world might eventually arrive, but he could not see " how to lead mankind from one point to the other." Here lay his motive for emigration. He and his friends might found a colony, as Penn had founded Pennsylvania, to win the world by example to a better order.

George's arguments weighed only in appealing to his emotions. He recoiled always from wounding people, and suffered when incurring displeasure and censure. But above all he was disturbed by Southey's determination to drive him, not only into a compromise with their original plan, but into a makeshift marriage. At twenty-two, a man does not lightly contemplate the union of his life with that of a woman he does not love. In Sara Fricker's case he had proved only too certainly that love was " a local anguish " ; unhappily not even the charms of Miss Brunton had been able to dislodge the image of Mary Evans. He told Wrangham in the last week of October that he was unwell and in low spirits; he was tortured by the prospect of remaining till the end of term at Cambridge and then proceeding to Bristol tamely to surrender to his fate with Sara. So in desperation he drove up to London on 8th November in a friend's phaeton, probably with the express intention of trying his luck with Mary Evans.

As usual, he procrastinated. It was more than a month before he ventured to plead his suit with Mary, and then he wrote rather than face her in person. The immediate motive of his departure for London may have been the acquittal on 5th November of Thomas Hardy, secretary of the Corresponding Society, who had been arrested, along with other members of the society, on a charge of high treason. Already in the provinces noted reformers had been tried for treason, and corrupt judges had sentenced them to transportation. Hardy's was a test case. If he had been convicted, his associates—including Horne Tooke, Thomas Holcroft, and John Thelwall—would have suffered the same fate on similar evidence, and the Government would have established a reign of terror in persecution of all opponents of its policy. William Godwin, as the author of *Political Justice,* knew himself to be a marked man; he had so far escaped arrest only because he avowed himself an opponent of force in any form, and therefore refused to associate in any society or union formed to urge its opinions by collective pressure. He took a bold course, attending the trials daily, and after the charges had been preferred against Hardy, he published in the *Morning Chronicle* an open letter to the Lord Chief Justice exposing the fallacy of the charges. Hardy and his associates were accused of endeavouring " to change the form of government established, by publishing or causing to be published, divers books and pamphlets and by belonging to political societies having the same object." Godwin

pointed out that the charge attempted to construct a treasonable plot out of individual acts which were not in themselves treasonable—in fact, " out of many facts, no one of which was capital, to compose a capital crime." Hardy's counsel adopted Godwin's arguments; in reply to the case of the attorney-general, Sir John Scott—later the detested reactionary Lord Chancellor Eldon—that Hardy and his friends had sought " to tread in the footsteps of the French Jacobins," he showed that they had only advocated radical parliamentary reform by constitutional means.

After Hardy's acquittal on 5th November, the Government rallied all its forces in a desperate assault on Horne Tooke on the 17th. Unlike Hardy, Tooke was a celebrity, who, all his life a sharp thorn in the seat of authority, had begun to write his witty and erudite *Diversions of Purley* during an imprisonment for promoting a subscription in aid of Americans " barbarously murdered at Lexington " in 1775. He was defended by Thomas Erskine, the greatest of Liberal lawyers; the Prime Minister himself was among the witnesses for the Crown, and Sheridan among those for the defence. " The self-possession, the wit and humour of Mr. Tooke . . . presently set the court in a roar "; the unpopular Pitt was caught tripping in prevarication on the evidence of Sheridan; and Erskine's eloquence so effectively disposed of the prosecution that the jury required only six minutes to return a verdict of acquittal. The venerable Tooke was embraced in open court by Miss Amelia Alderson, afterwards a popular novelist as Mrs. Opie, and the cheering mob unharnessed the horses from Erskine's coach to pull him in triumph through the streets.

Coleridge may have witnessed this scene, for Erskine was the subject of the first of his *Sonnets on Eminent Characters*, published on 1st December in the *Morning Chronicle*—the paper which had printed Godwin's open letter—and beginning

" *When British freedom for an happier land*
   Spread her broad wings, that flutter'd with affright,
   Erskine! thy voice she heard, and paus'd her flight
 Sublime of hope, for dreadless thou didst stand . . ."

He may have attended the court on 1st December, when Holcroft, against whom the attorney-general declined to submit evidence which had already failed to convict Hardy and Horne Tooke, left the dock on acquittal to sit beside Godwin, and Thomas Lawrence, elected R.A. that year, was so struck by the contrast between the two friends, the bent little philosopher and the angry aggressive actor, that he drew " a spirited sketch of them in profile." Little over a fortnight later he met Holcroft when dining with Perry, proprietor of the *Morning Chronicle*, to whom he had been introduced by George Dyer.

Holcroft was a man of fifty, fierce and irascible in manner, a restless agitator against injustice, from which he had suffered much in his career as radical politician, actor, playwright, and novelist. Himself ardent in pursuit of practical reform, he felt impatience with a clever young man who seemed to be wasting his energy on escapist and impractical ideas. He inveighed violently against pantisocracy, thinking it " not virtuous "; he argued in favour of atheism; he despised Bowles's sonnets as expressing " sentiments only fit for girls." This comment on his beloved Bowles so irritated Coleridge that he deliberately baited the older man, leading him to exhibit his little smattering of metaphysics and his comparative ignorance of scholarship. Coleridge no doubt shone, as only he could shine, in curvetting round a subject on the richly caparisoned charger of fluent argument. " Sir! " exploded Holcroft, " I never knew so much real wisdom and so much rank error meet in one mind before! " " Which means, I suppose," retorted the bright young man imperturbably, " that in some things, sir, I agree with you, and in others I do not." For Holcroft's " fierceness and dogmatism," Coleridge reported to Southey, " you receive little compensation either from the veracity of his information, the closeness of his reasoning, or the splendour of his language." More favourably impressed by Coleridge than Coleridge by him, Holcroft invited him to dine the following Sunday at his house, where he met Godwin. He was even less impressed than by Holcroft. Godwin seemed to him " to possess neither the strength of intellect that discovers truth, nor the powers of imagination that decorate falsehood; he talked sophisms in jejune language." Godwin's appearance was gnome-like, with a massive head mounted on stooping shoulders and a stout, short-legged body; he had a thin voice, no sense of humour, and his conversation was ponderous and pedantic; his vanity accepted most egregious flattery, and he inclined to appear patronising to his juniors. Coleridge had already composed his sonnet of eulogy to Godwin, but in any case it was inspired by admiration solely for the philosopher's valiant intervention in the trial of Hardy. Unlike Wordsworth and Southey, he had not accepted *Political Justice* as a prophet's voice in the wilderness, and the antagonism aroused at this first meeting decided him to write a refutation of Godwin's philosophy. In later years he revised his hasty judgment, writing in his copy of *Political Justice*, "I remember few passages in ancient or modern authors that contain more just philosophy, in appropriate, chaste or beautiful diction, than the five following pages. . . . Though I did it in the zenith of his reputation, yet I feel remorse *ever* to have only spoken unkindly of such a man." As for Godwin, he kept a terse diary, recording his daily comings and goings, to which he returned in after years to note what seemed to him the year's most important happenings. In his diary for 1794 he wrote: "It was in the close of this year that I first met with Samuel Taylor Coleridge, my acquaintance with whom was ripened in the year 1800." The significance of the note is illustrated by Godwin's inclusion of Coleridge, a man nearly seventeen years his junior, as one of "the four principal oral instructors to whom I feel my mind indebted for improvement."

The *Sonnets on Eminent Characters*, as poetry the most pedestrian of Coleridge's compositions, attracted attention, and provided the money to prolong his stay in London. They were his first professional excursion into political journalism, and reflect the extreme radicalism of his views. After Erskine, Dr. Priestley, Lafayette, the Polish patriot Kosciusko, Godwin, Sheridan, and Lord Stanhope (whose plea for peace negotiations attracted, besides Coleridge's sonnet, a "dedicatory epistle" in verse from Landor) were all apostrophised in terms of praise. The sonnet to Burke hailed his genius while lamenting his apostasy; only Pitt was assailed as " yon dark scowler," who " kiss'd his country with Iscariot mouth." The non-political subjects were Bowles, Mrs. Siddons, and Southey, who, then quite unknown, appeared incongruous in such distinguished company.

In the intervals of meeting notable people like Perry, Holcroft, and Godwin, Coleridge was established in his old quarters at the Angel and going every evening round the corner for conviviality to the Salutation and Cat in Newgate Street. Here, with Dyer and other old Christ's Hospitallers, he renewed acquaintance with Charles Lamb, whom he can scarcely have remembered as a backward boy more than two years his junior at school. But Lamb remembered the senior boy whom he had admired beyond everybody, and now began a devoted attachment which lasted, with one brief interruption, for life. Lamb was himself suffering mental distress; he had been recently crossed in love and was haunted by the horror of succumbing to the disease of madness in his family. He confided his troubles to Coleridge, who undoubtedly exchanged confidences with his customary spontaneity. Together they wrote sonnets, Lamb being largely responsible for that on Mrs. Siddons published as Coleridge's; together they drank an alcoholic beverage called " egg hot " and smoked " oroonoko ", while Coleridge talked endlessly, and Lamb, apart from occasional comments in his engaging stutter, listened.

Weeks passed. Always " to-morrow " Coleridge was going to see Mary Evans before moving to Cambridge or Bristol, and as he had remarked to Southey of his previous London sojourn, the intervening time was lost. He was writing more or less regularly to Southey. He read the poems of Southey and Lovell in proof, decided that Lovell had " no taste or simplicity of feeling," but lavishly praised Southey's poems, offering emendations, some of which were accepted. He had been reading Hartley and was become " a complete necessitarian "; he told of his meeting with Holcroft, and enclosed some of his sonnets and the lines " To a Young Ass." But as Christmas approached, Southey grew impatient for his presence at Bristol, and he realised that he must make his venture with Mary Evans or resign her for ever for Miss Fricker.

So at last, fearing to face rejection in person, he wrote to her. For four years he had "*endeavoured* to smother a very ardent attachment," he had thought of her incessantly, and her "image was blended with every idea." With convincing honesty and sincerity he described the development of his feeling for her. He knew she had regarded him "merely with the kindness of a sister," and as a homeless schoolboy he had loved her gratefully for her kindness. But he had then romanticised her in his mind till he really longed for her, and now feared the prospect of losing her as the centre of his thoughts. He had "clung with desperate fondness to this phantom of love, its mysterious attractions and hopeless prospects"; though it was "a faint and rayless hope," it had soothed his solitude "with many a delightful day-dream." He asked to be restored "to *reality*, however gloomy," and promised that he would not embarrass her "by even a *look* of discontent." His letter ended with the mysterious information that he was leaving the next day for Cambridge, and "in a few months" would "seek forgetful calmness" in "incessant and useful activity" at the Temple. Probably his brother George had proposed his reading for the bar since his religious opinions forbade his taking orders, and as his delicacy deterred him from reference to emigration, lest he might seem to be seeking to influence her decision by the warning of such a drastic consequence, he mentioned this forecast of his future to suggest that her rejection of him would not influence his career.

Her reply reached him on Christmas Eve. As he told her, its firmness did honour to her understanding, its gentleness to her humanity. She blamed herself—"most unjustly!"—for not having seen that he might be led to regard her as more than a sister. "To love you," he said, "habit has made unalterable," but, "divested as it now is of all shadow of hope," the passion would "lose its disquieting power." He begged forgiveness for having pained her, and ended, "May God infinitely love you!"

He then began a letter to Southey: "I am calm, dear Southey! as an autumnal day, when the sky is covered with gray moveless clouds." After paraphrasing passages in his final letter to Mary, he told Southey that his "ideal standard of female excellence rises not above that woman," but consoled himself that, if he had married her, the excess of his affection might have "effeminated" his intellect. He could rise above the "selfish pang" of losing her. "But to marry another, O Southey! bear with my weakness. Love makes all things pure and heavenly like itself,—but to marry a woman I do *not* love, to degrade her whom I shall call my wife by making her the instrument of low desire, and on the removal of a desultory appetite to be perhaps not displeased with her absence! Enough! These refinements are the wildering fires that lead me into vice. Mark you, Southey! *I will do my duty.*" He then replied to Southey's upbraidings, warning him that his sensibilities were tempestuous—that Southey felt indignation at weakness, and "Indignation is the handsome brother of Anger and Hatred." He promised to come to Bath on Saturday the 27th; he thought of walking down; he had written to Bristol, stating no definite time of his coming to avoid disappointment. He was delaying on account of Lamb— "who like me, is a Unitarian Christian, and an advocate for the automatism of man"—whose sister was dangerously ill.

Southey went to Marlborough on Saturday to meet the "appointed waggon," but "*no S. T. Coleridge was thereon!*" He decided to wait no longer. Coleridge's confession of his rejection by Mary Evans showed that he had meditated treachery to Miss Fricker—perhaps to pantisocracy, for what might have happened if Mary had accepted him! Southey went to the Salutation and Cat, and was directed to Coleridge's lodging at the Angel. He found that Coleridge's excuse was true; Mary Lamb was ill, and her devoted brother was finding comfort only in Coleridge's company. "When you left London, I felt a dismal void in my heart," Lamb wrote afterwards; "I found myself cut off at one and the same time from two most dear to me." Southey also found that Coleridge had good reason for thinking of walking down; he had spent all his money. But neither refinements of feeling nor financial impediments obstructed the practical man of action. Coleridge's conversation

had attracted so many customers to the Salutation and Cat that
the landlord offered him free quarters to stay and continue to
talk. But Southey would not allow him to stay, so Coleridge
had to leave his clothes in lieu of paying his score, Lamb was
left to find solace in solitude, and the truant departed in custody
" to Bath, and in a few days to Bristol."

3. ROMANTICS AT BRISTOL

Southey was now more gaoler than colleague to Coleridge.
He was the hardened conspirator guarding the weaker, under
suspicion of backsliding from his complicity in crime. While
upbraiding, he took no notice of Coleridge's objections to his
falling off from the pantisocratic ideal. On the contrary, he
coolly informed him that, as war with the United States was
threatening and there seemed no immediate prospect of raising
capital for emigration, he and Lovell and Burnett had decided to
abandon the idea and settle in common ownership of a farm in
Wales. To this plan he had been persuaded by his schoolfellow
Wynn, whose father, a baronet, had estates in Wales, though it
does not appear that he placed one of his farms at the disposal
of his son's friend.

Protesting against his treatment as a renegade, Coleridge
plaintively asked, " Wherein, when roused to the recollection of
my duty, have I shrunk from the performance of it? " He
objected that Southey now always said, " I, I, I, will do so and
so," instead of, as formerly, " It is all our duty to do so and so,
for such and such reasons." He could not understand how " the
principles and proposed consequences of pantisocracy " could be
set in practice by four or five men " going partners together " in
a Welsh farm, but if they were all agreed on the " utility of
aspheterizing in Wales," he was willing to surrender his opinions.
For once, he took the practical lead, proposing that, before
definitely deciding, they should discover what capital was required and whether a farm could be found with a house large

enough to hold them all. In Mrs. Lovell's opinion, the move to Wales would be impossible for three months at least, so Coleridge proposed to accept a reporter's post on the *Telegraph*, which he had been offered in London, live on a guinea a week, contributing the balance of his salary to the common fund, and at the same time finish his volume of *Imitations*.

But Southey had no taste for letting him loose again in London. When Coleridge pointed out the necessity of his visiting Cambridge to explain the reason for his not returning, he even insisted on accompanying him. When the Master of Jesus remonstrated on the "visionary and ruinous tendency of his conduct and schemes," which he attributed to vicious democratic doctrines, Coleridge replied, as he had explained to brother George, that he was "neither Jacobin nor Democrat, but a Pantisocrat." The college again showed patient tolerance of its brilliant but eccentric scholar. The Master gave him a whole term in which to reconsider his decision before in April referring his case to the Christ's Hospital almoners, who, doubtless prompted again by Boyer, then extended the reprieve till the end of the academic year in June. The kindly consideration received by Coleridge from College authorities contrasted strangely with the harsh treatment of his son at Oxford twenty-five years later.

Pausing only two days in London, Southey and Coleridge returned from Cambridge to Bristol and settled in lodgings with Burnett in College Street. They had no money. The small sale of *The Fall of Robespierre* had quickly petered out. Though he had canvassed 450 subscribers, Coleridge, influenced by George Dyer's counsel, abandoned his *Imitations* as unlikely to produce the windfall he needed. Southey's small volume of poems had not sold, and though Cottle had engaged to publish *Joan of Arc*, Coleridge's criticism had decided him to re-write the poem. Coleridge took the initiative in earning money. He was in close correspondence with Dyer, and transmitting through him the last of his *Sonnets on Eminent Characters* to the *Morning Chronicle*, he asked Dyer to find him newspaper work which he could do from the country, while through him Southey had inserted in the *Telegraph* an open letter to George Canning, who had seconded the royal address declining peace negotiations with the existing rulers of France.

They decided to give lectures in Bristol, Coleridge on morals and politics, Southey on history. The business arrangements were undertaken by Joseph Cottle, the bookseller. Coleridge delivered his first two lectures at the Corn Market in Wine Street before the end of January; he lectured again at the room in Castle Green in February. Spoon-fed on government propaganda, the locals were so incensed by his liberal opinions that he was compelled to print the text of his first lecture to disprove the rumours that "there was treason in it." Twenty-one years later he reprinted the lecture to clear himself of the charge of apostasy, since it had been cited as proof of his early Jacobinism, and remarked that his convictions had changed only on the doctrine of philosophical necessity, imbibed from his reading of Hartley and introduced in the conclusion of the lecture, as the means of acquiring "subdued sobriety of temper" necessary to avoid irritation to indignation and so to revolution. In this advocacy of avoiding resort to violence, he followed Godwin, as in his warning that "revolutions are sudden to the unthinking only," and "political disturbances happen not without the warning harbingers."

It was fashionable for Victorian critics, during that golden age of complacency, to dismiss Coleridge's early expressions of political opinion, like the plan of pantisocracy, as the impractical vapourings of an unformed mind. But to a generation unlucky enough to have witnessed two wars, as abominable in their inception as beyond belief more horrible in the mad fury of destruction and infliction of suffering than the war condemned by Coleridge as "unjust because unnecessary," these lectures, after a hundred and fifty years, read, as they read when first printed, with the novelty and freshness of truth shedding rays of enlightenment through the yellow fog of obtuse understanding. It is as incredible that they were composed thus long ago by a young man of twenty-two, as that the mass of mankind in the meantime has remained immobile in the mud of brutish stupidity.

The "treasonable" lecture began by citing the example of

France as a warning to Britain. The people, like Samson, were strong and blind; in pulling down monarchy and aristocracy, the twin pillars of Oppression's temple, the crash of which caused every European tyrant to tremble on his throne, they buried themselves in the ruins. The Girondists, the makers of revolution, were "men of enlarged views," but men of genius are rarely men of action, and in the emergency of their creation they were replaced by the Jacobins, men of lesser mind but of ruthless purpose. If Robespierre's "first intentions were pure, his subsequent enormities yield a melancholy proof, that it is not the character of the possessor which directs the power, but the power which shapes and depraves the character of the possessor."[1] Having thus dissociated himself from the Jacobins, Coleridge delivered himself of a dictum on democracy which must have occurred to him in argument with Southey: "The majority of democrats appear to me to have attained that portion of knowledge in politics, which infidels possess in religion . . . both, contemplating truth and justice 'in the nakedness of abstraction,' condemn constitutions and dispensations without having sufficiently examined the natures, circumstances, and capacities of their recipients."

Discussing the different classes of "professed friends of liberty," he cited those dependent "with weather-cock uncertainty on the winds of rumour . . . on the report of French victories they blaze into republicanism, at a tale of French excesses they darken into aristocrats; and seek for shelter among those despicable adherents to fraud and tyranny, who ironically style themselves constitutionalists." Another class comprised those sufferers under oppression stimulated by designing agitators to desire of vengeance. "To unenlightened minds, there are terrible charms in the idea of retribution, however savagely it be inculcated," said Coleridge: "The groans of the oppressors make fearful yet pleasant music to the ear of him, whose mind is

[1] " It is when men of authentic genius change that the spirit of Man is wounded, when they cease to ' fulfil the law and the prophets,' and become a law unto themselves; when the still small voice becomes a shout, when the gift of clairvoyance is transmitted into the sword-flash, and thereafter the star burns sultry, then black."—Henry Williamson on " The Tragic Spirit," *The Adelphi*, Oct.-Dec., 1943.

darkness, and into whose soul the iron has entered." A third class pursued " the interests of freedom steadily, but with narrow and self-centering views . . . Whatever is above them they are most willing to drag down." To these levellers Coleridge declared, " It is a mockery of our fellow creatures' wrongs to call them equal in rights, when by the bitter compulsion of their wants we make them inferior to us in all that can soften the heart, or dignify the understanding."

Here appeared the distinction between democracy and the creed he called pantisocracy. Democrats demanded equality " of *rights*, not of *condition*." A quarter of a century later he was to be accused as an apostate by Hazlitt and other liberals because he found no enthusiasm for parliamentary reform, but of what use was a vote to a man who could neither read nor write? To the unenlightened, the vote was a weapon likely to be self-destructive for want of instruction in its use, like a rifle to one who has never learned to shoot. " The over-worked labourer, skulking into an ale-house," was an unlikely agent for social improvement. Godwin advocated equality of opportunity as the means by which all men might arrive at the stage of enlightenment where they lived in fraternity with an equal sense of responsibility, but he agreed that, when that stage was reached, government would no longer be needed since the laws of morality would require no enforcing. Coleridge objected that " a distant prospect, which we are never to reach, will seldom quicken our footsteps, however lovely it may appear." To him, " in that barbarous tumult of inimical interests, which the present state of society exhibits, *religion* appears to offer the only means universally *efficient*."

To Coleridge, at an early stage of the Napoleonic wars, thus came realisation of the necessity that similarly appeared to men like Dick Sheppard in the war years following 1914 and to such different thinkers as Sir Richard Acland and Dr. C. E. M. Joad in those following 1939. Universal education, in an ever improving scale of scope, must be the objective of benevolent government, and its effects may be implemented by equality of opportunity and " aspheterism " of raw materials and public services (which Sir Richard Acland called "common owner-ship"), so tending gradually to equality of condition. But during the process, the little enlightened must have faith, for they are intellectually yet insufficiently strong to devise from philosophy a moral code. As we in our time have seen the revolutionists, bereft of religion, fasten their faith on supposed super-men—the Russians on Lenin, the Germans on Hitler—so Coleridge was to see the French revolutionists lose sight of their revolutionary principles in fanatical idolatry of Napoleon.

The doctrines of this first lecture he argued in private with Southey. When he lost comfort in his friend Seward's self-illusory delight in duty, Southey had embraced all that suited him in Godwin's doctrines. He declared himself a democrat in politics; on the evidence of Poole's statement and passages in Coleridge's letters, he was in religion an atheist. His son and biographer, a respectable parson, discreetly averred that "his opinions at this time were somewhat unsettled, although they soon took the form of Unitarianism." Under the influence of Unitarian divines like William Frend and Dr. Edwards, Coleridge became a Unitarian at Cambridge, and in daily intercourse with Southey, he soon accomplished his conversion. At the end of February he wrote to Dyer of how he looked forward to making him acquainted with Southey—"a Man of *perpendicular Virtue a downright upright* Republican!"—saying that "he is *Christian-ising* apace," and "I doubt not, that I shall present him to you right orthodox in the heterodoxy of Unitarianism." Thus he restored Southey to religion and at the same time revealed to him the cardinal defect in Godwin's doctrine. Soon his eloquence was similarly to convince Wordsworth, and finally, after some years, Godwin himself. "In my forty-fourth year," wrote Godwin, "I ceased to regard the name of Atheist with the same complacency I had done for several preceding years." Describing his "theism" as consisting "in a reverent and soothing con-templation of all that is beautiful, grand, or mysterious in the system of the universe, and in certain conscious intercourse and correspondence with the principles of these attributes, without attempting the idle task of developing and defining it," he added,

" into this train of thinking I was first led by the conversation of S. T. Coleridge."

Coleridge was finding the course of untrue love far from smooth. Good Joseph Cottle, who was disposed to avuncular benevolence in the astonishing delight of finding two young men of genius on his doorstep in the prosaic purlieus of Bristol, " observed at this time a marked coolness between Mr. Coleridge and Robert Lovell, so inauspicious in those about to establish a ' Fraternal Colony ', " and Coleridge told him that Lovell, having at first done all in his power to promote his " connexion with Miss Fricker," now opposed the union. To Dyer Coleridge confided more. " In expectation of emigrating on the Pantiso-cratic Plan," he had paid his addresses to a young lady, to whom he now considered himself " under particular Ties of Gratitude," since, " in confidence of " his affection, she had rejected the addresses of two other suitors, " one of them of large fortune," and " by her perseverent Attachment " to him she had " disobliged her Relations in a very uncomfortable Degree." She was " perpetually obliged to resist the entreaties and to endure the reproachful admonitions of her Uncle," and could not conceal from Coleridge how heavy her heart was with anxiety, " how disquieted by Suspense." Though, " with her usual Delicacy," she had kept silent about her predicament till his coming to Bristol, now her relatives were so pressing that " a short Time must decide whether she marries me whom she loves with an affection to the ardor of which my Deserts bear no proportion—or a man whom she strongly dislikes in spite of his fortune and solicitous attentions to her."

Apparently as a result of his laudatory sonnet to Thomas Erskine, he had been approached through Perry or Dyer with an offer of tutoring the sons of Erskine's brother, Lord Buchan, and he explained his entanglement with Sara Fricker so that Dyer might understand his declining such an advantageous appointment. If he could take lodgings in Edinburgh near the young gentlemen and live as a married man, he could accept the post; but if, as he supposed, living in the house with the Erskines was " a necessary accompaniment of Tutorage," did not Dyer think it his duty to decline the offer? Apparently Dyer, in simple sincerity always sympathetic and the least worldly minded of men, did think so, for Lord Buchan's sons did not receive the benefit of Coleridge's tutelage.

The plan of taking a Welsh farm had been speedily proved impracticable without capital, and according to Coleridge, Southey was "exerting his Influence to procure a situation in London." Southey had no influence, save through Bedford and Wynn; he had failed the year before with Bedford, on the grounds of his anti-ministerial politics, and as Wynn was still an undergraduate, his wire-pulling powers must have been limited. From Southey's letters to Bedford it appears that the only "situation" he tried for was a reporter's place on the *Telegraph*, which he hoped to obtain through Coleridge and as his colleague. "Hireling writer to a newspaper!" he exclaimed to Bedford, "'Sdeath! 'tis an ugly title: but, *n'importe*, I shall write truth, and only truth." But neither he nor Coleridge had the chance of expounding truth in the *Telegraph*, for that newspaper, after a short struggle on a circulation not exceeding seven hundred copies, was purchased by Daniel Stuart and absorbed into the *Morning Post*.

Ironically Southey, who only two months before had extracted Coleridge from London and insisted on his living at Bristol, was now convinced that "London is certainly the place for all who, like me, are on the world." But a few weeks later, before the end of March, he announced that, if he and Coleridge could get £150 a year between them, they proposed to marry and live in the country, where they could continue to write, while "practising agriculture," till they could raise enough capital for America—"still the grand object in view." Thus far, he regarded his fortunes as indissolubly linked with Coleridge's. "Coleridge is writing at the same table," he wrote to Bedford; "our names are written in the book of destiny on the same page," and he compared him with the most brilliant and admired of their Westminster schoolfellows.

Coleridge continued to lecture, though "Mobs and Mayors, Blockheads and Brickbats, Placards and Press Gangs" were

F

" leagued in horrible Conspiracy " against him. " Two or three uncouth and untrained Automata " uttered bloodcurdling threats against his life, and though the local democrats were sturdy in support, they were few in number. During one lecture some hooligans were " scarcely restrained from attacking the house " in Castle Green where the " damn'd Jacobin was jawing away." At quarter day, on the strength of his lectures, he asked Cottle for an advance of five pounds, as the three partners were over four pounds short of their lodging bill. Cottle then offered him thirty guineas for a volume of poems, making advances as required without waiting for completion of the work. He made the same offer to Southey, to whom he also engaged to give fifty guineas for *Joan of Arc*. Southey was occupied for six months in re-writing *Joan* under Coleridge's supervision, and he was not ready with his history lectures till May.

By this time he had fallen into a mood of despondency. He sat in his lodgings, writing and re-writing, dedicating his leisure to Edith and declining nearly all social engagements. He " almost offended by never calling on " one " very pleasant " family, " literary and accomplished," whom Coleridge visited three or four times a week. True to his habit, wherever he went, Coleridge made hosts of friends, many of whom, charmed by his conversation and convinced of his genius, were later willingly of service to him. Among them, besides Joseph Cottle and his poetasting brother Amos (" Oh, Amos Cottle!—Phoebus! what a name," wrote Byron in *English Bards*) were the Rev. John Prior Estlin, a Unitarian minister, and Josiah Wade, a faithful friend for twenty years, both of whom were enthusiastic admirers; John Morgan, who was to afford asylum to Coleridge during the saddest years of his life; Dr. Beddoes the scientist, founder of the Pneumatic Institution and father of the poet of *Death's Jest-Book;* Michael Castle and Charles Danvers. Of these, the last alone was a particular friend of Southey's.

Southey felt " the effort to join in conversation . . . too painful " and that the " torpedo coldness " of his countenance had a chilling effect on the company. Coleridge, buoyant with optimism, encouraged by admiration, applied " the medicine of argument " to his " misanthropic system of indifference," but it would not do—" a strange dreariness of mind," he told Bedford, had seized him. It is not unduly speculative to suppose that Southey felt some jealousy of Coleridge's social success. Among the mediocrities of his school and college acquaintance his brilliant talents had made him the pivot of any circle in which he found himself; it was he who astonished admiring listeners by brilliance and vehemence in expounding unorthodox ideas. Now, for the first time, he was decidedly second fiddle; his utterance seemed stilted after Coleridge's fluent eloquence, his knowledge scanty beside the variety of Coleridge's copious reading. He felt tongue-tied, overshadowed. Unable to compete, he withdrew from competition, and sitting at home, he fretted and, fretting, manufactured a grievance—it was unfair that he should stay at home working while Coleridge frittered away his time in talking.

At the end of May he was " dragged into a party of pleasure," with Coleridge, Edith, Sara, and Joseph Cottle as host, to visit Chepstow and Tintern. The night before he had been scheduled to deliver his fourth historical lecture, on " the Rise, Progress, and Decline of the Roman Empire," but he had deferred to Coleridge's desire to give this lecture. Unluckily Coleridge did not turn up, apologies had to be made to the audience, and Coleridge was found at home in his lodgings, smoking his pipe, having forgotten all about the lecture. After dinner at Chepstow, Southey took occasion to rebuke Coleridge for disappointing his audience, and when Coleridge passed it off lightly, he grew heated. The two girls fanned the flame by taking sides. The embarrassed Cottle " retired to a distant part of the room " and so failed to hear the end of the altercation, but apparently Southey, on the instance of this remissness, accused Coleridge of not pulling his weight in the partnership, which he hinted at dissolving. Characteristically, Coleridge thought nothing of the injustice of the charge in the light of his achievements by comparison with Southey's. He was only " greatly agitated, even to many tears," by his friend's threatened abandonment of their partnership and, consequently, of the Pantisocratic plan.

" A little cessation in the storm," enabled Cottle to intervene. The girls theatrically joined the hands of the disputants, and during the afternoon Southey assured Coleridge that his " suspicions were altogether unfounded," that their " differences were merely speculative," and that he would certainly join in a Welsh farming venture. Coleridge was " glad and satisfied." But, within a few weeks, on a " strawberry party " to Ashton, Southey informed Burnett that his own private resources would remain his personal property, and they would only aspheterise in the actual farm of five or six acres. Burnett reported the conversation to Coleridge, who " received the account with indignation and loathings of unutterable contempt." He told Burnett that Southey " had long laid a plot of separation," and was now developing it " by proposing such a vile mutilation " of their scheme as he knew Coleridge would " reject decisively and with scorn." Burnett was Southey's friend and disciple; not unnaturally, he regarded Coleridge with " gentle dislike " from feeling himself supplanted by him in Southey's regard. Coleridge said he would " adopt the full system or depart," and left Burnett to " choose his associate." Burnett related this to Southey, who answered that he was prepared to go to Wales or anywhere Coleridge liked, but without saying upon what terms.

4. THE PARTNERSHIP DISSOLVED

In the middle of June the death of Edmund Seward plunged Southey, already dispirited, into hysterical despondency. " How I loved poor Edmund: he taught me all that I have of good. . . . It is like a dream, the idea that he is dead. . . . There is a strange warning in my heart." It does not appear that Seward imparted more to Southey than a stimulus to the Stoicism he professed on going up to Oxford, and his influence had lost capacity for comfort months before Southey met Coleridge. But the early death of his friend made him magnify his debt to him, and forgetting the interval between the waning of Seward's influence and the waxing of Coleridge's, forgetting that Poole had been shocked by his atheism at a time when Coleridge's influence had not yet asserted itself, he began to attribute his present unhappy circumstances and state of mind to his alliance with Coleridge. Once he told Coleridge that he had " acted wrong "; Coleridge, in the fulness of his heart, understood the statement as a confession of his backslidings from the pantisocratic ideal, and regarded his subsequent " cold and gloomy " manner as a "relapse" from contrition instead of a progression of regret.

Accumulating grievances against Coleridge, Southey exaggerated his carelessness of punctuality into a charge of "indolence." Coleridge would always talk rather than work, and his instinct to procrastinate was intensified by illness. During this summer Cottle received at least one note, excusing himself from a social evening because " a devil, a very devil, has got possession of my left temple, eye, cheek, jaw, throat, and shoulder." His rheumatic pains continually recurred, and anyone who has known the pressing need to work under the affliction of physical pain can appreciate at once the temptation to rest in the hope of feeling better to-morrow and the anguish of conscience that Coleridge subsequently suffered from incapacity to concentrate on the matter in hand. During this time his intellectual activity was ceaseless. From the first he had taken the initiative in attempting remunerative work. Later he related his achievements—not "boastfully, but to excriminate" himself. He delivered eleven lectures, which he composed himself, " excepting a very few pages which most reluctantly " Southey, in the intervals of revising his *Joan*, "eked out." He assisted Southey in the composition of his lectures, writing " one half in *quantity*," while he claimed that in quality " all the *tug* of brain" was his, and Southey's share " little more than transcription." He contributed passages to *Joan of Arc*, which Southey acknowledged by omitting them in later reprints of the poem. He took pains in correcting and amending Southey's other poems. All this was in addition to his own poetical composition. But his facility in composition, as in conversation, was a source of umbrage to Southey, himself a fluent writer, and after two years of nourishing this grievance, forgetting that they had subsisted on advances from Cottle under precisely equal agreements, he could declare unblushingly that he supported himself, " and almost him, I may say, for what my labours earned was as four to one."

In August Southey's uncle, the Rev. Herbert Hill, came on leave to England. He was " deeply hurt" by the " misapplication " of his nephew's abilities and " high moral qualities," but believing him to have " everything you would wish a young man to have excepting common sense and prudence," he wrote begging him to reconsider his position and to return to Oxford with a view to taking orders. Southey confided the contents of the letter to Coleridge and Burnett, and at night Coleridge, not dreaming of hesitation " concerning so infamous a proposal," asked what answer he had returned. " None," said Southey; " nor do I know what answer I shall return." George Burnett, who had himself renounced taking orders under the influence of Southey's arguments, " sat half-petrified, gaping at the pigmy virtue of his supposed giant."

When the other two had retired to bed, Coleridge " performed the office of still-struggling friendship " by writing his " free sentiments " to Southey on his uncle's arguments. He did not reproach him for inclining to abandon the pantisocratic plan. " Pantisocracy is not the question : its realisation is distant—perhaps a miraculous millenium." Nor did he reflect on Southey's meditating resumption of his Oxford career after inducing both his friends to abandon their universities—in Coleridge's case, involving the sacrifice of his scholarship. The point was, could Southey " perjure " himself? There were ministers of the established church who disapproved its " peculiar dogmas," but, seeing in innovation " dreadful and unhealable consequence," they declined to " quit the Church for a few follies and absurdities." While he regretted their reasoning, Coleridge did not condemn the " hearts and consciences " of such men. But Southey definitely disapproved of all establishment. He had called it " iniquitous, a mother of crimes "; it was impossible that *he* " could uphold it by assuming the badge of affiliation." Coleridge did not wish Southey's decision to be influenced by any consideration of him; he assured him that he wrote " altogether disinterestedly," and that Southey's " desertion or adhesion " would " in no wise " affect his own " feelings, opinions, or conduct," and only " in a very inconsiderable degree " his fortunes.

Next morning Coleridge walked part of the way to Bath with Southey, and recapitulated his arguments. Southey declared that he had " little notion of guilt " and had " a pretty sort of lullaby faith " of his own. He thought that any difficulties at his ordination would be obviated by his uncle's intimacy with the bishop and the " hush " in which he would live in the interval. When Coleridge protested that his sentiments in *Joan of Arc* were " of the boldest order," and asked how he would reply to questions on belief in the Trinity and the Redemption, Southey answered, " Oh, I am pretty well up to their jargon, and shall answer them accordingly." He left Coleridge " fully persuaded " that he intended to take orders, an impression confirmed a week later, when Southey told Burnett to act independently of him and invited him to visit him at Oxford.

Southey did not return to the Bristol lodgings, but remained with his mother at Bath. He said afterwards that " finances no longer suffered us to remain at Bristol as we had done." It is true that they were living on advances from Cottle, but both Southey's and Coleridge's volumes of poems were now ready for press, and as Coleridge said, though their prospects were not bright, they were as bright as when the pantisocratic plan was first embraced. Apart from the significant coincidence of Southey's departure with his uncle's return to England, he revealed in a letter to Bedford treachery more complete than Coleridge suspected. " My uncle is in England," he exclaimed excitedly on 22nd August; " I am in daily expectation of seeing him again." Then he tells Bedford, " When next I see you it will not be for a visit: I shall fix my residence near you to study the law!!! " He explained that he could not defer to his uncle's wish that he should take orders, as " the gate " was " perjury," and he felt " little disposed to pay so heavy a fine at the turn-pike of orthodoxy," but he hoped to induce his uncle to agree to his studying law. It is easy to see how he feared to inform Coleridge and Burnett of such complete renunciation of his partnership with them; he preferred to let them think that the issue between himself and his uncle was only the question of his taking orders, rather than to confess that he contemplated driving a bargain with him.

Unaware of the full measure of intended treachery, but understanding that he contemplated perjury, Coleridge regarded Southey as " one *fallen back into the ranks.*" While they continued to meet regularly, he " studiously avoided all particular sub-jects," generalising, saying nothing of his own plans apart from his literary work, talking only as he would " to any other man of genius " who happened to be his acquaintance. When Southey complained of his " cold civility " and that he had withdrawn his confidence from him, he was merely more careful to avoid him. In the middle of September he visited Nether Stowey, where Tom Poole introduced him to his orthodox cousins, one of whom described " Coldridge " as " a young man of brilliant understanding, great eloquence, desperate fortune, democratick principles, and entirely led away by the feelings of the moment."

Robbed of the prop of Southey's decided personality, unable any longer to drift on the support of his counsels, Coleridge had to direct his own course. Sara Fricker was in love with him, and suffering the reproaches of her family for persisting in her attachment to the romantic but impecunious poet, whose estrangement from Southey deprived her of her sole ally in the family, her sister Edith.

> " *O ever present to my view!*
> *My wafted spirit is with you,*
> *And soothes your boding fears:*
> *I see you all oppressed with gloom*
> *Sit lonely in that cheerless room—*
> *Ah me! You are in tears!* "

So wrote Coleridge in the " Lines Written at Shurton Bars, near Bridgwater," during his visit to Poole in September. He could no longer brook delay in rescuing her from such durance, and when Cottle, delighted with the quality of the poems already submitted for the intended volume, proposed to pay him a guinea and a half for every hundred lines of verse he wrote, and to purchase all his prose besides, he decided on immediate marriage. Completely disillusioned with Southey and attributing his defection to mean reluctance from sharing with them the annuity promised to him by his rich friend Wynn on his coming of age, George Burnett gladly accepted an invitation to make his home with the newly married pair. Together he and Coleridge looked for a suitable cottage, and settled on one at Clevedon, near Bristol, apparently as early as 20th August, when " The Eolian Harp " was written in celebration of the decision to settle there.

As Burnett now accompanied Coleridge everywhere and Coleridge was avoiding Southey, their intimates soon asked why Southey was no longer with them. Coleridge replied that Southey was " quite undetermined " in his plans, " but had some thoughts of returning to Oxford." As Southey had no real intentions of returning to Oxford, he was doubtless occasioned some embarrassment in explaining it away, and he later vented his spleen by accusing Coleridge of " industriously trumpeting " his uncle's letter. Coleridge admitted that he had spoken " more particularly " to Danvers and Cottle, but Danvers was Southey's most intimate friend at Bristol and Cottle his publisher and benefactor, who could not be put off with a casual remark. Also, as Coleridge confessed, his " heart was very full."

Thus it was, with Coleridge much occupied on marriage plans, that Wordsworth " saw but little of him " after their meeting at Bristol in September. Coleridge's first personal impression of Wordsworth is unrecorded, but in borrowing the phrase " green radiance " from *An Evening Walk* for his " Lines Written at Shurton Bars," which he finally revised for the printer during the winter, he inserted a note of acknowledgment to " Mr. Wordsworth, a Poet whose versification is occasionally harsh and his diction too frequently obscure; but whom I deem unrivalled among the writers of the present day in manly sentiment, novel imagery, and vivid colouring."

On the morning of Sunday 4th October 1795, Coleridge married Sara Fricker at "poor Chatterton's church," St. Mary's Redcliffe, Bristol, and within three days they were "settled, nay quite domesticated" at Clevedon, their "comfortable cot." Burnett and one of Sara's sisters—probably Martha, to whom Burnett unsuccessfully proposed—lived with them. It was Martha who signed the register as Sara's witness. Coleridge's witness was neither Southey nor Burnett, but his friend and admirer, Josiah Wade.

Southey was out of the picture of pantisocratic bliss—he who had promoted the marriage, who had compelled Coleridge to sacrifice his Cambridge career to the pantisocratic plan, who, an apostle of impregnable virtue, had torn the errant disciple from the side of Charles Lamb at the Salutation and Cat. He was in an unenviable plight. Estranged from his friends, he waited the pleasure of his uncle's attention, while he escaped from his mother's plaintive reproaches and exhortations only to encounter Edith's tearful forebodings. In impatient suspense he feared that his uncle was offended and aggrieved by his continued objections to taking orders. Harrowed by the humiliating thought that, after breaking with Coleridge and Burnett on the chance of a bargain with his uncle, he might be deserted by him, he was embarrassed to exasperation by the need for evasive answers to inquiring friends, and in accordance with habit become instinctive, attributed all his woes to Coleridge. The egoist's self-importance overlooked the probability that his uncle, returning to England after several years' absence, might have old friends to visit and affairs more pleasant and pressing than tiresome negotiations with a recalcitrant nephew.

He resorted to jauntiness, to "bear a good face, and keep all uneasiness" to himself, but by the week following Coleridge's marriage, he was so worried over not hearing from his uncle that he thought of writing a tragedy with suspense as its subject. When, in the middle of October, his uncle eventually came to

Bath, he proved amenable, though disappointed that Southey persisted in refusing to enter a profession in which his influence could have served him. He was agreeable to Southey's adoption of the law as a profession, but insisted, as a preliminary to his legal studies, that he should accompany him for some months to Portugal, where he would be removed, not only from the dangerous influence of Coleridge and other political associates, but from the worse disaster of an " imprudent attachment." Southey's heart was " very heavy." He would have refused the proposition, but was " weary of incessantly refusing " all his mother's wishes, and Edith, though weeping at the prospect of parting, added her persuasions to accord with his uncle's wish. As usual, he dramatised his situation; there was " the advantageous possibility of being captured by the French," or he might become food for " the fishes on the road." Actually his fear of ship-wreck was a principal motive he assigned for his secret marriage to Edith Fricker on 14th November, the day of his departure from Bristol.

But his infatuation for Edith had been for two years the one objective from which his faith had never shifted. It had been indeed the controlling motive of all his conduct. Dissatisfaction with Oxford derived largely from separation from Edith; desire of her society doubtless accounted for his missing residence at Oxford during the Michaelmas term of 1793; impatience to be married excited disgust for the long years of waiting for a college benefice and influenced his decision against taking orders; visions of domestic bliss with Edith coloured his pictures of pioneer life in America, and he had driven Coleridge into Sara's arms because their union and emigration insured the prospect of his own union and emigration with Edith. Finally the realisation, after six months' alliance, that he and Coleridge together might have to wait long and laboriously before they earned the means to marry, roused despondency and dissatisfaction with his coadjutor. To separate from Edith for six months was hard enough, but to endure separation, knowing its motive was deadening of his desire for her, knowing that, at the end of the probationary period, his uncle might interpose further difficulties to thwart his design—the suspense would be intolerable. So, when his uncle required his company on a fortnight of visits to friends in Cornwall before embarking from Falmouth, he resolved on a secret marriage, and arranged with the accommodating Cottle that Edith should reside with his spinster sisters during her husband's absence.

Coleridge at Clevedon heard of the full extent of Southey's apostasy only on the eve of the marriage, when he wrote a letter of tremendous length, recounting the history of their friendship and exculpating himself from Southey's recriminations. If Southey had persisted in taking orders, his " motives would have been weak and shadowy and vile," but by changing his ground to the law, " they were annihilated," for " no man dreams of getting bread in the Law, till six or eight years after his first entrance at the Temple." " O selfish, money-loving man," he exclaimed, " what principle have you not given up? " To Lovell Southey assigned Coleridge's " indolence " as the reason for his abandoning pantisocracy; " supposing it true," said Coleridge, " it might indeed be a reason for rejecting *me* from the system. But how does this affect pantisocracy, that you should reject *it?* " And what had poor Burnett done to be thus summarily abandoned by the friend who had converted him, who had caused him to renounce his career for participation in the plan? Coleridge did not refer to his own renunciation, merely mentioning that duty had compelled him to refuse a " liberal proposal " from his brother George. Of Mary Evans, he remarked only on the fetter he had snapped like a sinew of his heart. He confessed that he first paid addresses to Sara " from principle, not feeling," but—" I love, and I am beloved, and I am happy! " In his letter's lines sounded one of those chords from the heart, deep in simple sincerity, that wring the hearts of his readers as they won those of his friends: " Never do I expect to meet another man, who will make me unite attachment for his person with reverence for his heart and admiration of his genius."

But Southey, with characteristic single-minded directness, had set his sails on a new course, and no berth was booked for

Coleridge. Already on 1st October, he had written to Bedford as if their friendship was a finished chapter: "My poetical taste was much meliorated by Bowles, and the constant company of Coleridge. He did me much good—I him more." He undoubtedly helped Coleridge by driving him, with his stronger personality, to efforts of work, and by supplying an anvil from which Coleridge struck sparks. Otherwise his only boon was the bestowal of a wife Coleridge had not wanted. His own account of his intellectual progress illustrates his debt to Coleridge. It was Coleridge who introduced Bowles's poems to his notice. "The frequent and careful study of Godwin was of essential service"; he had "read and all but worshipped," but had "since seen his fundamental error,—that he theorises for another state, not for the rule of conduct in the present." It was Coleridge who had demonstrated this defect in Godwin's philosophy. "For religion, I can confute the Atheist, and battle him with his own weapons." When he went a year before with Coleridge to Nether Stowey, he had been himself an atheist; he could now confute atheists with the arguments by which he had been himself confuted by Coleridge.

Protesting, he went to Cornwall, staying in the mansions of his uncle's influential friends, behaving boorishly by frequently seeking the solitude of his room to write to friends of his plight. He had written a preface for *Joan of Arc* on the eve of his marriage, and the poem was with the printer. It was due for publication on 1st December 1795, and that day Southey sailed for Portugal. Remote from distractions, he spent the next six months in deserving his uncle's good opinion.

PART FIVE

THE ARCHANGEL YET UNDAMAGED

I. THE PROPAGANDIST

CHARACTERISTICALLY Coleridge had sparsely furnished his Clevedon cottage with non-essentials, and two days after the marriage, Cottle received a long list of household requirements, varying from a kettle, carpet-brush, and dustpan, to nutmegs, currants, rice, and other cooking ingredients, in-cluding incongruously a keg of porter and a Bible. When Cottle, having supplied the requirements, rode over, he was delighted by the charming situation of the cottage and its con-venience. It had also the merit of cheapness, the rent being five pounds a year, with no taxes. It was truly a " comfortable cot," and pretty Sara proved an adequate housekeeper.

But they did not stay there long. The distance of thirteen miles was inconveniently far from Bristol. Coleridge needed to see Cottle regularly, and to borrow books from the public library. He missed his many friends, and to return in a single day entailed a walk too exhausting even for such a rapid and tireless walker, while, if he failed to return the next day, Sara was lonely and uneasy. He was also still lecturing. In November Pitt and Grenville utilised an attempt at assassination of George III to introduce bills curtailing liberty of the press and prohibiting public meetings, and he delivered two lectures, which he after-wards condensed into one and printed as *The Plot Discovered; or an Address to the People against Ministerial Treason*. In this lecture he differentiated between government *by* the people, which he hoped " will be the government of France," govern-ment *over* the people or despotism, and government *with* the people, which " ought to be a *progressive* government ascending from the *second* mode to the first." He argued that the present government, since members of Parliament belonged exclusively to the aristocratic, propertied and professional classes, verged on despotism, from which it was saved only by expression of the popular voice through the press.

Such activities demanded his presence at Bristol, and combining economy with convenience, he and Sara moved to her mother's house on Redcliffe Hill. Cohabitation with a mother-in-law is rarely conducive to domestic comfort, and Mrs. Fricker was a commonplace person incapable of intelligent listening, much less of contributing, to conversation. So Coleridge and Sara eagerly embraced an invitation in December to spend a few weeks with Tom Poole at Nether Stowey.

Coleridge had a weak man's admiration for strength of character. During his visit in the previous September he had recognised in Poole characteristics which had awakened admiration of Southey—self-confidence, integrity, inflexibility of opinion and purpose. He had talked of Poole on his wedding-night, and within three days wrote to him of his plans for the future. Poole had replied in terms of affectionate interest, inviting friendship. Worshipping books and devoting, from boyhood, his leisure to intellectual pursuits, surrounded by unsympathetic, ignorant, and politically antagonistic minds, he eagerly welcomed the opportunity of intellectual conversation. Without intention to flatter, he told Coleridge that " Providence has been pleased . . . to drop you on this globe as a meteor from the clouds." Recognising his genius, he regarded his society as a privilege which he may have dreamed of but never hoped to have the fortune to enjoy.

At Stowey, in pursuance of the pantisocratic ideal of living by manual labour, Coleridge learned to potter in the garden, while he was still revising his poems for Cottle. The *Religious Musings*, begun on that Christmas Eve of 1794 when he had finally renounced his hopes of Mary Evans, was utterly altered from the version already read to Cottle; he " tortured " the poem and himself with corrections. With Poole he discussed his plans. He had a notion of taking Sara to Cambridge, having first removed his name from the college books, to finish his " great

COLERIDGE IN 1796

(*from the portrait by Robert Hancock in the National Portrait Gallery.*)

work " of *Imitations* in two volumes. But Poole thought little
of this. The *Imitations* " never could be very popular," and while
they might achieve " a reputation of learning," " simply learned
men " were not very scarce—" *original* works of genius are your
forte." As long ago as the previous February, Coleridge had
planned with Southey a " Provincial Magazine," but the project
had been postponed and in the autumn abandoned by Coleridge,
partly because "I must be connected with R. Southey in it,
which I could not be with comfort to my feelings." Poole had
approved its abandonment, because, he said, " you were not born
to be a compiler." But from his lectures it was evident that
Coleridge had talent for commenting on current events; it was
the duty of the few enlightened minds to keep alight the torch
in the darkness engendered by government propaganda, and it
was necessary for Coleridge to earn money.

So, on his return to Bristol, he convened a meeting of his
friends—excluding Cottle, because " all who met were expected
to become subscribers to a fund," and he was delicately conscious
of being already deep in Cottle's debt—at the Rummer Tavern
to discuss the prospect of a periodical called the *Watchman*. The
" miscellany " was to be published, price fourpence, on every
eighth day to evade the stamp duty on weekly papers. It would
contain comments on current politics, parliamentary reports,
essays, poetry, and reviews. Its advantages included absence of
advertisements, so providing exceptional space for reading matter,
its adaptability for binding as an annual register, and whenever
ministerial and opposition papers differed in accounts of occur-
rences, the differences would " always be faithfully stated."
Coleridge himself was deputed to visit principal provincial towns
in search of subscribers, and in the second week of January,
armed with letters of introduction from Josiah Wade, Estlin,
Dr. Beddoes, and others, he set off for Worcester.

Apparently Wade was chairman of the committee of subscription, for Coleridge kept him punctually supplied with reports
of progress. After opening conversation on the coach by falling
over a fat man's stomach, who proved to be a " most violent
Aristocrat, but a pleasant humourous Fellow in other respects,

and remarkably well informed in agricultural science," he was well received at Worcester by a progressive manufacturer. But the aristocrats were "so numerous and the influence of the Clergy so extensive" that no bookseller would be persuaded to stock an unorthodox periodical. At Birmingham, though laid up for two days with a cold, he secured about a hundred subscribers. As Cottle said, everywhere Coleridge went, his hearers were "electrified by his extraordinary eloquence," and his host at Birmingham, a nonconformist friend of Estlin's, induced him to preach to his congregation. To comply with the custom of the chapel, he wore a gown, for which concession he had to exculpate himself to Wade, as it was his rule to defy convention by wearing in the pulpit his every-day clothes, usually a blue coat and white waistcoat. "Indeed I want firmness," he said, with his invariably shrewd insight. "I have that within me which makes it difficult to say, No! (repeatedly) to a number of persons who seem uneasy and anxious."

At Derby he was entertained by the brothers William and Joseph Strutt, sons of the colleague and successor of Richard Arkwright. With them he met Erasmus Darwin, who "bantered incessantly on the subject of Religion." Coleridge found that, as an atheist, he had no new arguments, but on any other subject he was "wonderfully entertaining and instructive," and "the first *literary* character in Europe, and the most original-minded man." The Strutts gave him introductions to influential radicals at Nottingham, where an "aristocrat" described the motto of the *Watchman*—"That all might know the Truth, and that the Truth may make us free"—as the words of a "seditious Dog," to which Coleridge's host delightedly retorted that "the *seditious Dog* was—Jesus Christ!" At Nottingham he received much kindness and hospitality, and "preached on Sunday to very good purpose, as far as the plate went." At Sheffield his host could promise no support, as, having been associated in the *Sheffield Iris* with James Montgomery, the poet, then in prison under the Libel Act, he declined to assist any rival periodical.

From Manchester he returned with a handsome subscription list, to be greeted with the encouraging news that Cottle had enrolled two hundred and fifty subscribers and another Bristol bookseller a hundred and twenty. The task of sustaining a periodical by the energies of a single writer requires qualities that Coleridge lacked and few have ever possessed. Addison and Steele succeeded with the *Spectator*, but they were collaborators and had also occasional colleagues. Though Johnson believed " a man may write at anything, if he will set himself doggedly to it," his *Rambler* was never " much a favourite of the public." As Poole said, Coleridge was not born to be a compiler; proverbially unpunctual, he was also temperamentally unable to write unless his heart was in his subject, while a bout of physical pain rendered him incapable of concentration. The first number of the *Watchman* appeared on 1st March 1796; the tenth and last, dated 13th May, gave the reasons for its discontinuance. Primarily, it did not pay expenses; principally because it fell between two stools. Those who needed a newspaper found it out-of-date, as they had already read the parliamentary debates in other mediums; those who wanted original composition found the supply meagre by comparison with magazines containing the miscellaneous work of many contributors. Charles Lamb's advice was sound when he said, " Leave out all articles of News, and whatever things are peculiar to News Papers, and confine yourself to Ethics, verse, criticism, or, rather do not confine yourself" but " let your plan be as diffuse as the Spectator." If he had thus given rein to his vein of vigorous criticism and vivifying imagination, he would have satisfied admirers of his personal eloquence, who were disappointed to find the dullness of the periodical enlivened only occasionally by the sparkle of his personality. Many of his supporters among serious-minded nonconformists—especially " *the Slang-men of Calvin's Superstition-Shops* "—were offended by the flippant essay on Fasts in the second number, with its ribald motto from Isaiah, " Wherefore my Bowels shall sound like an Harp."

The failure filled Coleridge with anxiety, for marriage had taught him " the wonderful uses of the vulgar article of life *Bread*," and there were " my wife, my wife's Mother and little Brother, and George Burnett—five mouths opening and shutting as I pull the string!" Friends rallied to the rescue. George Dyer sent him a loan for present expenses, and Perry of the *Morning Chronicle*, having just lost his associate-editor, wrote to Dr. Beddoes that, if Coleridge would "come to town and write for him," he would pay a salary sufficient to support himself and wife. As Cottle advised him to accept, he did so, though his heart was "very heavy, for I love Bristol and I do not love London." But already Tom Poole had initiated a fund, of which Estlin became treasurer, to which a number of Coleridge's friends subscribed five guineas each, with a promise to do so annually for six years. This they offered to Coleridge as a "trifling mark of their esteem, gratitude, and admiration," with the exhortation "to exert with kindness his argumentative powers, his forcible eloquence, his keen satire, his learning, in the support and dissemination of what he honestly believes to be the truth," and "above all, to invoke that Muse who is the source of his highest delight." Few young men of twenty-three can have received a tribute of admiration so generous. Few, too, can claim to have shown such appreciation of youthful genius and such confidence in their judgment as those plain, simple men of honest goodness, of whom Poole, Estlin, and Josiah Wade were different types.

Apparently Poole and Estlin counselled rejection of the place on the *Morning Chronicle* as condemning their *protégé* to the bondage of a "compiler," and conflicting with their hopes of his self-fulfilment. A selection of his lectures, anti-ministerial and pacifist, appeared as *Conciones ad Populum* (which Charles Lamb thought "the most eloquent politics" that ever came his way), and in April Cottle published the volume of poems, containing *Religious Musings* and the much-praised *Monody on the Death of Chatterton*, which was begun while Coleridge was still at school, much revised, and actually printed at Cambridge in 1794. The poems were well received, for the most wizen-souled reviewer must have recognised the rare array of rich variety, remarkable in range of conception, and the infallible ear for melody and rhythm. The *Monthly Magazine* "cataracted panegyric," the *Critical Review* (in which the reviewer seems to have been Francis Wrangham, though Lamb suspected Dyer)

" *cascaded* it," and the *Analytical Review* " dribbled it with very tolerable civility." Coleridge was pleased with one reviewer's praise of *Religious Musings* as " on the very top of the scale of sublimity," for the general tendency had been to prefer the lighter and more graceful poems, and to regard the *Musings,* in the words of Poole's brother, as " too metaphysical for common readers." The poem " was not written for common readers "; it was an attempt at expression of his personal faith, his deism, his pacificism, his belief in the brotherhood of man by means of freedom, beauty, love and happiness, and that " Life is a vision shadowy of Truth." Lamb saw something of its meaning to its author, and Coleridge rightly valued it, for it is a foretaste of what he might have accomplished in metaphysical poetry if the arteries of his poetic gift had developed in richness instead of desiccating.

But occasional verse and reviewers' praise do not earn money. A copy of the poems sent to George Coleridge had reopened relations with his family after eighteen months of silence following his abduction by Southey, but no financial aid came from that quarter. In May he stayed a week or so at Stowey, and fell more than ever in love with days spent at work in the garden before evenings in Poole's congenial company. When he left, he felt nostalgic longing for the " dear gutter of Stowey," the brook which bubbled down one side of the village's main street. In July came an invitation from a wealthy widow and enthusiastic admirer of his writings, Mrs. Elizabeth Evans, sister of William and Joseph Strutt of Derby, to live at Darley Hall as tutor to her children. Coleridge and his wife set off at once for Derbyshire, but on arrival, the lady greeted them with great agitation and embarrassment, explaining that her wishes had been over-ruled by her children's guardians, who apparently objected to the proposed tutor's political and religious opinions. Gracefully Coleridge begged her to feel no distress on his account, as he was content to have earned her acquaintance and esteem. " Say rather, my love and veneration," she exclaimed, and to recompense their disappointment entertained the young couple delightfully for ten days, driving them to Matlock, Ilam and

Dovedale, "a place beyond expression tremendously sublime."
When they left, she pushed notes amounting to £95 into Coleridge's hand and presented Sara, who was pregnant, with all her
baby clothes.

Returning through Derby, he was invited to open a school
there by an influential nonconformist, Dr. Crompton, who proposed to send his three sons for an annual fee of a hundred pounds
till Coleridge had secured twelve pupils at twenty guineas a year
each. Two hundred and fifty-two pounds a year "and my
evenings and mornings at my disposal" Coleridge thought
"good things." He took a house in Derby, which was to be
ready by October, and even persuaded the landlord to "Rum-
fordize" the chimneys—he had already proposed to the un-
enthusiastic Cottle that he should publish a pamphlet urging the
advantages of the adventurous Count Rumford's economic fire-
grates on the citizens of Bristol.

On his way from Derby to Bristol, he stayed a week with a
friend at Moseley, near Birmingham, where he formed a friendship with an enthusiastic admirer, Charles Lloyd, the twenty-
one-year-old son of a Quaker banker and already the author of
a volume of poems. Lloyd was talented but neurotic, an epileptic
whose disease later turned to lunacy. Passionately devoted to
poetry and letters and averse to a commercial career, he was a
problem to his parents, who, devoutly religious, welcomed his
attachment to a young man with reputation as an inspired lay
preacher. After his return to Bristol, he received a letter from
Lloyd, saying that his parents agreed to his plan of residing with
Coleridge as his pupil, but his father would like first to interview
him. Though Sara's confinement was imminent, she advised
her husband not to miss this chance of securing independence
through a rich and companionable pupil, and Coleridge was
accordingly absent when his first child, a son, was born on 19th
September 1796. Mr. Lloyd proved "a mild man, very liberal
in his ideas," who, after listening to Coleridge's eloquent conversation, expressed himself as "thankful to heaven" that his
son was to be with him. Charles Lloyd accordingly returned
with him to his wife's bedside.

To Poole Coleridge described in a letter his emotions on seeing his infant son, and later embodied them in a sonnet addressed to Lloyd.

> " *Charles! my slow heart was only sad, when first*
> *I scann'd that face of feeble infancy:*
> *For dimly on my thoughtful spirit burst*
> *All I had been, and all my child might be!*
> *But when I saw it on its mother's arm,*
> *And hanging at her bosom (she the while*
> *Bent o'er its features with a tearful smile)*
> *Then I was thrill'd and melted, and most warm*
> *Impress'd a father's kiss: and all beguil'd*
> *Of dark remembrance and presageful fear,*
> *I seem'd to see an angel-form appear—*
> *'Twas even thine, beloved woman mild!*
> *So for the mother's sake the child was dear,*
> *And dearer was the mother for the child.*"

Could he have foreseen the future of that elfin spirit, even less suited to worldly success than his own, and destined to find his only happiness in the half-pitying affections of illiterate dalesmen, his heart might have burst with anguish. He named him David Hartley, after the philosopher whose theory of the association of ideas had swayed his own thought for the past two years. His love for his son was almost maternal in its tenderness. Dearer doubtless " was the mother for the child," for he had never loved her for herself, and henceforth his feeling for her was for the mother of his children.

2. ABDICATION FROM PUBLIC LIFE

Mother and child were both " uncommonly well," and as soon as they could be left, Coleridge asked Poole to let him bring Lloyd to Stowey. His heart was " heavy respecting Derby ";

he needed Poole's advice on what to say to Dr. Crompton. Poole's counsel conformed with his own wishes; the drudgery of teaching accorded even less than that of hack-journalism with the hopes of the Poole-Estlin subscribers for the development of his genius. The stay at Stowey revived his desire " to live in a beautiful country, and to enure myself as much as possible to the labour of the field," and he asked Cruikshank, the local land-agent and Poole's friend, to obtain for him a house at Adscombe, near Stowey. To Lloyd, in the lines " To a Young Friend on his proposing to domesticate with the Author," he painted a delightful picture of their enjoyments together of the beauties of nature while they cultivated their minds on the green hill of knowledge.

But back at Bristol in November he was afflicted with agonising neuralgic pains " from my right temple to the tip of my right shoulder." He was " nearly frantic, and ran about the house naked, endeavouring by every means to excite sensations in different parts of my body, and so to weaken the enemy by creating diversion." By taking " between sixty and seventy drops of laudanum " he procured relief for one day, during which the pain " only *niggled*." But the next day it returned, and only by taking twenty-five drops of laudanum every five hours was he enabled to write Poole a " flighty but not exaggerated account " of his indisposition, which his doctor diagnosed as " altogether nervous," originating " either in severe application, or excessive anxiety." He had anxiety enough. The house at Adscombe was not to be had, and his hopes of rural delights were dashed. Then Lloyd's affliction and temperament suggested doubts of his proving a comfortable housemate. His epilepsy produced fits of morbid delirium, in which realities around him were distorted into grotesque features of nightmare, leaving behind a neurotic tendency to despondency. This Coleridge strove to combat in the stirring exhortation of the sonnet " To a Young Man of Fortune," containing the line, " What Nature makes thee mourn, she bids thee heal! "—an injunction which was ironically to torture his own conscience through many years of suffering. Further, Lloyd's father intimated that his son should remain with him only a year, so that he would then be deprived of Lloyd's fee of eighty pounds a year, a considerable contribution to his income. Other complications arose from Mrs. Fricker's aversion to leaving Bristol and her son's being not yet old enough for an apprenticeship. With Lloyd's delusions, Coleridge's neuralgia, a crying baby, and a mother-in-law fractious at the unsettled state of the household, the atmosphere was nerve-racking.

His present wretchedness pointed the contrast with his visions of peace and congeniality at Stowey, and he begged Poole to find him a house. Poole replied that there was no suitable house to be had—only an inconvenient cottage situated on the street at the west end of the village. To his consternation Coleridge immediately replied that he would take it for a year. " It is not a beauty, to be sure, but its vicinity to you shall over-balance its defects." He would like to move in at Christmas. He had decided not to undertake " the charge of Charles Lloyd's mind," and to counterbalance the subtraction of eighty pounds from his annual income, he would dispense with a servant and himself " work *very hard*—as Cook, Butler, Scullion, Shoe-cleaner, occasional Nurse, Gardner, Hind, Pig-protector, Chap-lain, Secretary, Poet, Reviewer, and *omnium-botherum* shilling-Scavenger." There would be no room for Mrs. Fricker, so she should have her wish of remaining at Bristol and Coleridge would allow her twenty pounds a year. Her furniture would have to remain with her, but Coleridge and Sara still had enough of their own to furnish one bedroom and a kitchen-parlour.

Poole knew that Coleridge, only a year before, had found Clevedon too far from Bristol for convenience. He had heard that Cottle and other Bristol friends frowned on the proposed move to Stowey and were urging on Coleridge a suitable house available near Bristol. It also seems that his own relations dis-liked the prospect of an extreme democrat as a near neighbour, and he feared that Coleridge and himself might suffer social ostracism and possibly petty persecution for their unpopular opinions. He therefore replied soberly, emphasising the prob-able, as well as the actual, disadvantages that Coleridge in his eager impetuosity appeared to overlook.

His letter gave Coleridge " unexpected and most acute pain ";
the " Damp " struck into his " very Heart." On hearing of his
disappointment with Mrs. Evans at Darley, Poole had written
in ardent sympathy, " By you, Coleridge, I will always stand,
in sickness and health, in prosperity and misfortune," and when
Coleridge had visited Stowey, he had expressed delight at the
possibility of his living near. It seemed to Coleridge that Poole's
opinions had suffered a " sudden revolution," probably because
his friends and relations disapproved of their friendship. He sat
down to pour out his anguish and reproach. Sara saw the working
of his face as he wrote, but he would not show her Poole's letter;
how could he let her think that his " most beloved friend " had
" grown cold " towards him? Mary Evans, Southey and Pantisocracy, the *Watchman*, the tutorship at Darley, Lloyd, and now
Poole and Stowey! " O my God! my God! when am I to find
rest! Disappointment follows disappointment, and Hope seems
given me merely to prevent my becoming callous to Misery! "
He was not merely lamenting the unkind fortunes of an adverse
fate. A few weeks before Charles Lamb (who, after nearly two
years' separation, continued a regular and copious correspondent),
writing that " I grieve from my very soul to observe you in
your plans of life veering about from this hope to the other, then
settling no where," had asked, " Is it an untoward fatality . . .
that does this for you . . . or lies the fault, as I fear it does, in
your own mind? " On the tinder of Coleridge's habit of self-
analysis the flint of the question struck a spark sufficient to keep
his conscience uncomfortably wakeful, and his eagerness to be
settled became frantic anxiety.

The devoted Poole, reminded of the pathetic sequence of
repeated disappointments, could not bear the charge of coldness.
He immediately wrote that the cottage was at Coleridge's disposal and he would make every preparation for his welcome,
even to supplementing his scarcity of furniture. Coleridge
apologised for " improper impetuosity," but Poole's previous
letter had inspired " the feelings of those distressful dreams where
we imagine ourselves falling from precipices "—he seemed to
be " falling from the summit of my fondest desires, whirled

from the height just as I had reached it." In his elation he was only deterred by doctor's orders from immediately setting out on the long walk to Stowey. His face was so "monstrously swollen" that his "recondite eye sits distent quaintly, behind the flesh-hill, and looks as little as a tom-tit's." He had a sore throat preventing him from eating "aught but spoon-meat without great pain," and also a rheumatic complaint in the back of his head and shoulders. Lloyd was, after all, to be a member of his household. He had gone to Birmingham, where his bouts of delirium had apparently convinced his father both of the danger of opposing his inclination and of the impossibility of his ever entering business life. So insistence on his return after a year was withdrawn and he was to reside indefinitely with Coleridge. He would furnish his own room, a "Press-bed" enabling it to serve as bedroom and parlour, would be his own servant, and contribute only the cost of his own maintenance.

In the latter months of the year Coleridge had written a few verses and sonnets, some of which had earned useful guineas on publication in newspapers and periodicals. On some paper surviving from the decease of the *Watchman* he had a sheet of sonnets printed, the cost of printing being defrayed by friends. And on the eve of departure for his new life at Stowey, in three days over Christmas, he wrote his *Ode to the Departing Year*, which was dedicated to Poole and published on New Year's Eve by the proprietor of the *Cambridge Intelligencer*, Benjamin Flower, a fervent pacifist and opposer of the government, who was to suffer imprisonment for alleged libel on that same apostle of convenient opinions, Bishop Watson, to whom Wordsworth addressed the protest he feared to publish. In the final epode of the *Ode* Coleridge upbraided his country for creating discord from the safety of insular isolation:

"*Abandon'd of Heaven! mad Avarice thy guide,*
At cowardly distance, yet kindling with pride—
Mid thy herds and thy corn-fields secure thou hast stood,
And join'd the wild yelling of Famine and Blood!"

With a warning that the accumulated resentment of aggrieved nations would one day wreak terrible retribution, he justified his own intellectual detachment as an objector to the war.

> " *I unpartaking of the evil thing,*
> *With daily prayer and daily toil*
> *Soliciting for food my scanty soil,*
> *Have wail'd my country with a loud Lament.*
> *Now I recentre my immortal mind*
> *In the deep Sabbath of meek self-content.*"

Having registered protest against the criminal folly of current politics, he had the right of individual integrity to retire to rural peace and, while seeking a modest livelihood, to cultivate his intellectual gifts for the benefit of human enlightenment. " I am not *fit* for *public* life," he wrote at this time to the political agitator, John Thelwall; " yet the light shall stream to a far distance from my cottage window."

3. SETTLEMENT AT STOWEY

The new year of 1797 found Coleridge settling into his inconvenient cottage at Stowey. In front, on either side of the door looking on the street, were two small, ill-lighted parlours; behind, a kitchen with an open hearth, and above three or four small bedrooms. A strip of land, half garden, half orchard, stretched at the back, but a path was opened from this to communicate with Poole's garden and thence with that of John Cruikshank, who, with his young wife, became close friends. Whenever he pleased, Coleridge resorted to Poole's spacious " book-room," and when spring came, he frequently worked in a jasmine-covered arbour in Poole's garden, where in the evening, over glasses of cider, he would read to Poole what he had written.

He was still meditating " a book of morals in answer to Godwin," in which he proposed, not only to expose Godwin's fallacies, "but to detect what appear to me the defects of all the systems of morality before and since Christ, and to shew that wherein they have been right, they have exactly coincided with the Gospel, and that each has erred exactly where and in proportion as he has deviated from that perfect canon." It is a cheap gibe that he made many plans which never approached, or could have approached, execution. It is true that his many literary schemes, if carried out, might have occupied a syndicate of assiduous workers through half a century of labour. But his philosophical plans were always defeated by the scope of their ambition. Not content with an answer to Godwin and a plain re-statement of the need for practical application of Christianity, he must expose the fallacies of all Godwin's predecessors, so involving himself in an interminable study of defective philosophies. He did not dally in indolence, as his critics averred. On the contrary, he read prodigiously, as the copious learning of his later work testifies, but to accomplish his ambitious programme was beyond the scope of a single lifetime. The immediate result of his reading for this "answer to Godwin" was to unseat his satisfaction in Hartley's theory of the association of ideas. As he said in *Biographia Literaria*, "I found myself afloat . . . the fontal truths of natural religion and the books of Revelation alike contributed to the flow; and it was long ere my ark touched on an Ararat, and rested." Temporarily his ark touched a shoal, for he became enthusiastic for Bishop Berkeley's notions of perception and interpretation.

In poetry he achieved more tangible results, working on his tragedy of *Osorio* and on the preparation of a second edition of his poems, to appear in the one volume with poems by Lamb and Lloyd. Poor Lloyd's ardently desired residence with Coleridge was brief. After spending Christmas with his parents, he was daily expected at Stowey, but in the middle of January he appeared unexpectedly in London and introduced himself to Charles Lamb, with whom he had corresponded through Coleridge. When dread of his disease was not warping his mental outlook, he had a gentle earnestness of manner and winning charm. He was moved to visit Lamb by Coleridge's account of

Mary Lamb's insanity, and Lamb, shunning all society and wretchedly lonely, felt gratitude that anyone should seek him out and sympathise with a sufferer from the same dreadful malady as shadowed his own life. From London he eventually arrived at Stowey, where his affliction became active. Five times in ten days he suffered prolonged fits of delirium, and Coleridge was up most of the night, exhausting himself physically in subduing his frantic struggles and mentally in witnessing his pitiable agony. Apart from the impossibility of keeping such an invalid in a confined household with a young mother and baby, Lloyd obviously needed expert treatment, and at the end of March he left Stowey for Erasmus Darwin's sanatorium at Lichfield.

Excepting the few weeks of Lloyd's unhappy stay, Coleridge enjoyed in these months the most undisturbed happiness of his life. He went to Bristol so rarely that repeatedly he had to apologise to Wade or Cottle for postponing engagements with them. Rising before seven, he worked in the garden; in the mornings he read and wrote till noon, when he fed the pigs and poultry; after dinner at two he wrote again till tea, and devoted the time between tea and supper to reviewing. After supper presumably—and probably earlier if opportunity occurred—he entertained Poole and other friends with his conversation. He grew potatoes and " all manner of vegetables," and enough corn to supply his household with bread; he kept ducks, geese, and two pigs. " A cow would not answer the keep," and Poole supplied all the milk they wanted. The mice played " the very devil " about the house, but Coleridge would not use traps, which seemed to him treacherous deception, like assassinating " too credulous guests."

Sometime after Lloyd's departure, he nursed another invalid, George Burnett, who repeatedly returned to Coleridge from unsuccessful efforts to earn a living, and suffered an attack of jaundice while at Stowey. During his convalescence, Coleridge seems to have exerted his influence to obtain for him the post of Unitarian minister at Yarmouth, where Southey, to make some amends to his former friend, sent to him his youngest brother as a private pupil. Estlin and his wife were other visitors, and Charles Lamb was invited for a holiday.

About the end of March, while Coleridge was still suffering from the stress of nursing Lloyd, Wordsworth came. Previously they had met only a few times at College Street eighteen months before, where Coleridge was too occupied by his estrangement from Southey and arrangements for his marriage to take much note of a new acquaintance. Naturally Wordsworth had been more impressed by him than he by Wordsworth, for Wordsworth's awkward manners had no attraction for casual acquaintances; Wordsworth had invited correspondence and then sent his *Guilt and Sorrow* for him to read. With his eager confidence in the capacity of human affection, Coleridge was ever ready to embrace new friendships and in Wordsworth's verse he recognised the same simple strength and spiritual quality to which he and Southey aspired. He not only sent Wordsworth's manuscript to Lamb, in the hope of introducing the two poets to each other, but quoted to Thelwall Wordsworth's preference for certain lines of *Religious Musings* as the opinion of " the best poet of the age " and " a very dear friend of mine." The correspondence continued, and recently he had apparently sent to Wordsworth a copy of the passage he had contributed to Southey's *Joan*, now altered and entitled " The Progress of Liberty," which he eventually omitted from the new edition of his poems on Lamb's objection to the incongruity of introducing Joan of Arc into a discussion of the inspiration of the French and American revolutions.

Lloyd's illness and departure left him in a mood of "depression too dreadful to be described," from which, he said, " Wordsworth's conversation, etc., roused me somewhat." Talking of Southey, Wordsworth said he wrote " too much at his ease," seldom expressing profound emotion. The criticism impressed Coleridge, who had himself sensed the weakness without diagnosing it, and inspired him to the prophetic opinion that Southey would make literature " more *profitable to him* from the fluency with which he writes, and the facility with which he pleases himself," but posterity would find his wreath " unseemly," his

beauties losing effect "from the bad company they keep."
Wordsworth also suggested to him that Southey inclined "to
rely too much on *story* and *event* in his poems, to the neglect of
those *lofty imaginings*, that are peculiar to, and definitive of,
the poet." He confided to Wordsworth Lamb's suggestion
that he should write an epic on the "Origin of Evil," and
evidently found that Wordsworth agreed with his massive
conception of such an undertaking, for he decided that he
would need not less than twenty years for its accomplish-
ment—ten to collect materials and "warm" his mind with
universal science, five to write the poem, and the last five to
correct it.

As Professor Harper supposed, "it must have been Wordsworth's natural gifts that won Coleridge's admiration; certainly
not his learning." It was, indeed, Wordsworth's lack of learning
that intensified his natural gifts in Coleridge's eyes. Here was a
poet, without culture, without his own wide reading, without
his searching speculations on metaphysics and religion, without
his dizzy flights of imagination, who had yet arrived at the
theory of poetic expression to which he and Southey had been
feeling their way! Here was a man of no more apparent intellectual equipment, and rather less ability to be colloquially arti-
culate, than Tom Poole, who had yet written poetry with simplicity of diction and strength of expression equal to the best of
his own achievements! Wordsworth's ruggedness, his egotistical
detachment, his very uncouthness, appealed to Coleridge, who,
weak and emotional himself, saw and admired in Wordsworth
the strength he had seen and admired in Southey, but with an
intensity deriving from difference in age and character—while
Southey had been younger than himself, little more than an
adolescent, Wordsworth was as much his senior, and had experienced emotional suffering. Many years later he said, "Of all
the men I ever knew, Wordsworth has the least femininity in
his mind. He is *all man*. He is a man of whom it might have
been said, 'It is good for him to be alone.'" Coleridge's more
complex nature had much of the feminine—his gentleness, res-
ponsiveness, spontaneity, quick sympathy, tender affection,

emotional fervour—and he admired in Wordsworth a masculinity unseasoned by his own subtle susceptibilities.

Poole saw it—perhaps not at first, for Poole's perception was slow, but with a certainty the surer for slowness. Always he deprecated Coleridge's enthusiasm for Wordsworth. For him Coleridge was always the genius transcending in brilliance all rivals, and his admiration for Wordsworth irritated Poole as unworthy self-abasement, a sullying of the shrine at which he himself worshipped with steadfast devotion. Cheap jealousy was not in Poole's nature, but he suffered sad moments, not untainted by resentment against Wordsworth, as he gradually realised that he was no longer the sheet-anchor to which Coleridge's frail craft was tethered.

G

PART SIX

PARTNERS IN POETRY

I. SUSPECTS AT ALFOXDEN

WORDSWORTH left Coleridge at Stowey with an invitation to visit him at Racedown. As soon as Coleridge had finally corrected his poems to his satisfaction, and sent them with Lamb's and Lloyd's to Cottle for the printer, he set off. On Sundays he frequently preached in the Unitarian chapels at Bridgwater and Taunton, usually walking and never accepting a fee for his sermons. On Sunday 4th June 1797 he preached at Bridgwater, breakfasted next morning at Taunton, and then walked the twenty miles to Racedown. The distance was nothing to him. Later in the summer he walked to Bristol and back, a distance of forty miles, in a single day—to make the personal acquaintance of " that great and excellent woman," Mrs. Barbauld, to whom he had sent a copy of his poems. He found Wordsworth and Dorothy alone, Mary Hutchinson having left only that morning for London. In old age they both remembered how Coleridge, eager to meet them and unfatigued by his long walk, " did not keep to the high-way, but leapt over a gate and bounded down the pathless field, by which he cut off an angle." That evening Wordsworth read his latest poem, *The Ruined Cottage*, and Coleridge then recited two and a half acts of his tragedy *Osorio*; next morning Wordsworth read *The Borderers*.

The Ruined Cottage, afterwards included in the first book of *The Excursion*, was the story of the simple cottage couple, whose happiness is withered by the poverty and famine induced by the country's going to war, impelling the husband to enlist, while the lonely wife loses first her growing boy as a farmer's apprentice and then her younger child by death. The simplicity of its telling, in unadorned blank verse, confirmed Coleridge's impression of Wordsworth's powers from his reading of *Guilt and Sorrow*. With wonderful fidelity he remembered his impressions in *Biographia Literaria*. Some harshness of versification, to his unfailing musical ear, remained—and always did remain—but " the occasional obscurities, which had risen from an imperfect control over the resources of his native language, had almost wholly disappeared, together with that worse defect of arbitrary and illogical phrases, at once hackneyed and fantastic, which hold so distinguished a place in the *technique* of ordinary poetry, and will, more or less, alloy the earlier poems of the truest genius." He saw that he and Southey, though led by Bowles and Akenside to seek their inspiration directly from nature, had pursued the shadow of the substance in valuing their manipulation of difficult metres, their hard-sought metaphors and similes, their artful allegories and brightly polished phrases. Here was " no mark of strained thought, or forced diction, no crowd or turbulence of imagery," such as had been held against his *Religious Musings*, and he was impressed by " the union of deep feeling with profound thought; the fine balance of truth in observing, with the imaginative faculty in modifying, the objects observed; and above all the original gift of spreading the tone, the atmosphere, and with it the depth and height of the ideal world around forms, incidents, and situations, of which, for the common view, custom had bedimmed all the lustre, had dried up the sparkle and the dew drops." Though he had before confessed that his critical vice was " a precipitance in praise," his admiration was spontaneous and unstinted. After three weeks at Racedown he wrote, " Wordsworth is a very great man, the only man to whom *at all times* and *in all modes of excellence* I feel myself inferior."

Aside from his personal attractions, his admiration of her beloved brother won Dorothy's heart, for she knew that such admiration was what Wordsworth most needed to dispel his despondency and encourage him to fresh efforts. In her adoration she extravagantly applauded his work—as her most fervent admirer, Professor de Selincourt, admitted, she became " a dangerously undiscriminating critic "—but Wordsworth knew that her praise was neither unprejudiced nor endowed with critical experience. Coleridge, however, was a poet whose gifts he recognised however unwillingly, and also the possessor of intellectual attainments compelling the admiration of all who knew him.

Ten years later Southey shrewdly diagnosed the vice of Wordsworth's intellect as being "always upon the stretch and strain," looking "at pileworts and daffydowndillies through the same telescope which he applies to the moon and the stars." For want of wider experience and of the moderating influence of taste and discrimination deriving from intellectual culture—a want intensified by narrowness of life and the habit of self-absorption—Wordsworth increasingly tended to magnify the trivial, and Dorothy, intent on sharing his impressions, lost her sense of proportion and likewise saw with distortion. To this tendency Coleridge was a corrective; his quick selective sense seized on the significant, and his eloquence as rapidly translated its meaning. The speed of his perception must have been a breath-taking revelation to Wordsworth and Dorothy. While Wordsworth mused over an idea, his mental energies labouring exhaustingly to move his sluggish imagination, Coleridge had only to take up the trend of his thought to provide the clue to the solution. His leaping imagination was a hare to Wordsworth's tortoise; he understood, and painted in a few swift strokes, the notion which Wordsworth would have sweated hours to sketch.

Probably Wordsworth never fully grasped the implications of the poetic theory that Coleridge eloquently expounded and of which he declared his poetry to be the purest practical example. He said with truth in old age that he "never cared a straw about the theory." But he did immediately realise that Coleridge's endless conversation enabled him to see with clarity where before he had groped unsteadily in baffling fog. Both he and Dorothy recognised, as the latter confessed, that Coleridge's conversation was necessary to his artistic development.

So when Coleridge at length tore himself away on 28th June, it was only to return from Stowey four days later with Poole's one-horse chaise, in which he was to drive Dorothy " over forty miles of execrable roads," while Wordsworth walked. Though he retained rueful recollections of his charger in dragooning days, and when he borrowed a mount from Poole to ride between Stowey and Bridgwater, he begged for a steed " of tolerable meekness," he was delighted after his venture to reckon himself " now no inexpert whip."

The Wordsworths were guests for a fortnight at Coleridge's cottage, which must have been overcrowded when Charles Lamb arrived for his long-promised visit on 7th July. Coleridge was laid up throughout his week's stay, for two days after the Words-worths' arrival, " dear Sara accidentally emptied a skillet of boiling milk " over his foot. One evening, when all had gone for a walk, leaving him alone in Poole's arbour, he wrote the first of his poems under Wordsworth's influence, *This Lime-Tree Bower My Prison.*

> " *Well, they are gone, and here must I remain,*
> *This lime-tree bower my prison! I have lost*
> *Beauties and feelings, such as would have been*
> *Most sweet to my remembrance even when age*
> *Had dimm'd mine eyes to blindness! They, meanwhile,*
> *Friends, whom I never more may meet again,*
> *On springy heath, along the hill-top edge,*
> *Wander in gladness, and wind down, perchance,*
> *To that still roaring dell, of which I told.*"

In imagination he accompanied their walk, seeing their delight in the beautiful scenery he had described to them, and especially he felt pleasure in picturing the gladness of his " gentle-hearted Charles," who had pined

> " *And hunger'd after Nature, many a year,*
> *In the great City pent, winning thy way*
> *With sad yet patient soul, through evil and pain*
> *And strange calamity!* "

In the last year of his life, with a full heart, he re-read the poem and wrote in the margin, " Ch. and Mary Lamb—dear to my

heart, yea, as it were my Heart—S.T.C. Aet. 63; 1834—1797—
1834=37 years!"

The simplicity of thought and diction, the preference of blank
verse to a complicated form, the complete absence of " man-
chineel " ornament, indicates the fresh influence of Wordsworth
and the speed with which Coleridge had learned his lesson. A
few days later, replying to Southey's request for a contribution
to a volume to be published for the benefit of Chatterton's sister,
he promised a preliminary essay and possibly a poem, but prohibited the reprinting of his *Monody*. " On a life and death
so full of heart-going *realities* as poor Chatterton's," he wrote,
" to find such shadowy nobodies as cherub-winged *Death*, trees
of *Hope*, bare-bosomed *Affection*, and simpering *Peace*, makes
one's blood circulate like ipecacuanha." The second edition of
his poems was in the press and published in the course of the
current month. They could not be altered; but he was so out
of love with his own compositions, so conscious of their defects,
that he felt irritated at the praise of reviewers. Unable to express
his self-criticism in a review of his own work, he published in
the *Monthly Magazine* the three sonnets under the pseudonym
of " Nehemiah Higginbottom," which he reprinted in *Biographia
Literaria*. The first sonnet was " to excite a good-natured laugh
at the spirit of doleful egotism, and at the recurrence of favourite
phrases, with the double defect of being at once trite and licen-
tious "; the second on " low creeping language and thoughts,
under the pretence of simplicity "; the third, " the phrases of
which were borrowed entirely from my own poems, on the
indiscriminate use of elaborate and swelling language and
imagery."

Though in later years professing a contempt for the country
as an inveterate Londoner, Charles Lamb valued every minute
of brief escape from the office-stool into the little intellectual
society gathered in the rural peace of the Quantocks. He felt
" improvement in the recollection of many a casual conversation," and " the names of Tom Poole, of Wordsworth and his
good sister, with thine and Sara's are become ' familiar in my
mouth as household words.' " On leaving, he forgot his

greatcoat, and writing for its return, expressed envy of " that greatcoat lingering so cunningly behind." As he travelled alone from Bridgwater to Bristol, heart-full at parting, he looked out for John Thelwall, who was daily expected at Stowey, but felt that if he had met him, going to the happy scene he was himself leaving, " it would have moved me almost to tears."

Thelwall was a notorious enthusiast for the French Revolution and opponent of the war and the government. At the age of thirty, in November 1794, he had stood in the dock with the veterans Horne Tooke, Hardy and Holcroft on a charge of high treason. If the accused had been found guilty, said the banker-poet, Samuel Rogers, they would certainly have been hanged, for " we lived in a reign of terror then." After his acquittal, he had campaigned courageously against Pitt's government, and when he held a mass-meeting in Marylebone Fields, his paper, the *Tribune*, was suppressed. Banned from holding meetings in London, he wandered about the country, lecturing on historical subjects, drawing pointed parallels with current politics. Often he was mobbed at lectures, and magistrates refused him the law's protection. Coleridge had opened correspondence with him in the spring of 1796 by sending him a copy of his poems. Thelwall returned the compliment with a present of his latest book, and they exchanged in friendly argument their views on religion and politics in an interesting series of letters. Months before, Coleridge had invited him to visit him at Bristol, but now for the first time Thelwall had the opportunity to meet in the flesh the man whose reputation and writings so much interested him. He arrived at Stowey on 17th July, at nine in the evening, and found Sara alone, as Coleridge was staying with the Words-worths at Alfoxden, about three miles away.

The Wordsworths were enchanted with the Quantocks. " There is everything here," wrote Dorothy, for while she found the brooks and woods as attractive as those of Cumberland, there was also the sea at hand and many " romantic " villages. Especially they liked the park of Alfoxden House, and indulging " dreams of happiness in a little cottage " near there, they made inquiries for such a place. Then came the news that Bartholomew,

the farm bailiff of the St. Aubyn family, was empowered to let
Alfoxden House furnished, with immediate possession, for the
astonishingly small rent of twenty-three pounds a year. Wordsworth immediately took the house on an annual tenancy, signing
the agreement with Bartholomew on 14th July, Poole witnessing.

Coleridge was assisting in his friends' installation when Thelwall arrived, while Sara remained at home to deal with the
accumulated laundry of her husband and guests. Thelwall slept
the night at Stowey, and was next morning conducted by Sara
to Alfoxden for breakfast. For three days the whole party
remained at Alfoxden, wandering about the beautiful gardens,
discussing poetry, the " moral character " of democrats and
aristocrats, and " pursuits proper for literary men " who were
" unfit for management of pecuniary affairs," like Rousseau,
Bacon, and Arthur Young. They were " a most philosophical
party," and Thelwall desired only the company of his wife to
complete his pleasure in a " delightful spot." Since his paper
had been suppressed and he seemed well advised to leave London
to escape the probability of another government prosecution,
Thelwall was looking for a small farm, and Poole and Coleridge
undertook to find something suitable for him in the neighbourhood.

But " Citizen " Thelwall was a marked man, and his presence
in the district excited suspicion of a seditious plot in the war-
fearful minds of neighbouring gentry. Though, as Coleridge
remarked, the coast from Clevedon to Minehead scarcely permitted the approach of a fishing-boat, it was suspected that this
convocation of " suspects " might indicate the proposed landing
of a French invasion. So, owing to " the grave alarm of a titled
Dogberry of our neighbourhood," Coleridge related in *Biographia Literaria*, " a spy was actually sent down from the
government *pour surveillance* of myself and friends." Coleridge
was actually interviewed by the disguised Bow Street runner,
who, readily drawing the friendly and talkative philosopher into
conversation, affected extreme democratic opinions, and was so
impressed by Coleridge's eloquent exposition of his familiar
arguments against Jacobinism that he shamefacedly confessed " he

had only *put it on*." The landlord of the inn at Stowey also confided to Coleridge how he was questioned by the spy about him and his mysterious friend at Alfoxden, and how finally he declared, " Why, folks do say, your Honour! as how that he is a *Poet*, and that he is going to put Quantocks and all about here in print; and as they be so much together, I suppose that the strange gentleman has some *consarn* in the business."

But the " strange gentleman," in his old age as Poet Laureate and the respected friend of all the Tory gentry, titled or untitled, lay or clerical, in the Lake District, felt that the story of his being once the quarry of a government spy, derogated from his dignity and respectability. He did not definitely deny its truth; he implied a doubt of its truth by stating that the facts related by Coleridge only came to his knowledge after he had left Alfoxden. Victorian biographers naturally supposed that no spy could enter the gossipping confines of a remote country village without every child's mother chattering of the phenomenon, and as Wordsworth was eminently respectable while Coleridge had certain regrettable foibles unhappily too often coincident with genius, respectability accepted, as always, the testimony of respectability. Even Coleridge's grandson, confronted with his grandfather's letters to Thelwall, referred to " apocryphal anecdotes about the spy " in *Biographia Literaria*.

Researches by Mr. A. J. Eagleston revealed records in the Home Office archives of a spy having been sent to Stowey, on representations from Lord Somerville, of Fitzhead Court, Taunton (curiously, a distant relative of Southey's), a landowner near Bridgwater named Sir Philip Hale, and a Bath physician named Lysons, who acted on the gossip of his cook, who had been formerly employed at Alfoxden. The spy lodged at Stowey during August, and reported that Poole protected " a mischievous gang of disaffected Englishmen," who had been visited by the notorious Thelwall. Ironically for respectability, Wordsworth was the chief object of suspicion, as he had no wife with him, but only a woman who " posed for his sister! " Coleridge, as he relates, was planning a poem to be called *The Brook*, and made many excursions with pencil and notebook to the stream running from Holford to Kilve; the following spy duly noted that he was "apparently taking observations" on the "river" in his "portfolio." On such momentous information some excited clerk in the Home Office must have had visions of the French fleet sailing into the bowels of Somerset, with dire consequences to the minnows and grayling! "Coldridge" was reported as "a man of superior ability," who kept a press in his house and was believed to print his own compositions. But the fact that Coleridge often preached sermons on Sundays must have weighed in his favour, and the spy regretfully decided that he was "respectable." And when Basil Montagu, described as "a great counsellor from London," came to see his son at Alfoxden, and such an eminently respectable Bristol citizen as Cottle visited Coleridge, the spy packed up in disgust.

In the nineteen-twenties, when a man with a beard appeared on a Labour platform during an election in a cathedral town, he was popularly reckoned a Russian in disguise. So, in country villages, young men in beards and corduroy trousers are labelled "a rum lot," and if they show no visible signs of making money by selling something for more than they bought it for, they will be objects of suspicion. Poole was locally notorious for revolutionary opinions, Coleridge was his friend, and now came a dark, gaunt young man, with a woman supposed to be his sister, but obviously showing to him more than a normal sisterly affection. They kept unconventional hours, and used each other's houses as their own. In Stowey Coleridge's friendliness and willingness to talk with anybody had won him the villagers' tolerant affection, but in the neighbouring villages his name was a subject for dark gossip. He once encountered a woman from George Burnett's village, who talked of him as "that vile jacobin villain" who had seduced "a young man of our parish"; he listened patiently, exclaiming at appropriate intervals, and so won her heart by his "civilities" that he "had not courage enough to undeceive her." As for Wordsworth, after half a century's residence in Cumberland, he was still regarded with dubious glances by the dalesmen; striding along, often muttering to himself, he was too lost in thought to notice their tentative greetings. As a stranger of unknown antecedents, he was big game for gossip in a country village.

Poole, as a man of important standing locally, suffered from his association with these eccentrics. " We are shocked to hear that Mr. Thelwall has spent some time at Stowey this week with Mr. Coleridge, and consequently with Tom Poole," wrote one of his orthodox cousins on 23rd July. " Alfoxden house is taken by one of the fraternity. . . . To what are we coming? " These virtuous relatives made representations to his aging invalid mother, who was alarmed at the possibility of her son's ostracism by neighbours with whom she had been friendly for fifty years. His work as organiser of the village benefit club and book society faced probable frustration, and even his business and credit were likely to be affected. He was therefore compelled to tell Coleridge that he could not risk the consequences of finding a farm for Thelwall.

Coleridge did not immediately abandon his efforts. His favourable impression of Thelwall in correspondence was confirmed by personal contact. " Thelwall," he said, " is a very warm hearted honest man—and disagreeing, as we do, on almost every point of religion, of morals, of politics, and of philosophy, we like each other uncommonly well." He believed him to be " perhaps the only *acting* Democrat, that *is* honest—for the *Patriots* are ragged cattle—a most execrable herd—arrogant because they are ignorant, and boastful of the strength of reason, because they have never tried it enough to know its *weakness*." Writing to Thelwall that " the aristocrats seem to persecute *even Wordsworth*," he assured him that " we will at least not yield without a struggle; and if I cannot get you near me, it shall not be for want of a trial on my part."

Though he had been ill the day before, he walked one day in September to Bridgwater to sound two of the principal land-agents. One was " powerless "; the other, a Mr. Chubb, was unable to see him on account of the assizes. Returning home, he wrote to Chubb, praising Thelwall's personality and even arguing as a reason for his settlement near Stowey, that, in the event of revolution, Thelwall might have great influence on the lower classes, in which case it would " prove of no mean utility to the cause of Truth and Humanity that he had spent some years in a society, where his natural impetuosity had been disciplined into patience, and salutary scepticism, and the slow energies of a *Calculating* spirit." But Chubb replied that he would find Thelwall a farm if Poole and Coleridge were agreed on the advisability of his settling there. As this again reposed responsibility on Poole, Coleridge had to inform Thelwall of his inability to serve him.

In excusing Poole's unwillingness and his own helplessness, he explained to Thelwall the local atmosphere of antagonism and suspicion. "Very great odium T. Poole incurred by bringing *me* here. My peaceable manners and known attachment to Christianity had almost worn it away when Wordsworth came, and he, likewise by T. Poole's agency, settled here. You cannot conceive the tumult, calumnies, and apparatus of threatened persecutions which this event has occasioned round about us. If *you*, too, should come, I am afraid that even riots, and dangerous riots, might be the consequence. Either of us separately would perhaps be tolerable, but *all three* together, what can it be less than plot and damned conspiracy—a school for the propagation of Demagogy and Atheism?" Yet the aged and respectable Poet Laureate could assert that at Alfoxden "annoyances I had none," and expressed himself so decisively that the restrained, though whimsically satirical, account in *Biographia Literaria* was for a century fancied a fiction of Coleridge's picturesque imagination!

Truly Wordsworth suffered no personal "annoyances." Poole suffered the annoyances and Coleridge the vexation of having implicated him by introducing Wordsworth. It was characteristic of Wordsworth that, unaffected by the village gossip in the seclusion of Alfoxden, he should be unperturbed by the inconvenience and discomfort endured by his friends on his account. He had a furnished mansion, with beautiful grounds, for at least a year at a nominal rent; he had an assured income from the annuity purchased with Raisley Calvert's legacy, supplemented by Montagu's fee for allowing his boy to educate himself. He had even discovered salve for his conscience in the decision of Coleridge and Thelwall to snap their " squeaking baby-trumpet of sedition " and retire from the unsavoury business of politics to the peace of rural seclusion. Former fretfulness over his impotence to combat the rising tide of war hysteria was now forgotten, and though he had not blown his trumpet-blast, like Coleridge and Thelwall, before retirement, but had removed his trumpet from his lips by leaving his letter to the Bishop of Llandaff in manuscript, he was capable of assuming virtue to himself in forbearance from futility. He was free to cultivate his fresh confidence in his poetic powers in Coleridge's society, which, as Dorothy wrote, was their " principal inducement " to taking Alfoxden.

Coleridge was easily distracted from worry over local politics by the delight of discussing poetry with a fellow artist; in fact, Alfoxden became for him a refuge from domestic and financial anxiety. As he told Thelwall, " I get nothing by literature." The second edition of his poems, including those of Lamb and Lloyd, was published in July or August, but he had probably forestalled its small profits in advances from Cottle. He had no means of subsistence apart from the fund organised by Poole and Estlin, and his hopes now rested on the possibility of Sheridan's accepting his tragedy for performance at Drury Lane. On completing and dispatching the manuscript of the tragedy on 16th October, feeling " no hope of its success, or even of its being acted," he wrote, " I suppose that at last I must become a Unitarian minister, as a less evil than starvation."

It may be supposed that Sara became eventually jealous and resentful of his habitual absences at Alfoxden. Coleridge did not conceal his delight in Dorothy's company. Wordsworth's " exquisite sister " was " a woman indeed!—in mind, I mean, and heart—for her person is such, that if you expected to see a pretty woman, you would think her ordinary—if you expected to find an ordinary woman, you would think her pretty!—But her manners are simple, ardent, impressive—

In every motion her most innocent soul
Outbeams so brightly, that who saw would say,
Guilt was a thing impossible in her.

Her information various—her eye watchful in minutest observation of nature—and her taste a perfect electrometer—it bends,
protrudes, and draws in, at subtlest beauties and most recondite
faults." Such praise must have brought petulant frowns to
Sara's pretty brow, for Coleridge's letters to her show that he
never discussed his intellectual acrobatics with her. She was
interested only in things and people, and Coleridge would make
frivolous references to some woman's evident admiration of him,
pointing the playfulness by immediately mentioning his ever-
present visions of her with his " sweet babe."

Later, Dorothy made no secret of her opinion that Sara was
an unworthy mate for Coleridge and that his unhappiness was
due to lack of a wife's sympathetic understanding. From the
first there can have been no love lost between the two women,
the one resenting her husband's delight in the other's company,
the other resenting the wife's possession of her husband. Dorothy's
fanatical devotion to her brother is generally supposed to have
been so exorbitant as to have excluded any natural feminine
passion for another man, but such supposition ignores the growth
and gradation of her devotion. Before she met Coleridge, her
fervent attachment to her brother was extravagant, but only after
she left Alfoxden, after she ceased to be daily in Coleridge's
company, did it become neurotic, disturbing and even dangerous.
Her early Grasmere journals show that she loved Coleridge, and
frustration of this natural passion excited her hysterically emotional temperament to vent her feelings in unnatural adoration
of her brother. If Coleridge had been free, she would undoubtedly
have married him. Practically it would have been a perfect
arrangement, since both she and Wordsworth so eagerly desired
his society that they gave up a house which cost them nothing;
she would have retained her brother and secured for him the
daily companionship of the one man whose intellectual stimulus
was necessary to his development. As certainly, Coleridge would

have married her; he admired her, felt tenderness for her, and his sentimentalising would soon have been construed by the emotional Dorothy into an avowal of passion.

Her middle-class upbringing prohibited the mere idea of her becoming his mistress, nor could she have consciously contemplated the possibility of falling in love with a married man. Her enthusiasm and admiration for Coleridge's attainments and her delight in his beneficial effect on her brother, developed a seemingly sisterly affection, which she only recognised as love after prolonged separation. On his side, the puritan in Coleridge combined with an under-sexed nature to preclude temptation to adultery. He craved sympathy, encouragement and maternal tenderness from women—not passion.

Nor had Dorothy's understanding yet awakened dissatisfaction in Sara's lack of it. He was still making the best of a bad job. Sara was a devoted mother, a tolerably efficient housekeeper, if inclined to muddle and bustle, and her admiration for her brilliant husband, amounting to astonishment at her possession of him, was not yet blurred by disappointment in his want of worldly success. While her plump prettiness was of the type that quickly develops middle age in commonplace dumpiness, as yet she retained her freshness and a superficial charm. She liked Thelwall and contributed to the success of his visit. Another visitor, Richard Reynell, thought her " indeed a pretty woman," saw at the cottage " domestic life in all its beauty and simplicity," and declared it " a treat, a luxury, to see Coleridge hanging over his infant and talking to it, and fancying what he will be in future days."

But domesticity could not compete with intellectual excitement, any more than could Tom Poole's ponderous praise and affectionate encouragement. Poole's arbour more rarely echoed Coleridge's chanting of his poetry, which he now preferred to repeat in the woods of Alfoxden. The garden grew neglected; weeds flourished during his absence at Racedown, and Coleridge had neither time nor inclination to clear them. Four and five days a week he spent at Alfoxden, frequently spending the night, and in the wooded groves expounded splendid plans for poetic achievement.

2. *THE ANCIENT MARINER*

The idea of an epic, first suggested by Lamb, recurred to Coleridge in his ambitious enthusiasm. His subject, *The Brook*, was to afford opportunities for " description, incident, and impassioned reflections on men, nature, and society " by tracing a stream from its source, past barns, sheepfolds, hamlet, town and factory, to the sea. To Wordsworth he recommended a similar theme, with the title of *The Recluse*. But wishing to collaborate with Wordsworth as closely as formerly with Southey, he planned the scheme and contents of a poem in three cantos on *The Wanderings of Cain*, of which he was to write the second while Wordsworth wrote the first canto, " and which ever had *done first*, was to set about the third." He completed a rough draft of his canto, but hastening to Alfoxden with the manuscript, found Wordsworth with a " look of humourous despondency fixed on his almost blank sheet of paper." Wordsworth had none of Southey's application or fluency. He could write only what and when he was in the mood to write, and his two long poems, *The Prelude* and *The Excursion*, both only parts of the original scheme of *The Recluse*, were the result of forced labour over many years, which explains their unevenness of quality. Later he was to condemn in Coleridge the inability to write to order—because Coleridge needed money from his writings, while he himself successfully evaded the necessity.

After this failure, their collaboration became limited to exchange of ideas and the joint-publication of their poems. The plan of the proposed volume, as explained by Coleridge, indicates the source of his fascination for Wordsworth and Dorothy. Their conversations " turned frequently on the two cardinal points of poetry, the power of exciting the sympathy of the reader by a faithful adherence to the truth of nature, and the power of giving the interest of novelty by the modifying colours of the imagination." Coleridge pointed out that " the sudden charm which accidents of light and shade, which moonlight or sunset diffused over a known and familiar landscape, appeared to represent the practicability of combining both." Such deductive interpretation of natural phenomena was new to the Wordsworths, who were accustomed to purely objective observation. Wordsworth felt on safer ground by persevering with the line he had already adopted. It was therefore left to Coleridge to attempt " the interesting of the affections " in incidents and characters " supernatural, or at least romantic," " by the dramatic truth of such emotions as would naturally accompany such situations, supposing them real."

The occasion for a first experiment occurred when Coleridge and the Wordsworths decided in November 1797 to walk to Lynton by Porlock, and see the wonderful wild moorland scenery of the seaboard and the celebrated Valley of Rocks—or Valley of Stones, as it was then frequently called. As their " united funds were very scarce," they proposed to defray the expenses of the trip by writing a poem for a magazine. Coleridge related a dream of his friend Cruikshank about a skeleton ship with a skeleton crew, and proceeded to discuss stories of superstition remembered from various books of travel he had read. One such story he recalled from Shelvocke's *Voyages* about a ship's mate who, persuaded that a long spell of adverse weather was due to the persistent pursuit of the ship by an albatross, shot the bird in hope of relieving their misfortune. According to Wordsworth, he then suggested that Coleridge should write a poem about the ghostly navigator of the phantom ship, who was doomed to his fate for the crime of killing an albatross.

That same " memorable evening " they began the poem together. But Coleridge's falcon imagination left the pedestrian Wordsworth's plodding hopelessly behind. After suggesting two or three lines, to which he afterwards pompously laid claim, Wordsworth decided that " our respective manners proved so widely different that it would have been quite presumptuous in me to do anything but separate from an undertaking upon which I could only have been a clog," and he left Coleridge to follow the flights of his imagination alone.

Thirteen years later, when he was living at Dove Cottage and reading books of travel, De Quincey came on the passage in Shelvocke and recognised the germ of *The Ancient Mariner*. He mentioned it to Coleridge, who, having forgotten that he had remembered the albatross incident from a previous reading of Shelvocke, denied that he had received the idea directly from reading the book. Wordsworth, however, remembered that Coleridge had derived the idea from some travel book, and now with curiosity noted the book, which De Quincey probably left at Grasmere and came to repose in Wordsworth's library at Rydal. After Coleridge's death, Wordsworth decided to appropriate to himself the albatross idea, and he told his adoring Miss Fenwick, " I had been reading in Shelvocke's *Voyages*, a day or two before, that while doubling Cape Horn they frequently saw albatrosses in that latitude, the largest sort of sea-fowl, some extending their wings twelve or thirteen feet."

Dutifully Victorian biographers accepted Wordsworth's word. But unluckily for Wordsworth's reputation as " a man of stern veracity," Professor Livingstone Lowes, in that extraordinary study of the mechanics of a poet's mind, *The Road to Xanadu*, discovered that his words to Miss Fenwick were almost precisely quoted from Shelvocke, produced proof that there was a copy of Shelvocke in the Rydal library, and fairly deduced that Wordsworth looked up the passage for Miss Fenwick's benefit. On another occasion, after the appearance of De Quincey's reminiscences of Coleridge, Wordsworth told Alexander Dyce that the " idea of ' shooting an albatross ' was mine; for I had been reading Shelvocke's *Voyages*, which probably Coleridge never saw."

The notion of Wordsworth's having ever read anything which Coleridge never saw is comic. He was never in his life a reader; after leaving Cambridge he lamented to Mathews his poverty of reading; at Racedown he read the *Gentleman's Magazine*; in a few years he devised the excuse from his eye trouble for his little reading as for leaving his correspondence to his women-folk. Coleridge, by contrast, read insatiably, and he had moreover dipped into many books of travel while contemplating emigration to America. From these facts Professor Lowes fairly deduced that Coleridge had the idea himself from Shelvocke; that his copy of the book was at Dove Cottage and was found there by De Quincey; that Wordsworth first heard definitely of the derivation from De Quincey, and retaining it in his mind, he informed Dyce and Miss Fenwick, after Coleridge's death, that he had read Shelvocke and suggested the subject to Coleridge!

Professor Lowes also produced circumstantial evidence that Coleridge derived other ideas from Shelvocke in the course of the poem, proving that he had first-hand knowledge of the book. But these details, Wordsworth, of course, did not " remember." Obviously Coleridge, who had never at that time experienced a sea trip, had gathered vivid impressions from reading books of maritime adventure. The greatest marvel of *The Ancient Mariner* is the vividness of its imagery, the verisimilitude of atmosphere, the accumulated effect of awful eeriness:

> " *Are those her ribs through which the Sun*
> *Did peer, as through a grate?*
> *And is that Woman all her crew?*
> *Is that a Death? and are there two?*
> *Is Death that woman's mate?* "

Critics have been content to accept *The Ancient Mariner* as a masterpiece in the fantastic, and biographers have hesitated to seek autobiography in its apparent unreality, though latterly some have ventured to read in the Mariner's haunted conscience a reflection of the discord in Coleridge's own mind. But the sense of discord, to find final agonised expression in *Dejection*, had not yet stricken Coleridge. He was still happy, unafflicted by consciousness of frustration, of inability to apply his powers and to appease his friends' hopes for him. He was content in a sense of achievement by having finished his tragedy.

The theme of *Osorio*—which had occupied his mind for more than six months past, and which probably first occurred to him from reading *Guilt and Sorrow*—was its later title, *Remorse*, which supplied the motive of the Mariner's hallucinations. Lately, too, he had been converted from his satisfaction in

Hartley's philosophy of the association of ideas by reading Bishop Berkeley, whose doctrines derive from the axiom that the act of seeing is in fact an act of interpretation, involving a rational process, and that ideas are to be interpreted through sensations. For some months while Lloyd lived with him, he had witnessed— and striven to comprehend and combat—the morbid hallucinations of an unbalanced mind. He had realised how the act of interpretations, when governed by an irrational instead of a rational mind, created distorted visions incredible to rational sight. So, in his Mariner, he visualised a mind unbalanced by remorse and fear, fanned to frenzy by the awful circumstances of men dying of thirst on a ship becalmed. The reality of its unreality, the incredibility of its horror, and the conviction of its possibility prove the success of the poem in achieving its creator's design of treating the supernatural, " so as to transfer from our inward nature a human interest and a semblance of truth sufficient to procure for these shadows of imagination that willing suspension of disbelief for the moment, which constitutes poetic faith." It is the supreme masterpiece in successful projection of metaphysical speculation into narrative poetry.

The last lines, often condemned as superfluous moralising, contain a statement of Coleridge's faith.

> " Farewell, farewell! But this I tell
> To thee, thou Wedding-Guest!
> He prayeth well, who loveth well
> Both man and bird and beast.
>
> He prayeth best, who loveth best
> All things both great and small;
> For the dear God who loveth us,
> He made and loveth all."

This is the faith of the pacifist, the convinced and literal Christian who declines to differentiate between individual murder, punishable by the laws of society, and wholesale murder, encouraged and embellished with the trumpery of glory by governments

and peoples at war. It was likewise the faith of the true lover of
nature, whose tenderness forbade him to set traps for the mice
which plagued his household. It was a completer faith than the
idolatry of beauty, which, as Mr. Herbert Read has pointed out,
was seized upon by young men like John Stuart Mill, whose
religious beliefs were shaped by the materialism of the Industrial
Revolution and whose emotional senses found a substitute for
religion in Wordsworth's poetry, and again by young men even
more spiritually derelict in consequence of direct contact with
war. This idolatry was a form of intellectual escape, available
only to the trained mind; Coleridge's was the simple doctrine
of Jesus Christ, realisable alike by the illiterate and the intellectual.

3. THE INSPIRED PREACHER

Soon after returning from Lynton, while *The Ancient Mariner*
was advancing and expanding far beyond the bounds of the
originally intended magazine poem, Coleridge heard at the
beginning of December 1797 that Sheridan had rejected *Osorio*
on account of the obscurity of the last three acts. The news
confirmed his conviction that he could not live by literature,
and he faced the choice between a journalistic job and accepting
a post as a Unitarian minister.

Through Poole or Dr. Beddoes, he had become acquainted
with Thomas and Josiah Wedgwood, wealthy sons of the
famous potter. Thomas, an incurable invalid and an enthusiast
for chemical research, was a patient of Dr. Beddoes; Josiah lived
at Cote House, Westbury, near Bristol, and had country estates
in the management of which he accepted advice from Poole.
During the autumn Thomas came to Stowey and visited the
Wordsworths, whose spacious accommodation at Alfoxden was
more suited to hospitality than Coleridge's modest cottage.
Coleridge, on a visit to Cote House, met James Mackintosh,
eminent as a political journalist and champion of democracy
since his able reply to Burke's *Reflections on the French Revolution*,

and Mackintosh's brother-in-law, Daniel Stuart, proprietor of the *Morning Post*, offered him a guinea a week for verses. His first contribution under this arrangement, the lines " To an Unfortunate Woman at the Theatre," appeared on 7th December.

But this newspaper engagement revived memories of his difficulties on the *Watchman*, and reminded him of Poole's remark that he was " not born to be a compiler." The mere consciousness of being under an obligation to write punctually to order froze his faculties. " Something must be written and written immediately—if any important Truth, any striking beauty, occur to my mind, I feel a repugnance at sending it garbled to a newspaper: and if any idea of ludicrous personality, or apt anti-ministerial joke, crosses me, I feel a repugnance at rejecting it, because *something must be written*, and nothing else suitable occurs." He felt that the longer he continued " a hired paragraph-scribbler," the more powerful he would find these temptations. Besides, " of all things I most dislike party-politics," and his employer especially welcomed contributions with " a *tang* of personality or *vindictive* feeling."

There were moral and intellectual objections to his becoming a Unitarian minister. Though he had regularly preached in the chapels at Taunton and Bridgwater, he had declined payment for his services, and he disliked the idea of " becoming an hired Teacher in any sect " because " it makes one's livelihood hang upon the profession of *particular opinions*: and tends therefore to warp the intellectual faculty." Also, he had observed that a minister depending for revenue on collections from the congregation inclined " to adapt his moral exhortations to their wishes rather than to their needs." A minister at Derby had been compelled to resign " on account of his sermons respecting Riches and Rich Men." On the other hand, there were compensations. As a Unitarian minister, he had only to retain his belief that " Jesus Christ was the Messiah—in all other points I may play off my Intellect *ad libitum*." Further, " by law I shall be excepted from military service—to which, Heaven only knows how soon we may be dragged," for he thought it likely " that in case of an invasion our government will serve all, whom they choo ss to suspect of disaffection, in the same way that good King David served Uriah—' set ye Uriah in the forefront of the hottest Battle, and retire ye from him, that he may be smitten and die '."

All things considered, the pulpit seemed preferable to the press, and when Estlin advised him that he might have the place of the retiring Unitarian minister at Shrewsbury, where the living was endowed and not dependent on the congregation's approval, he decided to accept. A temptation to revoke his decision was immediately inspired by a cheque for a hundred pounds sent by the Wedgwoods to relieve his present necessities and to prevent his deciding hastily under duress. At first he gladly accepted the prospect of " tranquillity and leisure of independence for the next two years," but after a week's " fluctuations of mind " and sleepless nights, he decided that acceptance would only temporarily postpone the evil of financial anxiety. " A permanent income not inconsistent with my religious or political creeds, I find necessary to my quietness—without it I should be a prey to anxiety, and anxiety with me always induces Sickliness, and too often Sloth." So he returned the cheque, and in the second week of January set off for Shrewsbury.

On Sunday 14th January 1798 Coleridge preached in Shrewsbury's Unitarian Chapel, and among the congregation was William Hazlitt, the nineteen-year-old son of the Unitarian minister in the neighbouring town of Wem. Cottle once heard Coleridge preach at Bath to a meagre congregation, which yawned through a sermon amounting to little more than a lecture on the Corn Laws. But either Coleridge was depressed by his small and unresponsive audience or Cottle was no great connoisseur of sermons. Young Hazlitt was so intrigued by the romantic notion of a poet and philosopher as a preacher of the gospel that he walked ten miles through mud to hear him, but his impression is consistent with Coleridge's reputation for eloquence and with the eager invitations to preach he received from ministers. As he gave out his text—" And he went up into the mountain to pray, himself, alone,"—" his voice ' rose like a stream of rich distilled perfumes, and when he came to the two

last words, which he pronounced, loud, deep, and distinct,"
it seemed to young Hazlitt " as if the sounds had echoed from
the bottom of the human heart, and as if that prayer might
have floated in solemn silence through the universe," so that
the idea of St. John, " crying in the wilderness," came to his mind.
" The sermon was upon peace and war; upon church and state—
not their alliance, but their separation—on the spirit of the world
and the spirit of Christianity, not as the same, but as opposed to
one another." He inveighed against those who " inscribed the
cross of Christ on banners dripping with human gore," and " to
show the fatal effects of war, drew a striking contrast between the
simple shepherd boy, driving his team afield, or sitting under
the hawthorn, piping to his flock," and " the same poor country-
lad, crimped, kidnapped, brought into town, made drunk at an
ale-house, turned into a wretched drummer-boy . . . and
tricked out in the loathsome finery of the profession of blood."
It was more than Hazlitt had hoped for—" Poetry and Philosophy
had met together, Truth and Genius had embraced, under the eye
and with the sanction of Religion "—and he went home satisfied.

The following Tuesday Coleridge went to Wem to dine and
stay the night with Hazlitt's father. For two hours he conversed
" with William Hazlitt's forehead," for Hazlitt, shy, diffident,
tongue-tied, was " shoe-contemplative," as Coleridge afterwards
described his habitual demeanour when entering a room full of
people. But while Coleridge talked, Hazlitt noted his appearance.
" His forehead was broad and high, light as if built of ivory,
with large projecting eyebrows, and his eyes rolling beneath them,
like a sea with darkened lustre." His face had a faintly purple
tinge, as in the pale thoughtful complexions of Murillo and
Velasquez. " His mouth was gross, voluptuous, open, eloquent;
his chin good-humoured and round; but his nose, the rudder
of the face, the index of the will, was small, feeble, nothing."
His hair, " black and glossy as the raven's . . . fell in smooth
masses over his forehead." The impression tallies with Coleridge's
self-description in a letter to Thelwall of a year before, but
Hazlitt's memory failed in describing his person as " rather above
the common size, inclining to the corpulent." He was picturing

Coleridge's figure as it became in middle age; when Dorothy Wordsworth first saw him, he was " pale and thin."

Coleridge talked familiarly and agreeably on a variety of subjects, mentioning Godwin and Mary Wollstonecraft, Burke and Mackintosh, Holcroft, Wordsworth, and Tom Wedgwood. He flattered Hazlitt by seeming to take much notice of him, and eventually drew him out on the subject of Burke.

When Hazlitt came down to breakfast next morning, he found Coleridge with a letter from Josiah Wedgwood, saying that he and his brother had " a considerable superfluity of fortune," of which they regarded themselves " rather as Trustees than Proprietors," and having " canvassed " Coleridge's past life, his present situation and prospects, and his character and abilities, they asked him to " accept an annuity for life of £150," to be regularly paid by them, " no condition whatever being annexed to it." It was a princely offer, even in those days when wealthy men still retained a just sense of the responsibility of riches, and it is not surprising that Coleridge, as Hazlitt said, " seemed to make up his mind to close with this proposal in the act of tying on one of his shoes."

Hazlitt " felt very little gratitude for Mr. Wedgwood's bounty," for he had looked forward to having a pastor so gifted only ten miles away. But he was more than appeased, even overwhelmed, by an invitation from Coleridge to visit Stowey. He walked with him six miles of the distance to Shrewsbury, and noticed—as did Carlyle long afterwards—that Coleridge continually crossed him " by shifting from one side of the foot-path to the other," as if " unable to keep on in a straight line." It struck Hazlitt only as an odd movement; he did not then " connect it with any instability of purpose or involuntary change of principle," as he did twenty-five years later. All the way Coleridge talked of English philosophers. He drew the difference between a subtle and an acute mind, the one characteristic of a philosopher, the other a mere shop-boy's quality. Significantly, he " dwelt particularly " on Berkeley's *Essay on Vision* " as a masterpiece of analytical reasoning."

Hazlitt's habitual reserve was so far overcome that he talked of his own proposed thesis on " The Natural Disinterestedness of the Human Mind." Coleridge " listened with great willingness," and Hazlitt returned home with renewed zeal for his work. For, " till the light of his genius shone into my soul," he had been " dumb, inarticulate, helpless," and " that my understanding . . . did not remain dumb and brutish, or at length found a language to express itself, I owe to Coleridge. . . . He was the first poet I had known, and he certainly answered to that inspired name. I had heard a great deal of his powers of conversation, and was not disappointed. In fact, I never met with anything at all like them, either before or since." Thus another man of genius—following Southey, Lamb, Lloyd, and Wordsworth—fell under the spell of the archangel, not yet " a little damaged."

Josiah Wedgwood's letter was accompanied by one from Poole, showing that his influence had weighed with the brothers in inspiring their offer and urging Coleridge to accept. In Poole's opinion, he could accept the annuity and still enter the ministry if he wished. But Coleridge, despite appeals from his Unitarian admirers and exhortations from Estlin that " the cause of Christianity and practical Religion demands your exertions," felt that he could not accept both the annuity and a minister's living, since the Wedgwoods would not have made the offer if he had already had other means of subsistence. He argued fairly that he could serve the cause of Christianity as effectively outside as inside the ministry, and that, while he had preferred— " as more *innocent* in the first place, and more *useful* in the second place "—the ministry to the press as a trade, the necessity for bondage to either was now removed. Thelwall's comment, on receiving a letter in which Coleridge did not make clear that he had decided against entering the ministry, had shrewdness and humour: " I suppose he did not . . . accept the cure of Unitarian souls . . . for I know his aversion to preaching God's holy word for hire, which is seconded not a little, I expect, by his repugnance to all regular routine and application. I also hope he did not, for I know he cannot preach very often without travelling from the pulpit to the Tower. Mount him but upon

his darling hobby-horse, ' the republic of God's own making,'
and away he goes like hey-go-mad, spattering and splashing
through thick and thin and scattering more *levelling* sedition and
constructive treason than poor Gilly[1] or myself ever dreamt of."

Another reason for Coleridge's rejection of the ministry
appeared in a letter written from Shrewsbury to Wordsworth:
" But dismissing severer thoughts, believe me, my dear fellow!
that of the pleasant ideas which accompanied this unexpected
event, it was not the least pleasant, nor did it pass through my
mind the last in the procession, that I should at least be able to
trace the spring and early summer at Alfoxden with you, and
that wherever your after residence may be, it is probable that
you will be within the reach of my tether, lengthened as it now is."

4. POETS IN CONTRAST

Coleridge stayed three weeks at Shrewsbury. He was " talking
at a great rate to his fellow-passengers " when he arrived, " he
did not cease while he stayed," and, added Hazlitt, " nor has he
since, that I know of." He was certainly an unqualified success
and would have received the living if he had wanted it. Even
some of the Anglican clergy were " eminently courteous " and
went to hear him preach. He had reason to think that he would
have " doubled the congregation almost immediately," though
he may have been deceived by the many who came from
curiosity to hear the unusual young preacher and would have
stayed at home when lure of novelty lapsed. Though he declined
even payment of his travelling expenses, the Shrewsbury Unit-
arians begged his acceptance of " a small compensation," for
while they expressed disappointment at the deprivation " of
that pleasure and edification we had so much reason to promise "
themselves, they were " not so selfish as not to feel also the most

---

[1] Gilbert Wakefield, who spent two years in Dorchester gaol for writing and
publishing what Wordsworth wrote but did not publish—a ' seditious ' reply to
Bishop Watson.

lively satisfaction " in the good fortune that placed him in " a
situation more conformable to your inclinations and Views."

He arrived at Bristol on 30th January, full of eager joy at
the prospect of returning to Stowey and determined " to settle
and persevere in some mode of repaying the Wedgewoods thro'
the medium of Mankind." On 3rd February he walked with
Dorothy Wordsworth over the hills and watched the mist
drifting over the sea. During his absence at Shrewsbury Dorothy
had begun to keep a journal, in which she recorded impressions
of scenery and weather effects. Her object was the preservation
of these impressions for future use by Wordsworth and Coleridge.
In later years Wordsworth depended more and more on her
journals, and of their tours together he used at home the notes
she had written in the freshness of the moment. The impressions
were not necessarily Dorothy's own, but those she derived in
company with Coleridge or Wordsworth, mutually com-
pounded and clarified; a specially happy descriptive phrase would
be noted. Walking with Coleridge, she noticed how " the
withered leaves danced with the hailstones "; the notion was
probably his, and was not improved in Wordsworth's lines:

> " But see! where'er the hailstones drop
> The withered leaves all skip and hop."

So, on 27th February, when Coleridge walked with her from
Stowey to Alfoxden on " a very bright moonlight night," they
saw how " the sea big and white, swelled to the very shores,"
and Coleridge wrote in *The Ancient Mariner:*

> " The harbour-bay was clear as glass,
> So smoothly it was strewn!
> And on the bay the moonlight lay,
> And the shadow of the Moon.
> . . . .
> And the bay was white with silent light,
> Till rising from the same,
> Full many shapes, that shadows were,
> In crimson colours came."

Together, too, they saw the "hornèd moon," "star-dogged", and on 24th March, "a duller night than last night," they noticed "a sort of white shade over the blue sky," and Coleridge wrote in *Christabel:*

> " *The night is chilly, but not dark.*
> *The thin gray cloud is spread on high,*
> *It covers but not hides the sky.*"

From February to April few days passed without Dorothy's walking with Coleridge, and all the time he was buoyed on the full tide of imaginative creation. To Cottle he wrote cryptically on 18th February: " I have finished my ballad—it is 340 lines. I am going on with the Visions. . . ." The " ballad " cannot have been *The Ancient Mariner*, which ran to 658 lines. Those who suppose *Kubla Khan* to have been written in the summer or autumn of the previous year may read here a vain determination to finish that " vision," but the " visions " were more likely those of the Mariner. The first part of *Christabel* comprised 331 lines, but it seems improbable that he had progressed so far with that poem, and the " ballad " may have been a first draft of *The Three Graves*. On 23rd March Dorothy noted that Coleridge " brought his ballad finished," and this may have been *The Ancient Mariner*.

" I gave him the subject of his *Three Graves*," said the oracular Wordsworth after Coleridge's death, " but he made it too shocking and painful, and not sufficiently softened by any healing views." The criticism is just; into the story of a mother's passion for her daughter's lover Coleridge instilled the dramatic horror of Webster and Tourneur. The simple fireside story, based on material of village gossip, was used by Wordsworth in the ballads he was writing at this time—*We are Seven, The Thorn, The Last of the Flock, Goody Blake and Harry Gill, The Idiot Boy*, and *Simon Lee*. The form and treatment is that of the modern short story, and it may be fairly argued that the subjects are better suited to prose than verse. In *The Thorn*, for instance, as Coleridge pointed out, Wordsworth falls into bathos by putting the telling of the tale into the mouth of a dull and garrulous narrator. Prosaic narrative was outside Coleridge's conception of poetry. To him it was instinctive to seek beneath the surface; his treatment was subjective where Wordsworth's was objective. It is doubtful if Wordsworth ever grasped Coleridge's application to poetry of Berkeley's theory that vision is individual interpretation. His own earthbound imagination being incapable of accompanying Coleridge's metaphysical flights, he conceived the intangible as " supernatural," and as an attempt at practical proof of his argument against Coleridge, he wrote *Peter Bell* to show " that the Imagination not only does not require for its exercise the intervention of supernatural agency, but that, though such agency be excluded, the faculty may be called forth as imperiously and for kindred results of pleasure, by incidents within the compass of poetic probability, in the humblest departments of daily life."

Very soon Coleridge was to realise that Wordsworth had " hurtfully segregated and isolated his being." Beginning with an escapist's desire to deaden his conscience about Annette, about his motiveless inactivity, and about his failure to serve the political cause in which he fervently believed, he had acquired a detachment almost inhuman, which, while it enabled him to live entirely with his thoughts and so to concentrate on creative work, gradually deadened his faculty of sympathy. Because he knew that great thoughts depended upon subtle and sensitive perception, and because he saw that Wordsworth was imaginatively incapable of projecting himself into the minds and senses of others, Coleridge encouraged him to write an auto-biographical poem, as the only medium through which he could describe the metaphysical experience regarded by Coleridge as the richest matter for poetic expression. So, while writing his ballads on rustic subjects according to his own inclination, Wordsworth also in these months began *The Prelude* at the instigation of Coleridge, who informed Cottle on 8th March that Wordsworth had written " more than 1,200 lines of a blank verse, superior . . . to anything in our language which in any way resembles it," quoting Poole's opinion as confirming his own that it was "likely to benefit mankind much more than anything Wordsworth had yet written."

To everybody Coleridge sang Wordsworth's praises. He was "a great man," "a tried good man," a poet "the latchet of whose shoes I am unworthy to unloose." When Tom Wedgwood and Mackintosh ventured to aver that they saw nothing in Wordsworth's conversation to justify such applause, Coleridge told them, "He strides on so far before you that he dwindles in the distance!" After this objection by Wedgwood and Mackintosh, he forestalled the adverse impression of Wordsworth's awkward manners and stilted speech. "His genius is most *apparent* in poetry," he warned Estlin, "and rarely, except to me in *tête-à-tête*, breaks forth in conversational eloquence." By belittling himself in comparison, he created among his friends, who recognised him as the greatest genius of their acquaintance, a legend about Wordsworth's genius, which in time became rooted in their minds, and in the course of a decade or so, without any praise in the press, Wordsworth became accepted by an influential minority at Coleridge's valuation.

While at first intimate communion with Wordsworth stimulated Coleridge to poetic achievement, his extravagant admiration unsettled the always unstable foundations of his self-confidence. Wordsworth's obstinate preference for his rustic ballads and his confusion of the metaphysical with the "supernatural," which he regarded as inferior to the realistic, caused him to imagine in himself a deficiency from which Wordsworth was immune. Wordsworth must have expressed to him freely in conversation the disparaging opinion he afterwards avowed: "Not being able to dwell on natural woes, he took to the supernatural, and hence his *Ancient Mariner* and *Christabel*, in which he shows great poetical power; but these have not the hold on the heart which Nature gives, and will never be popular poems, like those of Goldsmith or Burns." Coleridge could not withstand the disapproval of his idol, and more than a year before he had arrived at the depths of despair that found expression in *Dejection*, he told Francis Wrangham that Wordsworth "is a great, a true Poet—I am only a kind of a Metaphysician."

Yet in those fruitful early months of 1798 Coleridge's poetic achievement outweighed Wordsworth's. This fact is rarely recognised, largely because the joint volume of *Lyrical Ballads* contained nineteen poems by Wordsworth and only four by Coleridge, and because Coleridge, as usual, pushed Wordsworth into prominence at his own expense. "I wrote *The Ancient Mariner*, and was preparing, among other poems, the *Dark Ladie* and the *Christabel*, in which I should have more nearly realised my ideal than I had done in my first attempt," he related. "But Mr. Wordsworth's industry had proved so much more successful, and the number of the poems so much greater, that my compositions, instead of forming a balance, appeared rather an interpolation of heterogeneous matter." Wordsworth's "industry" was more successful because he concentrated—with a single-minded intensity of purpose of which Coleridge was inherently incapable and which he consequently admired as a symptom of Wordsworth's superiority—on his chosen function of giving "the charm of novelty to things of everyday," while Coleridge was distracted by the multiplicity of ideas crowding upon his more fertile imagination. The conceptions of *Christabel* or the *Dark Ladie* were each more ambitious in length and scope than anything attempted by Wordsworth, but they were unfinished and therefore excluded from the volume. *The Three Graves* required little addition for completeness, but it was thrown aside probably because Coleridge had no heart to finish it after Wordsworth's adverse criticism. The composition of these ballads was interrupted by a number of completed poems, none of which fell within the scope of Coleridge's function of lending human interest to the supernatural or romantic. *Frost at Midnight*, in which Coleridge, musing over the cradle of his infant son, fondly pictures for him a happier boyhood than his own, was written in February: *The Old Man of the Alps*, *Lewti*, and *The Recantation*, afterwards called *France: An Ode*, were published in the *Morning Post* during March and April, while *Fears in Solitude* was written in the latter month. All these were extraneous from the scheme and therefore excluded from the volume, though they had claims for inclusion at least equal to

H

Wordsworth's *Expostulation and Reply* and *Lines written in Early Spring*.

"It was dear Coleridge's constant infelicity that prevented him from being the poet that Nature had given him the power to be," said Wordsworth. "He had always too much personal and domestic discontent to paint the sorrows of mankind, he could not—

> "*afford to suffer*
> *With those whom he saw suffer.*"

As Wordsworth well knew, Coleridge's subsequent unhappiness dried up the fount of his poetry. But he was never capable of the egotistic detachment that enabled Wordsworth to wrestle with harrowing emotions in imagination and then retire to bed to relax and be read to sleep by Dorothy—a detachment eventually deepening to an insensibility fatal to his poetry in its turn. Coleridge could not "afford to suffer," and so suffered the more acutely. While Wordsworth was now content in his own pursuits, Coleridge, despite his contempt for politics and politicians, felt anguish at the unnecessary sufferings inflicted by materialistic and amoral governments upon their people. His fading faith in France as the European pioneers of liberty finally vanished when the French invaded the Swiss cantons and instituted military dictatorship under the thin disguise of democracy.

In the five stanzas of the ode originally called *The Recantation* he traced the transition of his political faith. He told how he had loved the spirit of liberty, had welcomed the French Revolution and abhorred England's joining "the dire army" against it, had regarded the atrocities of the Terror as inevitable excesses of violent revolution and retained the hope that France would eventually establish the ideal government; but how he now saw their government competing with the corrupt monarchies for dominion over lesser nations, and was forced to the conclusion that the ideal of freedom was attainable by no community under any form of government, but only by the individual, "so far as he is pure, and inflamed with the love and adoration of God in Nature." He was now confirmed in the belief with which he had retired to Stowey sixteen months before. Witnessing with disgust the jealous dissension among democratic leaders, the want of principle preventing their unity in common endeavour, he concluded that men of principle and enlightenment had no place in politics. He now recognised in "the *Rulers* of France . . . nothing that distinguishes them to their advantage from other animals of the same species." Landor, his junior by over two years, who had declined political employment and likewise retired to rural contemplation, exclaimed in his violent way, "As to the cause of liberty, this cursed nation has ruined it for ever." But, though he never forgave the French, he continued throughout his long life to regard hopefully every revolutionary movement as potentially pregnant with the betrayed ideals of the French Revolution. Coleridge, however, while he too felt lasting bitterness against the French for their betrayal, no longer believed in the ability of popular movements to promote the people's improvement. Contrasting the disinterested integrity of men like Grey and Stanhope with the unscrupulous careerism of intriguing demagogues, he inclined to regard aristocrats as more likely to govern for the general benefit.

Godwin justly argued that " government, even in its best state, is an evil," and therefore it is desirable to " have as little of it, as the general peace of human society will permit." But this was among the arguments instanced by Coleridge when he convinced Southey that Godwin was dogmatising for a future state of civilisation. In his Bristol lectures he had plainly expressed the opinion that the people were not ripe even for representative government. "I regard governments," he now wrote, "as I regard the abcesses produced by certain fevers—they are necessary consequences of the disease, and by their pain they increase the disease; but . . . not only are they physically necessary as effects but also as causes they are morally necessary in order to prevent the utter dissolution of the patient."

Though "no Whig, no Reformist, no Republican," he remained a bitter opponent of Pitt's government, whose policy he condemned for having coerced the French into military aggression and created democratic unrest at home. In *Fears in*

Solitude, written in April 1798, when invasion was considered imminent, he regarded the threatened calamity as just retribution for imperialist ambition and for the war against France:

> " *We have offended, Oh! my countrymen!*
> *We have offended very grievously,*
> *And been most tyrannous. From east to west*
> *A groan of accusation pierces Heaven!*
> *The wretched plead against us; multitudes*
> *Countless and vehement, the sons of God,*
> *Our brethren!* "

When Sheridan and Tierney were accused of " recanting " because, after originally supporting the French Revolution, they now condemned the revolutionists for betrayal of its principles, he published in the *Morning Post* on 30th July *Recantation Illustrated in the Story of the Mad Ox*. The French Revolution is represented as an ox, which, being released from work in " yoke and chain," frisked gladly in the field, till the stupid rustics, seeing its gambols, declared in a panic that it had gone mad, and started to hound it down.

> " *The frighted beast scamper'd about—*
> *Plunge! through the hedge he drove:*
> *The mob pursue with hideous rout,*
> *A bull-dog fastens on his snout;*
> ' *He gores the dog! his tongue hangs out!*
> *He's mad, he's mad, by Jove!* ' "

A " man that kept his senses " sought to stop the hunt, but the mob cursed him—" What? would you have him toss us all? "—till he withdrew protesting. Goaded and terrified, the ox at last turns on his pursuers and plays havoc among them, whereupon the wise man joins in organising its capture, to the indignation of the mob.

> " ' *A lying dog! just now he said*
> *The Ox was only glad—*
> *Let's break his Presbyterian head!* '

> ' Hush! ' quoth the sage, ' you've been misled;
> No quarrels now! let's all make head,
> You drove the poor Ox mad! ' "

So Coleridge defended the apostasy of himself and others, but
he could not reconcile his conscience with the revised policy
admitted by his reason. He described himself as

> " The humble man, who, in his youthful years,
> Knew just so much of folly, as had made
> His early manhood more securely wise! "

who, in the peace of rural retreat, had

> " With many feelings, many thoughts,
> Made up a meditative joy, and found
> Religious meanings in the forms of Nature! "

And the anguish of his soul cried out:

> " My God! it is a melancholy thing
> For such a man, who would full fain preserve
> His soul in calmness, yet perforce must feel
> For all his human brethren—O my God!
> It weighs upon the heart, that he must think
> What uproar and what strife may now be stirring
> This way or that way o'er these silent hills."

In imagination he suffered the agonies of the maimed and
wounded, the bereaved wife and mother, the frightened or
starving child. As Wordsworth said, with his temperament and
circumstances, he could not afford so to suffer. Wordsworth was
untroubled by such sufferings at second hand; having determined
on detachment in rural seclusion, he banished the world and its
troubles as outside his perspective. He allowed Coleridge to
argue him out of respect for Godwin's doctrines, because he no
longer needed the moral support of Godwinism. From Coleridge,

too, he absorbed a smattering of Hartley's philosophy of association, as appeared in his prefaces and part of *The Prelude*, but idleness reinforced his inclination to avoid philosophical speculation.
What might be deemed deficiency in others became, as always,
virtue in Wordsworth. " It is his practice and almost his nature,"
lauded Coleridge, " to convey all the truth he knows without any
attack on what he supposes falsehood, if that falsehood be inter-
woven with virtues or happiness." When he first met Coleridge,
he was " a republican, and, at least, a *semi*-atheist," but by the
spring of 1798 Coleridge could declare, " He loves and venerates
Christ and Christianity. I wish he did more." But this was the
" one subject " on which " we are habitually silent; we found
our data dissimilar, and never renewed the subject." Wordsworth's " data " remains unrevealed, but doubtless differed little
from that assembled by many a materialist. Christianity well
suited Coleridge's expansive nature, which excited him to
friendliness with all and sundry and to unrewarded and often
uncomfortable exertions on their behalf, as when he tried to
find a farm for Thelwall. But Christianity would have been an
embarrassment to Wordsworth, who cultivated only such friends
as could practically serve him. Morally weak, Coleridge needed
some supporting faith; but Wordsworth was a man of moral
strength, whose masculinity despised weakness as feminine.

The time was soon to come when Wordsworth became a
steadfast and respected supporter of the established Church.
His health or occupation often prevented his own attendance
at Sunday observance, but he was always careful to be represented by his women folk. But the Church had no closer
affiliation to Christianity than the Pharisees to Jesus Christ; it
was a respectable British institution, to which Wordsworth
necessarily subscribed when he became articled to respectability.
When Coleridge declared his belief in religion as the only
" universally *efficient* " cure for social ills, Wordsworth might
have retorted with his own argument against Godwin—that
he was dogmatising " for a future state," as eighteen hundred
years after Christ the prospect of a Christian world seemed as
remote as ever.

But Wordsworth had no desire to expose his data to Coleridge's scrutiny. Instead, he absorbed from Coleridge's conversation a smattering of philosophy sufficient to disguise his devout study of Nature as a substitute religion, of which he became the prophet accepted by materialists, like himself, whose faith required to rest in the tangible and external. As a poet, Wordsworth became Nature's apostle; in his preface of 1815 he explained how poetry emerged from exact observation and description, coloured by sensibility, reflection and imagination. He gathered from Coleridge enough of Berkeley's theories to understand that vision was interpretation; but with him interpretation was a decisively rational process, originating from impressions of photographic exactitude. Imagination began its function only after conception of the impression; he could not grasp Coleridge's notion of actually seeing with imagination—of a subjective as opposed to an objective process. His art, therefore, was realistic where Coleridge's was romantic and symbolic, and his realism, with its basis in the tangible, recommended itself to the materialist mind in search of a faith unmisted by mysticism. It is not remarkable that a purely aesthetic attitude of mind—which was actually Wordsworth's only religion—should be accepted by his disciples as a substitute religion. For the aesthetic sense has always played a potent part in the externals of religious observance; the severe simplicity of recalcitrant nonconformity is a reaction against the obscuring of religion by elaborate ritual, and the superstitious awe excited by aesthetic window-dressing in cathedrals has been exposed in Hugh Walpole's *The Cathedral* and *The Inquisitor*.

But Coleridge's intellectual vision could not be hypnotised nor his spiritual requirements satisfied by an aesthetic attitude. Suffering the more because he could not afford to suffer, he was now about to embark on a long pilgrimage in search of spiritual and mental peace.

PART SEVEN

THE APOSTATES

I. EPISODE OF CHARLES LLOYD

SOUTHEY duly spent his six months in Portugal, where he learnt something of Spanish and Portuguese and accumulated material for a travel book. His uncle found him "perfectly correct in his behaviour, of the most exemplary morals, and the best of hearts," but was disappointed at his continued determination not to take orders and his perseverance in democratic opinions and romantic ideals. He returned to England in May 1796, to be met with the news of the sudden death from fever of his brother-in-law, Robert Lovell. Harassed by the winding up of the *Watchman* and the uncertainty of his future plans, Coleridge sustained the intimate burden of this bereavement and the mourning of the Fricker household. Southey decided, with less than his usual practical sense, to raise something for Lovell's widow "by publishing his best pieces, if only enough to buy her a harpsichord." Coleridge's payment of twenty pounds a year to Mrs. Fricker probably proved more useful.

In accordance with his idea of settling near his friend Bedford to study law, Southey spent some weeks at Brixton, but not even the society of Bedford and Wynn could prevent "an unspeakable loathing" for London, and he began married life with his Edith in lodgings on the outskirts of Bristol, whence in half an hour he could be "among rocks and woods, with no other company than the owls and jackdaws, with whom I fraternise in solitude." All thought of pantisocracy was now banished from his plans. He had only a few months to wait for Wynn's promised annuity of £160, and he made practical plans for a conventional career. "How does time mellow down our opinions!" he reflected. "Little of that ardent enthusiasm which so lately fevered my whole character remains. I have contracted my sphere of action within the little circle of my own friends, and even my wishes seldom stray beyond it." As Coleridge was still resident with Mrs. Fricker, it was impossible for Southey to avoid meeting him, and he made overtures to sink their differences, which were accepted. But there was no "enthusiasm of friendship" between them. "The cause of the difference was solemn, and 'the blasted oak puts not forth its buds anew,'" wrote Coleridge. "We are acquaintances, and feel kindliness towards each other, but I do not esteem or love Southey as I must esteem and love the man whom I dared call by the holy name of friend." Southey felt less "kindliness" than Coleridge thought ; feeling the cause of grievance to be wholly on his side, he resented Coleridge's avoidance of a return to their former intimacy.

He occupied himself with a volume of Letters from Spain and Portugal, to be published by Cottle and to pay his expenses during the six months before he received Wynn's annuity. This and contributions to the Monthly Magazine he recognised as hack work, and felt that the writing of his Welsh epic Madoc— the idea of which he had conceived, along with the transposition of pantisocracy from the Susquehanna to a Welsh farm, on a visit to Wynn in 1794—was "almost necessary" to his happiness. Deprived of Coleridge's conversation, he "declared war against metaphysics," and believed that "all the moral advantages said to result from them . . . are fairly and more easily deducible from religion, or even from common sense." Yet, at the age of twenty-two, he declared, "No man ever retained a more perfect knowledge of the history of his own mind than I have done," and "I look forward to the writing of this history as the most pleasing and most useful employment I shall ever undertake."

He finished his Letters for publication by the end of the year, and also a volume of poems, a copy of which he sent to Coleridge. He turned off occasional verse with the easy fluency he was soon to acquire in prose, but fluency and fertility left him little time for meditation on meaning or interpretation, or for the meticulous

SOUTHEY IN 1796

(*from the portrait by Robert Hancock in the National Portrait Gallery.*)

correcting and selection of the right expression that characterised Coleridge's work and Wordsworth's early work. Acknowledging the gift of the book, Coleridge wrote a critical letter, mostly suggesting obviously advantageous emendations, and to Thelwall he confided that " an admirable poet might be made by *amalgamating*" Southey and himself. " I *think* too much for a *poet*, he too little for a *great* poet." But he felt that Southey's worst fault was that " he abjures *feeling*," and six months later he found that Wordsworth shared this impression.

A chill delayed Southey's departure to London till February 1797, when he entered at Gray's Inn and, in accordance with the terms of Wynn's annuity, began to read law. With George Dyer as introducer, he went into literary society, but was even less impressed than Coleridge had been over two years before. Godwin had " large noble eyes, and a *nose*—oh, most abominable nose! Language is not vituperatious enough to describe the effect of its downward elongation." Godwin also loved London (a grave defect in Southey's eyes) and literary society, and talked " nonsense about the collision of mind " to the accompaniment of admiring applause from a blue-stocking audience. Southey admired Mary Wollstonecraft as " a first-rate woman," but Gilbert Wakefield had " a most critic-like voice, as if he had snarled himself hoarse." After meeting Basil Montagu and discussing legal prospects, he decided to specialise in chancery rather than common law, as he could not bring himself to appear in a criminal case and " plead against the life of a man." " Were I to be instrumental in bringing a murderer to the gallows, I should ever after feel that I had become a murderer myself." Nourishing no ambition to shine as a legal luminary, he wished only " to obtain enough to retire into the country."

Economic considerations luckily coincided with hunger for the country and a sight of the sea, for " the price of everything is nearly doubled since the commencement of the war," and believing that he could read law in the country as well as in London, he took Edith to Hampshire and eventually found lodgings for the summer at Burton near Christchurch. Besides contributing to the *Monthly Magazine*, he completed more hack work in translating Necker's memoirs of the French Revolution. But in the country, he worked slowly but satisfactorily on *Madoc*, revised both his poems and *Joan of Arc* for second editions, and also wrote a tragedy on the subject of *Joan*. When Cottle came to stay with him and told him that Chatterton's sister and niece were destitute, he undertook an edition of Chatterton's works. This occasioned his writing to Coleridge, who cordially invited him and Edith for a visit, conveyed Wordsworth's offer of " a suite of rooms " at Alfoxden, and on the strength of his successful driving of Dorothy from Racedown, even offered to fetch them from Hampshire in Poole's one-horse chaise. But Southey was not disposed to fraternal familiarity. In the same week as he received this invitation, he wrote to John May, a Lisbon acquaintance, a garbled account of his former alliance with Coleridge, ending with the accusation that Coleridge uttered " every possible calumny " against him over his renunciation of pantisocracy.

He was in this frame of mind when, in August 1797, he received an unexpected visit from Charles Lloyd and Charles Lamb. Apparently the delirious fits that occasioned Lloyd's departure from Stowey in March had abated under Dr. Darwin's treatment at Lichfield. He returned home to Birmingham, where he contrived to entangle himself with a girl named Sophia Pemberton. Probably he was only attracted by a charming feminine sympathiser with his tales of woe, but the " Rousseauish " sensibility, emotional tenderness, and effacing modesty that had charmed Coleridge and Lamb, allied with his elegant manners and wistful demeanour, won the girl's heart, and when her parents, finding his father's wealth insufficient compensation for his own mental infirmity, opposed their marriage, she intimated her readiness to marry without their consent. The consequence of his philandering immediately infected Lloyd with a fever of foreboding and self-distrust, and he took refuge with Lamb in London " to gain a little time and a little peace, before he made up his mind . . . wishing earnestly that he had never entered into engagements which he felt himself unable to fulfill, but which on Sophia's account he could not bring himself to relinquish."

Apparently he had opened correspondence with Southey, as with Lamb, and when he proposed that Lamb should accompany him to Southey "for a day or two," Lamb, who was at a loss to know how to advise or comfort him, eagerly welcomed relief from his embarrassment.

Lamb could only be out of town for one night, so Lloyd proposed to return to London with him and then travel to Stowey to ask Coleridge's advice. But Southey's impetuous and decisive personality immediately overwhelmed Lloyd's weak and timid character. He himself had defied family disapproval to marry the girl of his choice; Lloyd must not hesitate to do likewise. He readily convinced Lloyd that the conscientious, introspective Coleridge was no such adequate adviser as a man of action like himself, and Lamb returned alone to London, leaving Lloyd already so far strengthened in resolve as to write "an explicit letter to Sophia."

Lamb left them on Tuesday 15th August; on Saturday the 19th he received a letter from Lloyd, dated from Bath, saying that he was on his way to Birmingham with Southey "for the purpose of persuading Sophia to a Scotch marriage." Lamb wrote off the news to Burnett, who informed Coleridge. Naturally hurt that Lloyd should have preferred advice on a delicate matter of such importance from a stranger like Southey rather than himself, Coleridge immediately asked confirmation from Lamb. From what Lloyd had told him of Sophia's character, Lamb suspected that she would not consent to a "Scotch marriage," and apparently it so happened; though he did eventually marry her, the event was deferred. Lloyd returned with Southey to Hampshire, and when the Southey's left Burton for Bath in mid-September, Edith and her mother-in-law travelled under Southey's brother's care, while Lloyd and Southey walked, making "a pilgrimage to Stonehenge on the way." Lloyd remained nearly four months at Bath as a "boarder" with Southey's mother, leaving for London in the new year of 1798.

Before his association with Southey Lloyd's affection for Coleridge was unabated. He told Lamb that if he went to Coleridge for advice about his marriage, he could never have brought himself to leave him. They continued in close correspondence till late in July 1797, when Coleridge sent him a manuscript of *This Lime-Tree Bower My Prison*. But, wounded by Lloyd's neglecting his counsel for that of Southey of all people, of whom Lloyd knew nothing save the fact that he and Coleridge were estranged, Coleridge delayed answering his letters. Lloyd's neurotic sensibility was readily prone to grievance at such neglect. A few weeks later he was plaintively lamenting that Southey's brother Tom had neglected to write to him, and in September he complained of Coleridge to Lamb, who wrote to Coleridge: " You use Lloyd very ill, never writing to him. I tell you again that his is not a mind with which you should play tricks."

Confiding his complaints to Southey as to Lamb, Lloyd found his grievance growing in massive distortion as he listened to Southey's version of the pantisocratic partnership. Soon his unbalanced mind conceived his former dearest friend as a treacherous enemy, making use of friends like himself and Southey and then maligning them behind their backs. It is generally assumed that the three sonnets of " Nehemiah Higginbottom," in which Coleridge satirised the characteristics of his own early poetry and incidentally of his disciples, Southey, Lamb, and Lloyd, excited Lloyd's indignation at his " treachery " and inspired him to revenge in cruelly caricaturing Coleridge in his novel, *Edmund Oliver*. But the " Higginbottom " sonnets appeared in the *Monthly Magazine* for November 1797, and on the 11th of that month Southey wrote to his brother, " Do you know that Lloyd has written a novel, and that it is going immediately to the press? " *Edmund Oliver* was therefore written without the provocation of the sonnets; it was written, moreover, while Lloyd was living under the same roof as Southey.

Between November and the novel's publication in the spring of 1798, Lloyd may have added in his spleen a few more pointed passages, but the story and character of the hero of *Edmund Oliver* are based on Coleridge's life and character. Edmund's " love-fit," leaving college, and going into the army were Coleridge's own experiences, related by him to Lloyd, who confessed in the preface that " the incidents relative to the army were given me by an intimate friend, who was himself eye-witness to one of them, and can produce testimony to the truth of the other two." Edmund was even endowed with Coleridge's appearance, with " his large glistening eye," " his dark eyebrows" and " dark hair." Worst of all, Lloyd betrayed the knowledge—acquired by living in the same house—of Coleridge's habitual recourse to laudanum, Edmund being made to write: " I have at all times a strange dreaminess about me, which makes me indifferent to the future, if I can by any means fill the present with sensations,—with that dreaminess I have gone on here from day to day; if at any time thought-troubled, I have swallowed some spirits, or had recourse to my laudanum."

Though Southey countenanced what Lloyd had written and knew how he himself had fermented Lloyd's feelings, he did not hesitate to express outraged indignation on discovering that Coleridge was " Nehemiah Higginbottom." Doubtless he owed the discovery to Cottle, for the identity of Coleridge with his own satirist was so little known that Dr. Beddoes warned a mutual acquaintance against mentioning the sonnets to Coleridge, as he was likely to be " as sore as a boil" about them. On 8th December Coleridge replied to Southey that he was " very sorry" for having written the sonnets, " but ' sorry' would be a lame word to express my feelings, if I had written them with the motives which you have attributed to me." He denied that he had ever " been in the habit of treating our separation with levity," or that the sonnets were directed against Southey. " I am sorry to perceive a disposition in you to believe evil of me," and " I feel myself wounded and hurt and write as such." He nevertheless felt so little animosity that he provided Lloyd and Southey with an introduction to Daniel Stuart of the *Morning Post*, which enabled Southey to secure the same terms as himself, a guinea a week, for contributions of verse. Southey made many more guineas from this source than Coleridge, continuing to contribute verse till 1803. Many of his best short poems appeared in the *Morning Post*, including, in August 1798, that most popular of unpatriotic poems, *The Battle of Blenheim.*

Lamb declined to believe that Coleridge's sonnets were not intended to satirise Southey, but his affection for Coleridge was too deep to be uprooted on such slight pretext. At Christmas his sister was seriously ill with mental disorder, and on hearing of this, Lloyd, with the best intentions and unconscious that his own tendency to derangement might render his company painful in the circumstances, insisted on leaving Southey and going to London to offer consolation to Lamb. He settled in lodgings with Lamb's friend, James White, where Southey found him in January 1798, with "a vast number of new acquaintances, a false tail, a barber to powder him every morning, and . . . as happy as he wishes to be."

Lloyd and Southey together failed to rouse Lamb against Coleridge on account of the sonnets. In fact, Lloyd's well-meant attentions exasperated him. Lloyd tried to force his mind " from its natural and proper bent," continually inviting him out to dinners and suppers to distract him from worry over his sister, and complaining of being hurt when Lamb declined. At one such party, when Lloyd was playing the piano to a convivial audience, Lamb felt suddenly so overwrought that he rushed away to the solitude of the Temple, where, in surroundings reminiscent of much in his past, he wrote his poem, *The Old Familiar Faces*, in which he apostrophised Coleridge as " Friend of my bosom, thou more than a brother! " Irritation excited by Lloyd's misdirected efforts at consolation inspired comparison with the comfort imparted by Coleridge when he was similarly suffering three years before, and he wrote to Coleridge on 28th January: " To you I owe much under God. In my brief acquaintance with you in London, your conversations won me to the better cause, and rescued me from the polluting spirit of the world. I might have been a worthless character without you ; as it is, I do possess a certain improbable portion of devotional feelings."

But he confessed that, in his state of distressful anxiety, he was " very querulous " and " full of little jealousies and heart-burnings." He was thus a ready prey for malicious tattle. Lloyd must have shown him *Edmund Oliver* in proof or manuscript;

he would naturally expostulate against the betrayal of Coleridge's confidences, and Lloyd would seek to justify himself by a recital of imagined injuries. Then, in March, hearing of a projected third edition of Coleridge's poems, Lloyd wrote to Cottle, requesting that Coleridge should be " persuaded to resign " the use of his contribution to the previous volume. Cottle tactlessly forwarded the letter to Coleridge, who found it " curious that *I* should be applied to to be ' persuaded to resign and in hope that I might ' *consent to give up* a number of poems which were published at the earnest request of the author," adding tartly, " I have no objection to any disposal of Lloyd's poems except that of their being republished with mine."

Presumably Cottle likewise forwarded this letter, which was calculated to excite Lloyd's morbid sensibility to hysteria. Prejudiced in sympathy with Lloyd from his liability to his own sister's malady, critical of Coleridge's insufficient tolerance of Lloyd's weakness, and uneasy in his own conscience for having rebuffed Lloyd's well-meant efforts at consolation, Lamb angrily accepted the rejection of Lloyd's poems as equally applicable to his own—an attitude in which he was confirmed by receiving from Coleridge what Lloyd described as " a very odd letter," probably asking if he wished to associate himself with Lloyd in withdrawing his poems. Lloyd regarded Lamb as acting in concert with him when he informed Southey on 4th April, " I don't know what may be his [Coleridge's] sentiments with regard to our conduct, but I can perceive that he is bent on dissociating himself from us—particularly Lamb I think he has used unkindly." He was also able to show Lamb a letter from Coleridge containing the remark, " Poor Lamb, if he wants any *knowledge*, he may apply to me." Knowledge of what? Lamb did not ask the question, did not suspect that Coleridge might have been suggesting that he might ask of him the truth respecting some perversion of Lloyd's, or that the " poor " might be expressive of affectionate sympathy with his afflicted condition. Accepting Lloyd's misrepresentation, he interpreted the words literally to mean that Coleridge condescendingly offered himself as an encyclopaedia for ready reference—as a fatuous pretender, but nobody of Coleridge's intellectual equipment, would have done. He forgot the debt of gratitude he had acknowledged only two months before. He forgot Coleridge's "many kind letters" during his recent trouble and a generous invitation that Mary Lamb might spend her convalescence at Stowey. As he afterwards admitted, he allowed Lloyd to "alienate" him from Coleridge, and Lloyd—to cement the mischief he had made and again to emphasise that he was not alone in considering himself aggrieved—wrote to Dorothy Wordsworth that Lamb intended no further correspondence with Coleridge.

It seems that Coleridge received this intimation about the same time as a copy of *Edmund Oliver*—at the beginning of May 1798—and that he then fled for solitude to a lonely farm at Culbone, where he wrote *Kubla Khan*. In the preface to the poem, Coleridge related how, "in the summer of 1797, the Author, then in ill health, had retired to a lonely farm-house between Porlock and Linton," and how, after a dose of laudanum, he fell asleep in his chair after reading this passage in the *Pilgrimage* of Samuel Purchas: "In Xamdu did Cublai Can build a stately Palace, encompassing sixteen miles of plaine ground with a wall, wherein are fertile meddowes, pleasant Springs, delightfull Streames, and all sorts of beasts of chase and game, and in the middest thereof a sumptuous house of pleasure." During a sleep of three hours he composed a poem of two to three hundred lines, and on waking, immediately began to write them down. Before he could finish, "he was unfortunately called out by a person on business from Porlock," who kept him over an hour, and when he returned to the manuscript, he could remember no more than he had already written.

In a note written in 1810, he stated that his retirement to the farmhouse, and his recourse to opium for relief from mental trouble, were occasioned by his breach with Charles Lloyd, the nervous disquietude and misery that he suffered preventing his finishing *Christabel*. He never had much pretension to precision in dates. Habitually he cited his own birthday as the 20th instead of the 21st October, and at fifty-six, even when describing himself as feeling ten years older than his age, he declared himself as fifty-four. It was a simple slip to write, after a dozen years, "the summer of 1797" instead of 1798, when the trouble with Lloyd reached its head.

Sir Edmund Chambers unearthed yet another note on a manuscript of *Kubla Khan* belonging to Lord Crewe: "This fragment with a good deal more, not recoverable, composed in a sort of Reverie brought on by two grains of Opium, taken to check a dysentry, at a Farm House between Porlock and Linton, a quarter of a mile from Culbone Church, in the fall of the year, 1797." Enthusiasm for his discovery led Sir Edmund Chambers to suggest that this seemed "to outweigh the inference drawn from the notebook entry of 1810," and that Coleridge wrote *Kubla Khan* at Culbone before he informed Thelwall on 16th October 1797 that he had just "been absent a day or two." But Coleridge's smattering of medical knowledge combined with a frequent sufferer's preoccupation with his own ailments to make him confide in correspondents very particularly about his symptoms, and if he had been ill with dysentry as recently as "a day or two" before writing to Thelwall, he would certainly have said so. Further, as the late E. H. Coleridge objected, "it would, indeed, have been altogether miraculous if, before he had written a line of *Christabel*, or *The Ancient Mariner* . . . it had been 'given to him' to divine the enchanting images of *Kubla Khan*, or attune his mysterious vision to consummate melody," and the objection applies as eligibly to October as to the summer of 1797. Nor is there any reason why Coleridge should have associated the writing of *Kubla Khan* at Culbone with his trouble over Lloyd if there was no such association. He muddled dates —he had the drug addict's subterfuge in devising excuses for drug-taking, and may have been momentarily moved to think dysentry a better excuse than mental stress—but, as Dykes Campbell said, he was always a trustworthy recorder when he synchronised events by association.

The problem in detection is thus narrowed to May of 1798. Coleridge returned on 18th April from a visit of three or four days to his brother George at Ottery, and for the next ten days

was continually between Stowey and Alfoxden. Dorothy
Wordsworth's journal is irritating in its neglect of the significant.
She can record that " William went to have his picture taken,"
that she walked with him and that " Coleridge and he drank tea,"
but there appears no word of Lamb or Lloyd or *Edmund Oliver*.
For a week before 6th May she noted nothing; then Coleridge
was at Alfoxden on three successive days; on the 9th, though she
had seen him the day before, Dorothy " wrote to Coleridge."
After a week's silence, she wrote on Wednesday 16th May,
" Coleridge, William and myself set forward to the Cheddar
rocks."

It is possible, but improbable, that Coleridge went to Culbone
on 9th May, and that the interrupting " person on business from
Porlock " came to apprise him of the approaching birth of his
second child, Berkeley. But on Sunday 13th May he walked to
Taunton " to perform the divine services for poor Dr. Toulmin,"
whose daughter had committed suicide, and was back at his wife's
bedside when, at half-past one in the morning of Monday the
14th, she gave birth to her second son, christened Berkeley
after the philosopher who had supplanted Hartley in Coleridge's
intellectual esteem. At three in the morning he wrote letters to
Poole, Estlin, and his brother George, without mention of any
recent absence at Culbone.

The journey to Cheddar on the 16th was partly for pleasure,
but Wordsworth's " main business was to bring back poor
Lloyd, whose infirmities had been made the instruments of
another man's darker passions." Clearly Coleridge had confided
to the Wordsworths his emotion on reading *Edmund Oliver;*
they had discussed Lloyd's letter to Dorothy about Lamb, and
had rightly decided that Southey's " darker passions " had
played on Lloyd's hysterical temperament, which had since
worked on Lamb's feelings. It was almost certainly Wordsworth's suggestion that a meeting between Coleridge and Lloyd
would effect a reconciliation between them, and so between
Coleridge and Lamb. Like Neville Chamberlain in later history,
he believed in the policy of personal contact to compose mis-
understanding, and fourteen years later he proposed to effect

reconciliation between himself and Coleridge by " confronting " him with the third party to their difference. Apparently he proposed to interview Lloyd on Coleridge's behalf and persuade him to return with him to Stowey.

Lloyd was visiting Southey at Bristol, but when Coleridge, Wordsworth and Dorothy reached Bridgwater, where they spent the night of the 16th, they found—" by a letter that met us on the road "—that Lloyd was " off for Birmingham." Next morning they went on to see the Cheddar caves, and slept the night at the village of Cross. On Friday the 18th, Wordsworth proceeded to Bristol, carrying a letter from Coleridge to Estlin. He thought that Lloyd might possibly not yet have left, and he also wished to see his own Bristol friends. Returning home, Coleridge was shocked by news of the death of Poole's brother. He spent Saturday in " distressing perplexity " whether to call and offer consolation or whether to wait till the first pangs of grief had subsided. On Sunday morning he sent a note to Poole, assuring him that in all his sorrows as well in his joys he was " a true and faithful sharer," and offering to call, to stay with him, or to leave him alone, according to Poole's wish. Poole felt deeply the loss of his brother, to whom he had been more than ordinarily devoted; he probably saw Coleridge, and intimated a wish to be left alone for a few days to calm his mother's grief.

Coleridge was thus isolated in a state of accumulated trouble. " So many unpleasant and shocking circumstances have happened to me in my immediate knowledge within the last fortnight," he told Poole, " that I am in a nervous state, and the most trifling thing makes me weep." Writing to Estlin on the 14th he said: " I have had many sorrows and some that bite deep; calumny and ingratitude from men who have been fostered in the bosom of my confidence! " After finding his fireside confidences publicly paraded in *Edmund Oliver*, he had heard from Dorothy of Lamb's decision to break with him. Then after the distressing experience of comforting old Dr. Toulmin over his daughter's suicide, he had been afflicted to choking and " an agony of tears " on hearing of " the horrid manner " of another old acquaintance's death. Finally came Poole's bereavement. As always in distress, he tortured himself with self-analysis, wondering if, after all, he had done wrong in not becoming a stated minister. "For want of habit my mind wanders, and I cannot *pray* as often as I ought," he told Estlin: "Though Christianity is my *passion*, it is too much my *intellectual* passion, and therefore will do me but little good in the hour of temptation and calamity." Whether he had become a minister or not, he could never have acquired the unquestioning faith of the unimaginatively devout. He had arrived at the adoption of Christianity by intellectual reasoning—it was to him the supreme philosophy of life, the basis of all subsequent philosophical systems—and his instinctively inquiring mind was as incapable of *faith* (as distinguished from *belief*) in Christianity as in Wordsworth's substitute religion of Nature.

So it seems likely that he now sought refuge in solitude, where he found in laudanum relief from the mental distress that prayer failed to compose. Poole was inaccessible and Wordsworth away; in Wordsworth's absence gossip and the conventions forbade visits to Dorothy; Sara, uncomprehending and inclined to impatience with self-harrowings beyond the ken of her limited imagination, was naturally absorbed in her week-old baby, and satisfied in having negotiated her second confinement even more easily than her first. He went to the wild scenery of Exmoor that had so fascinated him in the previous November. Probably he had made friends of the farmhouse folk at Culbone when staying there with Wordsworth and Dorothy.

Before he left or after his return, he wrote to Lamb an undated letter which, even for Coleridge, represents a miracle of unerring insight and intuitive sympathy. Lamb's anger with him caused him "little pain," not for lack of love and esteem, but because he realised that Lamb "would not without struggles abandon" him at Lloyd's persuasion, and had confidence that "although you do not think as a wise man, you feel as a good man." On Lloyd's account he felt alarm, because clearly "his feelings are vitiated" and "his ideas are in their combination merely the creatures of those feelings." The pain he had himself inflicted on Southey by the Higginbottom sonnets deterred him from "too hastily" condemning Lloyd for the caricature in *Edmund Oliver*. He confessed to "some brief resentments," but from these "resulted only a sort of fantastic scepticism concerning my own consciousness of my own rectitude. As dreams have impressed on him [Lloyd] the sense of reality, my sense of reality may be but a dream." This extraordinary revelation of imaginative introspection was probably little better understood by Lamb than by Wordsworth. It shows that, pondering Berkeley's theory of vision as interpretation, from picturing in *The Ancient Mariner* the hallucinations of an unbalanced mind, he had now arrived at speculation on how far a supposedly rational mind might be derationalised by self-deception, so unconsciously distorting interpretation. Wordsworth, who would have regarded as lunacy a suggestion that his own mind was not immaculately rational, deprecated such speculation as digression into the supernatural. If he could have followed further the trend of Coleridge's thought, he might have warned him against possible loss of mental balance, for, as illustrated in Galsworthy's *Maid in Waiting*, madness is precipitated by fear of its approach. Coleridge's sanity was too deep-seated for subversion, but metaphysical speculation was to set him feeling for phantoms in a self-imposed martyrdom of blind man's buff.

He told Lamb that Lloyd's letters showed that he had "mistaken the heat and bustle and swell of self-justification for the approbation of his conscience," and explained that his last unanswered letter was written only to ask that Lamb should press upon Lloyd the propriety of a personal interview to resolve his grievances. Shrewdly he reasoned that both Lamb and Lloyd knew him first when they were suffering mental stress, and clothed his image in "a suit of notions and feelings which could belong to nothing human." But while Lamb was "restored to comparative saneness" and "merely wondering what is become of the Coleridge with whom" he was "so passionately in love," Lloyd had changed his disease and was "arraying his ci-devant Angel in a flaming San Benito—the whole ground of the garment a dark brimstone and plenty of little devils flourished out in

black." Against Southey he said nothing, but he clearly recognised that Southey's influence had perverted Lloyd. Ironically
the trouble might never have arisen if he had used Lloyd with
Southey's egotistical self-righteousness. His fault lay in a sympathy beyond Lloyd's experience, and his "kindness" and
"affectionateness" were mistaken for "wheedling."

2. HAZLITT AT STOWEY

It is possible that the fatal interrupter of *Kubla Khan*, the
"person on business from Porlock," came with a message of
reminder from Sara that Hazlitt was expected at Stowey. He
had been asked to postpone his proposed visit "for a week or
two," obviously on account of Sara's confinement, and is
reckoned to have eventually arrived—having walked all the
way from Wem, by Worcester, Gloucester and Bristol—at
the week-end of 26th–27th May. Wordsworth was still at
Bristol, but Coleridge took advantage of Hazlitt's chaperonage
to visit Dorothy on the afternoon of his arrival. They stayed
the night, and after breakfast next morning, strolled in the park
till, seated on a fallen tree, Coleridge "read aloud, with a
sonorous and musical voice," not his own poems, but Wordsworth's. They returned to Stowey late in the evening, and
passing "through echoing grove, by fairy stream or waterfall,
gleaming in the summer moonlight," Coleridge lamented that
"Wordsworth was not prone enough to believe in the traditional
superstitions of the place, and that there was a something corporeal,
a *matter-of-fact-ness*, a clinging to the palpable, or often to the
petty, in his poetry, in consequence." He emphasised that this
objection applied only to his descriptive poetry, for "his philosophic poetry had a grand and comprehensive spirit in it, so
that his soul seemed to inhabit the universe like a palace, and to
discover truth by intuition, rather than by deduction."
Next day, Wordsworth arrived at Stowey from Bristol,
"gaunt and Don Quixote-like," dressed incongruously with

current fashion " in a brown fustian jacket and striped pantaloons."
He walked with a rolling, lounging gait; " there was severe,
worn pressure of thought about his temples, a fire in his eye
(as if he saw something in objects more than the outward appearance), an intense, high, narrow forehead, a Roman nose,
cheeks furrowed by strong purpose and feeling, and a convulsive
inclination to laugh about the mouth, a good deal at variance
with the solemn, stately expression of the rest of his face."
Some forty years later, Wordsworth was annoyed by the suggestion that his forehead was narrow. " I went through three
large magazines of hats in Paris, before I could find one large
enough," he said, " and yet my skull is almost cut away behind! "
He liked the bust of himself by the fashionable sculptor Sir Francis
Chantrey, because it was idealised to suggest the soul of poetry
and so flattered him; Coleridge said of it that it was more like
Wordsworth than Wordsworth himself was! Hazlitt, a good
judge, thought that Haydon's head of him, in the huge historical
picture of " Christ's Entry into Jerusalem," was " most like his
drooping weight of thought and expression."

He talked " naturally and freely," Hazlitt noting " a strong
tincture of the norther *burr*," though he remarked in Coleridge's
intonation none of the Devon accent that Farington the diarist
professed to detect. Next day at Alfoxden Wordsworth read his
Peter Bell, " and the comment made upon it by his face and
voice was very different from that of some later critics! " There
was a " *chaunt* " in the recitation of both Coleridge and Wordsworth, but Coleridge's manner was full, animated, varied,
Wordsworth's more equable, sustained and internal—the one
more dramatic, the other more lyrical.

Three weeks Hazlitt stayed at Stowey, enjoying—like Lamb,
Cottle, and Thelwall in the previous summer—delightful after-
noons in Tom Poole's arbour, quaffing " flip " and listening to
the humming bees when not listening to Coleridge. During his
stay, he and Coleridge, with a Nether Stowey man named John
Chester, walked to Lynton. Chester was a simple countryman
and looked it—a short, bow-legged man, walking with a drover's
dragging slouch and wearing boots and corduroy breeches. He

234 THE FIRST ROMANTICS

was one of Coleridge's devoted disciples, and trotted at his side
to keep up with him, "like a running footman by a state coach ";
" he scarcely opened his lips, much less offered an opinion the
whole way," except to confide aside to Hazlitt that Coleridge
was " a wonderful man." When, on Lynmouth beach, Coleridge
acknowledged Hazlitt's argument that likeness was not mere
association of ideas, Chester listened in astonishment that anybody
could suggest anything to Coleridge that he did not already
know. Poor Chester's name survives only as Coleridge's humble
friend. He left nothing to mark his time on earth; yet Hazlitt
fairly said that, if he had to choose to be one of those three, he
would have been John Chester. For the other two were of the
few who must daily suffer in the ceaseless working of mind and
imagination, pursuing to the end truth's elusive shadow. They
could never know even the self-complacency of the city shopkeeper, with his blunted sense of right and wrong, much less the
stolid serenity of countrymen like Chester, living on the land,
untroubled save by the vagaries of the seasons.

Hazlitt's memory of their route was at fault, for if they passed
Blue Anchor beach (where the surf must still have been white,
unbrowned by Bridgwater's sewage), they must have made a
wide detour to pass Dunster on their right and look down on
it beneath them, before coming to Minehead. Presumably
Coleridge took them to the farm at Culbone, for they descended
from the moorland into " little sheltered valleys close by the
sea-side." A thunderstorm threatened while they were at Lynton,
and Coleridge ran from the inn bareheaded " to enjoy the com-
motion of the element " in the Valley of Rocks, which, he
told Hazlitt, was to have been the setting of *The Wanderings
of Cain.*

A day or two after returning from this excursion, Hazlitt left
on a Sunday morning. Coleridge was preaching that day for
Dr. Toulmin at Taunton; when he parted from Hazlitt, he had
not yet thought of the text for his sermon, which he composed
during his walk alone. They met at Bridgwater in the evening,
and walked to Bristol next day. After spending Tuesday with
Estlin, he travelled to Brentford, where he stayed with Poole's

friend, Samuel Purkis. On Thursday evening he was received
"with joy and affection" by the Wedgwood brothers at Stoke
d'Abernon in Surrey.

3. FAREWELL TO ALFOXDEN

The main object of his visit to the Wedgwoods was to discuss
the possibility of his going in the autumn to Germany, to learn
the language for the purpose of studying the German philosophers. The Wordsworths were under notice to quit Alfoxden
at the end of their twelve months' tenancy in July, the owner
having refused to renew the letting. "I was not refused a continuance," said Wordsworth after his accession to respectability:
"I never applied for one." After the spy's visit to Stowey,
having received representations from Lord Somerville and other
notable busybodies, Mrs. St. Aubyn upbraided her agent so
wrathfully that Tom Poole wrote to her in his defence, assuring
her that her agent had let the house to Wordsworth on his
recommendation. He confessed that he had not known Wordsworth long, but the fact that his uncle Cookson was a Canon
of Windsor was "sufficient" evidence of "the respectability
of Mr. Wordsworth's family!" He also confessed that the
notorious Thelwall had visited him, but Wordsworth had no
previous acquaintance with him. Begging her "to hearken to
no calumnies, no party spirit, nor to join with any in disturbing
one who only wishes to live in tranquility," he pledged himself
"in every respect that you will have no cause to complain of
Mr. Wordsworth," who, "of all men alive, is the last who will
give any one cause to complain of his opinions, his conduct,
or his disturbing the peace of anyone." But even with Poole,
of whom and whose family she had familiar knowledge, as
sponsor, Mrs. St. Aubyn declined to harbour an undesirable
tenant longer than she could help. Dorothy's journal records
on 3rd April a walk "to Crookham, with Coleridge and Wm.,
to make the appeal"—an appeal which can only have been an
application to the agent for renewal of the tenancy. Both

Wordsworth and Dorothy were reluctant to leave, and the " man of stern veracity " wrote to Poole in the following October, asking him to keep an eye on Alfoxden, for, " if any series of accidents should bring it again into the market, we should be glad to have it, if we could manage it."

Coleridge contemplated the loss of their society with anxiety amounting to alarm. Spending five days a week in their company, he had shared all his thoughts with them, and he recoiled in horror from the barren prospect of intellectual loneliness to which he would be left by separation. Delight in Dorothy's companionship had shown him the awful hollowness of a marriage, which, with cheerful optimism, he had tried for more than two years to make a success. He had tried to inspire Sara with enthusiasm for his pursuits as he had inspired other lesser minds. He had even attributed to her his own verses on " The Silver Thimble," in the hope of encouraging her taste for poetry. But he had been forced to recognise that her mind was commonplace as the suburban villa in which she was brought up. Visiting Southey at Keswick in the winter of 1811–12, young Shelley found Mrs. Southey " very stupid; Mrs. Coleridge worse." To Coleridge, Sara was the mother of his babies. He could be affectionate and playful with her in the children's company for a few hours, but he feared lest even this communion might become impossible if he was deprived of regular intellectual companionship.

The Wordsworths were willing to travel—William thought it would be " a great advantage to him to be acquainted with the German language," as " translation is the most profitable of all works "—and Coleridge viewed with eager joy the delight of sharing with them his impressions of a foreign country. Tom Wedgwood, who delighted in " metaphysicizing " with Coleridge, approved the plan of his studying the German philosophers, but the money question deferred a final decision till August. According to Cottle, the publisher stayed a few days at Alfoxden before the Wordsworths left in July, and accompanied Coleridge and Wordsworth to Lynton to be shown the " Valley of Stones." During the visit, the volume of *Lyrical Ballads* was planned.

Cottle offered them thirty guineas each for their tragedies.
Coleridge might have accepted for *Osorio*, but Wordsworth, in
spite of the summary rejection of *The Borderers* by the Covent
Garden management, still thought that it might achieve stage
success in " happier times," and " to throw away this chance for
a mere trifle, would be to make the present moment act fraudu-
lently and usuriously towards the future time." Wordsworth
also objected to Cottle's plan of publishing his poems in two
volumes, on the ground that " they would want variety," and
Coleridge argued " if this apply in his case it applies with ten-
fold more force to mine."

So at length they decided on publishing only the joint-volume
of *Lyrical Ballads*, for which Cottle paid thirty guineas. It was
to consist of " sundry shorter poems, and, for the most part, of
pieces more recently written." Wordsworth had to leave out
Peter Bell, which remained unprinted for twenty years, and
could include only the extract called *The Female Vagrant* from
Guilt and Sorrow. These sacrifices were balanced by the omission
of all Coleridge's recent reflective poetry. Cottle disliked the
volume's anonymity, but " Wordsworth's name is nothing to a
large number of persons," said Coleridge; " mine stinks." Probably poems like *Fears in Solitude* and *France: An Ode* were omitted
lest their political sentiments should prejudice the volume's
chances of fair criticism. For in July, George Canning clumsily
satirised, "C——dge and S——th—y, L——d, and L——be and
Co." in the *Anti-Jacobin*, while that paper's successor, the *Anti-
Jacobin Review*, contained in August a cartoon by Gillray,
depicting the revolutionist sympathisers, led by the Duke of
Bedford, pressing to worship Justice, Philanthropy, and Sensibility (qualities with which Canning and his friends had scant
acquaintance), and among them Coleridge and Southey as
donkeys, the one offering a volume of " Dactylics," the other
of " Saphics," with Lloyd and Lamb behind as a toad and a
frog. Their political opinions being well known among the
intelligentsia, Coleridge and Southey were fair game for the
bright young Tories. But Lloyd and Lamb had engaged in
no political activities—Lamb's employment by the East India

Company forbade participation in politics—and their only claim to inclusion in the cartoon was having published poems in the same volume as Coleridge's. Hence Coleridge probably feared that Wordsworth might suffer from association with his name or political opinions—a view likely to be fervently endorsed by the author of the unpublished reply to Bishop Watson.

4. BROTHER AND SISTER

Bidding farewell to Alfoxden on 26th June, the Wordsworths stayed a week with Coleridge at Stowey and then a week with Cottle at Bristol, before making a short walking trip in South Wales, where on 13th July, Wordsworth drafted the *Lines Composed a Few Miles above Tintern Abbey*, recalling his visit of five years before, on his way from Salisbury Plain to visit his friend Jones in Denbighshire, reflecting on how in the meantime he had found sanctuary from disturbing emotions in Nature-worship, and finally paying tribute to the boon of Dorothy's companionship. The most effective poem of reflection he had yet completed, it endorsed Coleridge's opinion that his genius flamed brightest in philosophical poetry, and encouraged Coleridge to emphasise his exhortations to perseverance with *The Recluse*.

Returning " after a ramble of four or five days," the Wordsworths settled temporarily at Bristol to be near the printer. There at the beginning of August they were joined by Coleridge, who had now convinced himself that the trip to Germany was " of high importance to my intellectual utility " and therefore " to my moral happiness." Apart from the hazards of wartime travel, he would have had to borrow money to take his family with him. Subject to Sara's consent, he therefore proposed to go alone, to stay the three or four months necessary to learn the language, and then either to return or, if " a scheme of weighty advantages " offered, to fetch over his family. Leaving Poole to broach this proposition to Sara, he made a " dart into

Wales" with Wordsworth and Dorothy, visiting Thelwall at the farm he had found in the Wye valley.

Returning by boat from Swansea to Bridgwater, he presumably found Sara indisposed to enthusiasm at his going abroad in Dorothy's company while she remained under Poole's protection with the children, but her consent was gained when faithful John Chester requested the privilege of accompanying him. The Wordsworths remained at Bristol till *Lyrical Ballads* was printed, and Coleridge and Chester joined them in London in September. Wordsworth's former publisher, the radical Johnson, was so charmed by Coleridge that, " purely out of affection conceived for me, and as part of anything I might do for him," he presented him with an order for thirty pounds on a Hamburg banker, enabling him to send Sara that sum out of the money he had with him. Johnson also undertook to publish in a quarto pamphlet *Fears in Solitude, France: An Ode,* and *Frost at Midnight,* which duly appeared under Coleridge's name before the end of the year.

The *Lyrical Ballads,* with whose publication literary historians mark the dawn of " The Romantic Movement " in English literature, slipped unobtrusively upon the world a few days before Coleridge, Chester, and the Wordsworths left London for Yarmouth on 14th September 1798. A few months later, on a visit to her mother at Bristol, Sara peevishly informed Poole that " the Lyrical Ballads are not liked at all by any."

They sailed from Yarmouth on the morning of Sunday 16th September, and arrived in Hamburg—" an ugly city that stinks in every corner "—on the following Wednesday afternoon. " Chester was ill the whole voyage; Wordsworth shockingly ill." Dorothy " was consigned to the cabin " before sailing, and did not quit it till they were on the Elbe's still waters. Only Coleridge was " neither sick nor giddy, but gay as a lark," and entertained himself and the other passengers with his usual volubility, as he describes in the first of *Satyrane's Letters.* Of the first few days at Hamburg Dorothy kept a journal; a livelier account by Coleridge appears in *Satyrane's Letters.* They were introduced to Klopstock, with whom Wordsworth conversed easily in French, while Coleridge had to rely on Latin and the German's few words of broken English. A tear blinded Coleridge while considering Klopstock " as the venerable father of German poetry; as a good man; as a Christian; seventy-four years old; with legs enormously swollen; yet active, lively, cheerful, and kind and communicative." But he disliked his powdered wig and wished he had worn his own grey hair, for the contrast of a snow-white wig with the colour of a wrinkled old face was disgusting—" his powder and periwig were to the eye what *Mr.* Virgil would be to the ear."

Coleridge decided to pursue his studies at Ratzeburg, and went over to find lodgings there for himself and Chester, the thirty-five miles taking nearly as long to cover as the hundred and twenty-six from London to Yarmouth. He returned to say good-bye to the Wordsworths, who wished to travel farther afield, and left again with Chester on 1st October. The Wordsworths went to Goslar, where they spent the coldest winter of the eighteenth century. Nor was the cold of the weather relieved by the hospitality they had hoped for from local society. They had forgotten that the many friends they had made and entertained at Alfoxden were introduced by Coleridge. Now they were alone again, Wordsworth's awkward stiffness deterred friendly advances. When he complained of their loneliness, Coleridge pointed out that he had two things against him—his dislike of smoking and his sister. Writing home, Coleridge spoke more plainly: it was " next but impossible for any but married women, or in the suit of married women, to be introduced to any company in Germany," as " sister here is considered as only a name for mistress." Nevertheless, " male acquaintance he might have had," said Coleridge, " and had I been at Goslar I would have had them." But what he kindly called Wordsworth's " unseeking manners " isolated him, and it was " no wonder " that he spent more time in writing English than studying German, " for he might as well have been in England as in Goslar."

Wordsworth learned little German and attempted no " profitable " work of translation, but he wrote English at Goslar to some purpose. Among the poems written there were *Ruth*, *Lucy Gray*, *Nutting*, and the several exquisite short poems addressed to the mysterious Lucy. Characteristically unable to do in Rome as Rome did, even by smoking a pipe, he dramatised his loneliness as he had dramatised his affair with Annette, as if it had been an infliction instead of an intended pleasure of his own seeking, and so far from enjoying the experience he had always desired from travel, he brooded over the past and hungered for Windermere and the Quantocks.

> "*I travelled among unknown men,*
> *In lands beyond the sea;*
> *Nor, England! did I know till then*
> *What love I bore to thee.*
>
> '*Tis past, that melancholy dream!*
> *Nor will I quit thy shore*
> *A second time; for still I seem*
> *To love thee more and more.*"

Though still capable of bathos in occasional lines of bald prose, the Lucy poems, *Ruth*, and even the lively lines, "A plague on your languages, German and Norse," show how much he had learned of melody and rhythm from Coleridge. But even more they reveal the depth of Dorothy's inspiration. At Racedown, dramatising the disaster of his love for Annette, he had exacted Dorothy's consolation as for a lover parted from his mistress. At Alfoxden he had been at first too busy developing his latent powers under the invigorating influence of Coleridge's inspiration, too happy in the first experience of sympathising genius and genuine friendship, either to dramatise himself or his relations with Dorothy. But the green streak of jealousy ran thick athwart his nature, as appears in his inevitable disparagement of all contemporaries, and he must have suffered frequent pangs in daily contact with Coleridge's bright genius, endowed with charms beyond his own attainment. He saw Dorothy's admiration and frank affection for Coleridge, her delight in his

I

company. He must have realised that, if Coleridge had been unmarried, Dorothy might well have become his wife. He felt jealousy that her devotion and her faith in his genius were now divided with another, and in self-defence he began again to dramatise himself—not now in connection with Annette—but directly with Dorothy herself. Werther-like, he talked of their separation as if impending, and pictured himself as prematurely aged and broken by sorrow, sustained only from disintegration and despair by her devotion.

> " *Oh! yet a little while*
> *May I behold in thee what I was once,*
> *My dear, dear Sister! and this prayer I make,*
> *Knowing that Nature never did betray*
> *The heart that loved her.*"

So he portrayed his pose at Tintern Abbey, before proceeding to pathetic visions of their possible separation.

It is possible that jealousy of Coleridge on Dorothy's account inspired his determination to dawdle gloomily away their time at Goslar instead of sharing Coleridge's lively life at Ratzeburg.

The Lucy poems baffled Victorian critics, who, according to whether their taste in sentimentality tended to Dickens or to Miss Yonge, imagined Lucy to be the heroine of calf-love in the Cumbrian hills or identified her with his future wife. Thanks to the discretion of Wordsworth's episcopal biographer they knew nothing of Annette, and prudery forbade the suggestion of Dorothy. But the Lucy poems continue the theme of the concluding passage of the Tintern Abbey lines, with death now dwelt upon as the cause of separation. In " Strange fits of passion have I known," the lover, riding to his mistress by moonlight, sees the moon sink behind her cottage:

> " *What fond and wayward thoughts will slide*
> *Into a Lover's head!*
> ' *O mercy!* ' *to myself I cried,*
> ' *If Lucy should be dead!* ' "

And again:

> " She lived unknown, and few could know
>   When Lucy ceased to be;
> But she's in her grave, and, oh,
>   The difference to me! "

Deliberately he tortured Dorothy with such forebodings and protestations of dependence on her devotion. Often, as appears from notes in her Grasmere journal, he indulged moods of morbid hysteria, the calming and comforting of which taxed her highly-strung nerves to exhaustion. Her always easily excitable emotions were torn between a natural affection for Coleridge and an un-natural devotion to her brother, an unnaturalness aggravated by the necessary repression of her feeling for a married man. During the four years between Goslar and Wordsworth's marriage, in 1802, Dorothy lived under tense emotional strain, which told its tale in the mental breakdown that wrecked her declining years. The contrast of expressions in her letters to Jane Marshall from Forncett and Racedown with her journal at Grasmere point the change of feeling towards her brother established at Goslar. The former reveal an emotional girl's hero-worship, loyal affection and admiration, and defiant belief in abilities disparaged by others; but the Grasmere journal betrays the extravagant passion of a wife or mistress rather than a sister. When Wordsworth had a good night's rest, she was " cheerful and happy "; she was " in low spirits " when he was unwell. When he went away for a few days she slept badly owing to her thoughts being " full of Wm.," and wrote to him daily. Once, when at parting he warned her to be looking well on his return, she wrote: " I *will* look well and be well when he comes back to me. O the Darling! Here is one of his bitter apples. I can hardly find it in my heart to throw it into the fire. . . . Sate down where we always sit. I was full of thought about my darling. Blessings on him."

Only a supremely selfish egoist could be blind to the un-naturalness of such emotion. A more subtle and sensitive under-standing would have recognised the dangers of accepting it, the injustice of encouraging it. Wordsworth cannot be blamed for luring his sister into an unnatural passion and depriving her of sexual fulfilment; he was too obtuse and too selfish to recognise his crime against her. He was always a taker, never a giver. He took from Dorothy, from Coleridge, from his wife, and from his daughter, without regard for their welfare. At Goslar he was full of self pity, exacerbated by sexual frustration. Essentially masculine, he was feeling the effect of five years of sex-repression, and since he could not bring himself to sacrifice association with his sister by taking a mistress, he sublimated his relation with her to vent his repression. The idea of incest could occur to neither, but their mutual state of sexual repression, having created their unnatural relation, intensified it till Wordsworth escaped by marriage, leaving Dorothy to degenerate into the neurosis of a withered virgin.

5. COLERIDGE IN GERMANY

By contrast with the Wordsworths' lonely tedium at Goslar, Coleridge's life at Ratzeburg was busy and eventful. He was a giver as Wordsworth was a taker. In every association, every friendship, he exerted himself to offer the fullest enjoyment of his personality. The Germans liked smoking, so he smoked with the same gusto as he had puffed Oroonoko with Lamb at the Salutation and Cat. " When my friends come to see me," he told Wordsworth, " the candle nearly goes out, the air is so thick."

In letters to Poole and Sara he never failed to record yearning for home and children, which he felt with full sincerity as he wrote, for then his vivid imagination transported him to Stowey and he all but breathed its air. Not that his letters to Sara disclose the revealing quality of those to other correspondents; he wrote down to her intelligence, retailing flippancies and reporting trivialities—the price of sticking plaster, the type of playing card used in Germany, amusing advertisements, and so forth. When he facetiously recounted his conquest of " a very beautiful little woman—less, I think, than you," the tone of her reply represents the superficiality of their sympathy: " I am very proud to hear you are so forward in the language, and that you are so gay with the ladies. You may give my respects to them, and say that I am not at all jealous, for I know my dear Samuel in her affliction will not forget entirely his most affectionate wife."

While he genuinely hungered for home, as he wrote his letters, he was at other times too busy for homesickness. He went everywhere, met everybody, and studied hard. By January he could read German as English, " without any *mental* translation as I read." But while Wordsworth had lived more cheaply at Goslar than he could at home, Coleridge had not lived at less than two pounds a week. Feeling the need, therefore, " to unite the advantages of advancing in German and doing something to repay myself," he planned to write a life of Lessing, which could incorporate a survey of the rise of German literature to its present state. To collect materials for this work, he proposed, instead of returning to England with the Wordsworths, to spend three months at Gottingen, where he optimistically expected to live on fifteen shillings a week. He was determined to exclude " all waverings about other works," for, he said, with astonishing insight, " that is the disease of my mind—it is comprehensive in its conceptions and wastes itself in the contemplations of the many things which it might do."

But he was an incorrigible drunkard in his thirst for knowledge; he could never resist invitations to fresh avenues of speculative thought. To Josiah Wedgwood he wrote copious accounts of his studies. In one long letter to him, he mentioned " six huge letters " lying by his side unposted from consideration of expense in postage. His cynical biographers have not failed to suggest that the letters existed only in imagination, but Professor Griggs has discovered and printed one—an erudite discussion on the origins of German civilisation—and as the letters comprised apparently expanded notes from his reading, there is less reason to doubt their existence than to wonder that there were not more. One lost letter was an analysis of Malthus's *Essay on Population*. He did not think that Malthus had succeeded in confuting the " extravagancies " of Godwin and Condorcet, but though unconvinced by Malthus, he was not convinced to the contrary. He was sceptical concerning " the possibility of universal plenty and wisdom," but his doubts of Malthus rested on other grounds laid out in the lost letter. " Is the march of the human race progressive, or in cycles? " he wondered. On such speculations his mind was busy. He had never believed in democracy as a political system, and since the experiment of the French revolution had apparently failed, he was derelict on the waters of doubt, distrustful that the wind of any political party could bring him to a desirable port.

Poole fervently believed in the potentialities of the sojourn in Germany to complete Coleridge's intellectual equipment for the task of a great philosophical work, and he was continually exhorting him to allow no worries or longings about his family to distract his concentration. When little Berkeley was ill with smallpox, he counselled Sara to say nothing to Coleridge till the child was better. When Coleridge heard of the illness and the child's recovery, he cried himself " blind . . . when I ought to have been on my knees in the joy of thanksgiving," but reassuring Poole's fears of his agitation, he declared himself " quite well, calm, and industrious." But the child, debilitated by struggle with disease, fell into a decline and died. After months of devoted nursing ending in heart-rending grief, Sara's belittling of all but her own loss is understandable. " You will feel and lament the death of your child," she wrote, " but you will only recollect him a baby of fourteen weeks, but I am his mother and have carried him in my arms and have fed him at my bosom, and have watched over him by day and by night for nine months." She could not understand that Coleridge's sensitive imagination transported him into the feelings of others, and that he would live over her sufferings, not simply as she suffered, but as she would have suffered with sensibilities like his own.

Poole knew him better. He wished that Coleridge should not be told of the child's death till his return to England, but when

Sara insisted on unburdening her grief, he wrote to soften the effect. "Let your *mind* act, and not your *feelings*," he implored. "Don't conjure up any scenes of distress which never happened. Mrs. Coleridge felt as a mother and . . . did all a mother could do. *But she never forgot herself.* She is now perfectly well."

On receiving the news, Coleridge walked out into the fields, oppressed, not by his feelings, "but by the riddles which the thought so easily proposes—and solves, never!" Wondering at his mental state, he compared his present emotions with those he had experienced on hearing of the baby's illness and supposed recovery. "At the time, in which I read Sara's lively account of the miseries which she herself and the infant had undergone, all was over and well—there was nothing to *think* of—only a mass of pain was brought suddenly and closely within the sphere of my perception, and I was made to suffer it over again. . . . But Death—the death of an infant—of one's own infant! . . . I cannot truly say that I grieve—I am perplexed—I am sad— and a little thing—a very trifle—would make me weep—but for the death of the baby I have *not* wept." And returning to his rooms, he wrote down reflective fancies on life, consciousness, and personal identity.

When the Wordsworths passed through Gottingen, he felt inclined to pack and accompany them to England. But he was deterred by the reflection that, without materials for his *Life of Lessing* completed, he would be without means to face embarrassment and debt. Thought of spring in England inspired homesickness and he longed to be at Stowey. The Wordsworths were "melancholy and hypp'd," Wordsworth being "affected to tears" at the thought of not living near Coleridge and begging him to settle near them in the Lake district. Astonishingly, Wordsworth, who read nothing, declared "the vicinity of a library absolutely necessary to his health, nay, to his existence." But Coleridge, aware of his dependence on him for mental stimulation during the year at Alfoxden, thought that Wordsworth must live near him, unless he could find another "who can feel with and understand him, can reciprocate and react on him."

From the records left by two of his English friends at Gottingen, Carlyon and Greenough, it can be realised how Coleridge spent far more than he ought. He was the central figure of convivial parties, and joined in walking tours, including a trip to the Harz Mountains. Continually his work was in his mind, and the whole party would divert the course of a tour to enable his visiting a library for research. Continually, too, he had moods of impatience to be at home. In the warmth of conviviality he planned fresh pleasure trips, even proposing a walk through Denmark, Norway, and Sweden, but when his friends had decided on the personnel of the party, he suddenly determined to return home. He left Gottingen on 3rd July and reached England after an absence of almost exactly ten months.

6. RE-UNION OF THE PANTISOCRATS

During Coleridge's absence abroad, a volume ironically entitled *Beauties of " The Anti-Jacobin "* followed up the attacks of the previous summer with pseudo-biographical notes on apostles of "The New Morality." Of Coleridge it was said that " to the disgrace of discipline, and a Christian University, this avowed Deist was not expelled " from Cambridge; that starvation compelled him to enlist in the army, and when applying to the recruiting sergeant, he asked, " Are you one of the cut-throats of the despot? "; that he had " now quitted the country, become a citizen of the world, left his little ones fatherless, and his wife destitute." Such slander afflicted him to despondency, for he had truly told Thelwall, " I am not fit for public life." It was always his weakness that he could not bear the idea of people's thinking ill of him. " I pine, languish, and waste away to be at home," he wrote in despondent mood to Poole, " for though in England only I have those that hate me, yet there only I have those whom I love." Among his first acts on returning to Stowey in July 1799 were offers of reconciliation to Southey, Lloyd and Lamb.

When Lloyd left Bristol for Birmingham in May 1798, so missing the opportunity of reconciliation with Coleridge, he had been staying with Southey, who at the same time went on a visit to George Burnett at Yarmouth, where he made a lasting friendship with William Taylor of Norwich. On his return, he took a house at Westbury, near Bristol, where he worked on *Madoc*, prepared for publication a second volume of his shorter poems and a second edition of *Letters from Spain and Portugal*, edited the first volume of the *Annual Anthology*, and usefully supplemented his income by journalism. *Joan of Arc* had made him a reputation far above anything Coleridge had achieved. As one of the few ambitious attempts at epic narrative since Pope's time, with its topical interest in eulogising liberty, it was lavishly received. Anna Seward, " Swan of Lichfield " in her day as Marie Corelli was goose of Stratford in hers, was " drowned in tears " while reading the poem, and recording her emotions in a notebook, transcribed them in a *Philippic on a Modern Epic* for the *Morning Chronicle*. Even the *Anti-Jacobin Review*, reviewing the second edition of *Joan*, acknowledged Southey as a poet of genius, though reviling him " for violating the laws of patriotism and criticism " and condemning the poem as " anti-English." Rated the most promising of rising poets, he could command as many booksellers' commissions as he could undertake. He reviewed for the *Critical Review*, and while Lamb reproached him for disparaging *The Ancient Mariner* in his notice of *Lyrical Ballads*, he was the only reviewer to praise Landor's *Gebir* on its appearance.

His house at Westbury was taken only for a year, and he was on the move, preparatory to settling again at Burton in Hampshire, when Coleridge returned from Germany. On 29th July Coleridge begged that, when they met, they should not " withhold from each other the outward expressions of daily kindliness; and if it be no longer in your power to soften your opinions, make your feelings at least more tolerant towards me." Southey replied with his old grievance that Coleridge had calumniated him. Coleridge's first impulse was to repeat his former particular account of their difference over pantisocracy, but deciding that

" this was neither wise nor delicate," he assured him that " I never charged you with aught but your deep and implacable enmity towards me, and that I founded this on the same authorisation on which you founded your belief of my supposed hatred to you." He referred Southey to Wordsworth and Poole as witnesses that, even " during the affair with Lloyd under suppositions of a highly irritating kind," he had never spoken of him without " affection and respect," nor charged him with anything but " restless enmity." Poole duly testified that " in the many conversations I have had with Coleridge concerning yourself he has never discovered the least personal enmity against, but, on the contrary, the strongest affection for you stifled only by the untoward events of your separation."

On this, Southey reconciled an estrangement embarrassing to his wife and Coleridge's. He and his wife completed a walking tour through Lynton and Lynmouth as far as Ilfracombe, and on their return, stayed with the Coleridges at Stowey before accompanying them on a visit to South Devon. " I have three brothers, that is to say, relations by gore," wrote Coleridge to Poole. " Two are parsons and one is a colonel. George and the colonel, good men as times go—very good men—but alas! we have neither tastes nor feelings in common." Formally forgiven by the family three years earlier for leaving Cambridge without a degree or approved profession, he had made a gesture to restore the old affection between himself and his brother George in the much admired dedicatory lines prefixed to the second edition of his poems. But George " was displeased and thought his character endangered " by this public association of a head-master and Church of England clergyman with the unconventional work of a Unitarian and opponent of the Government. As he did not scruple to disclose his feelings, Coleridge was deeply hurt and resigned all hope of intimacy with his family.

Southey felt respect for George Coleridge as a steadfast devotee to duty; he told Southey in a sentence summarising his life and character, that " from the age of eighteen he had never had leisure to read a book through." Southey's opinion of Edward endorsed Coleridge's old objections to his brother's jeering style in argument—he seldom talked " much to the purpose " but " only to confuse and misunderstand." They argued about " the equalitarian doctrines of the gospel," and Coleridge's aged mother, unable to " hear what was going on, but seeing Samuel arguing with his brothers, took it for granted that he must have been wrong, and cried out, ' Ah, if your poor father had been alive, he'd soon have convinced you! ' " Of James, the colonel, Southey reported nothing; he was doubtless—in Hazlitt's phrase —mumchance, too conscious of his dignity and importance to bandy words with his youngest brother.

Coleridge returned from Ottery to Stowey, while Southey remained a fortnight in lodgings at Exeter before going to Burton. Southey had laid aside *Madoc* and begun *Thalaba the Destroyer.* Coleridge proposed to write an epic on *Mahomet,* but got no farther than fourteen lines. He also proposed to finish *Christabel* " with all speed," but having spent more than his allowance in Germany, he had to write a " money-book " first. This was to be an anonymous " school book," as he was resolved to publish nothing under his name till " my Great Work," the *Life of Lessing.*

7. SOCKBURN AND LONDON

During the next month at Stowey, besides a visit to Josiah Wedgwood at his new Somerset home, Coleridge paid sundry visits to Bristol, making the acquaintance of Humphry Davy, who had joined Dr. Beddoes in supervision of the Pneumatic Institution, and assisting Cottle in winding up his publishing business. Of all Cottle's undertakings, only Southey's publications had brought him profit, and he sold all his copyrights to Longmans. On being told by Longman that the copyright value of *Lyrical Ballads* was " reckoned *as nothing,*" Cottle asked for the return of its copyright, so that he might present it to the authors. With generosity as remarkable as egotism, Wordsworth ascribed the failure of *Lyrical Ballads* to the inclusion of *The Ancient Mariner,* which " no one seemed to understand."

Persisting in the opinion more than thirty years later, he ascribed the failure " to the unintelligibleness of *The Ancient Mariner,* and to the want of a Preface "—a curious remark in apposition to his assurance that he only wrote a preface to the second edition " out of sheer good nature " to oblige Coleridge.

Towards the end of October Coleridge " was called up to the North by alarming accounts of Wordsworth's health." Cottle accompanied him, but on arriving at Sockburn, where Mary Hutchinson lived with her brother and sister, they found —" thank God! "—that the health rumours were " little more than alarms." Wordsworth was indeed well enough to set out on a walking tour of the Lakes with his brother John, Coleridge and Cottle. To Dorothy he wrote that " Coleridge was much struck with Grasmere and its neighbourhood," while he himself conceived a " mad " plan of building a house by the lakeside. He added, however, " There is a small house at Grasmere empty, which, perhaps, we may take." This was Dove Cottage, formerly a wayside inn, which he and Dorothy duly took, moving in on 21st December 1799.

At Sockburn Wordsworth certainly found nobody who could " feel with and understand him," who could " reciprocate and react on him." He stayed so many months because it was convenient and comfortable, and because Dorothy doubtless found the placid companionship of the Hutchinsons a relief from her brother's morbid moods when alone with her. George Hutchinson was a plain north-country farmer, and his eldest sister Mary was well suited to become a comfortable farmer's wife. Though they accepted " Daddy " Wordsworth's assurance that the lines " She was a phantom of delight " were addressed to his wife, even the sentimental Victorians admitted " an entire absence of romance in Wordsworth's courtship." To them it was a boy-and-girl attachment begun when they attended together the dame's school at Penrith, which endured unemotionally till its culmination in a comfortable marriage, untainted by passionate complications and conforming admirably with respectable conventions. Wordsworth " loved Mary Hutchinson; he had always loved her "; and their engagement " seemed somehow to be

just the natural sequel to their early unromantic regard." Evidence
that Wordsworth often asked Dorothy to write for him to Mary
was disconcerting, but then Wordsworth " detested correspondence," and was after all a genius. Mary was " a noble Cumbrian
maiden, with a clear intellect and an unsophisticated heart, a
gentle, tranquil, unambitious soul, very tender-hearted, sympathetic, and full of tact. Had she possessed a larger or wider
culture, she would not have been any more perfectly fitted for
him "—complacent, comfortable, capable, she was the ideal
housekeeper for a man of " high vocation."

De Quincey, who liked her, described her fairly. She was " a
tallish young woman," of " tolerably good " figure and a fair
healthy complexion, " generally pronounced very plain " but
with a pleasant expression and frank, homely manner. She had
little conversation, and Clarkson, the slave-trade abolitionist,
averred that she could only say " God bless you! " " Her intellect
was not of an active order, but, in a quiescent, reposing, medita-
tive way, she appeared always to have a genial enjoyment from
her own thoughts." A restful person, she was fond of the
gushing, excitable Dorothy, and listening with a complacent
smile, readily accepted her estimation of Wordsworth's talents
and personal worth.

Her younger sister Sarah was a livelier personality, short, fair,
and plump, with an attractive smile and light in her eyes; she
had common sense, quick understanding, a cheerful temper, a
sense of fun and humour, and her sister's simple frankness of
manner, without the sobriety of her stolidity. There was an
understanding that she and Wordsworth's brother John, the
sailor, might make a match of it, but both she and Mary had
heard much of Coleridge, and on meeting him and feeling his
inevitable charm, she did not conceal her liking for his conversation and company.

Finding his fears of Wordsworth's health unfounded, Coleridge
was like a boy released from school. His re-union with Sara
had been trying. According to her conception, he had been
enjoying himself abroad while she had suffered alone an anxious
burden of nursing followed by the tragedy of her baby's death,

and it was her nature to emphasise her misfortunes by magnifying her emotions. Coleridge was probably made to feel, if not that his absence had invited the tragedy, at least that he had heartlessly under-estimated her pathetic plight. He was also left in no doubt that he had failed her worldly expectations. She did not conceal her petulant disappointment at the failure of *Lyrical Ballads*, and now, after spending abroad more than he could afford, he returned without any work ready for publication. Aggrieved, she made the most of her grievance, her reproaches doubtless not uncoloured by comparison with her sister's lot as wife of the industrious Southey.

So Coleridge came to Sockburn, as he had formerly escaped regularly to Alfoxden, eager for the intellectual pleasure of the Wordsworths' companionship, and he was warmed by the cordial hospitality of their simple friends. He enjoyed the sensation of " affectionate reception from a stranger who is the dear friend of your dear friend! How often you have been the subject of conversation, and how affectionately! " Feeling himself in company prepared to like and admire him, he exerted himself to inspire liking and admiration, and succeeding, he achieved a sense of well-being, of content, which was his closest approximation to self-confidence. And so, after a particularly happy party on 24th November, warmed by the intimacy of fireside confidences, he felt a stirring of tender love for Sarah Hutchinson.

There was no thought of philandering, of an adulterous connection—even if Sarah would have entertained such an affair. But, though he had tried sincerely to love his wife and find in her the content obtainable from woman, he had been forced to recognise that such content was impossible without intellectual sympathy and companionship. It was not in his nature to be content with the conventional Victorian marriage, by which a man divorced domestic life from his active life. He found pleasure in Sarah Hutchinson's company as formerly in Mary Evans's, and in time he idealised her in absence as he had idealised Mary. The emotions inspired by Sarah found expression in the poem called *Love*, first published in the *Morning Post* on 21st December 1799 as the Introduction to the *Tale of the Dark Ladie*, the ballad begun about the same time as *Christabel*, and like *Christabel*, never finished.

At Sockburn he received—doubtless on representation from the Wedgwoods—an offer from Daniel Stuart to write regularly for the *Morning Post*, and in spite of his former reluctance to enter London journalism, he accepted for " four or five months," as a means of clearing the embarrassment of his having anticipated his allowance in Germany. Perhaps because Wordsworth joined with Southey in deprecating the plan, the " school book " was abandoned, and he disliked Southey's suggestion that he should publish his descriptive letters from Germany, if only because it would take " more trouble to fit 'em up, than they are worth." He went to London at the end of November, found lodgings at 21 Buckingham Street, Strand, and was joined there by Sara and little Hartley by 9th December.

" I am employed from I-rise to I-set," he wrote on Christmas Eve to Southey; " (that is, from nine in the morning to twelve at night), a pure scribbler." His mornings were given to " booksellers' compilations," by which he hoped to make the amount of his next year's anticipated allowance. After dinner he worked for Stuart, who paid all his living expenses. Stuart received good value for his money, for, besides political leaders which became the most influential in contemporary journalism, Coleridge produced his graceful *Ode to Georgiana, Duchess of Devonshire* (which the famous beauty neglected to acknowledge with the material bounty bestowed by great ladies in the days of Congreve, Gay and Pope), *A Christmas Carol*, and the maliciously satirical epistle from *Talleyrand to Lord Grenville*.

Southey was suffering from dyspepsia and debility resulting from assiduous application to work. Concerned for his health, Coleridge was active as his agent, inviting contributions to his anthology, interviewing publishers on his behalf, and optimistically proposing schemes of collaboration. He was advised he had a " clear case " for libel against the publishers of *Beauties of " The Anti-Jacobin "*, but no action was taken, doubtless because he found himself deceived in a first impression that his advisers offered to undertake the prosecution, " so as that I shall have

neither trouble nor expense." He resumed his friendship—never
again interrupted—with Lamb, made good new friends in John
Tobin, the dramatist, and his brother James, and began an intimacy with Godwin of mutual intellectual value. Still insisting
that Godwin was "no great things in intellect," he found him
now "in heart and manner . . . all the better for having been
the husband of Mary Wollstonecraft." Godwin's children found
a playmate in little Hartley, who one day gave Mr. "Gobwin,"
as he called him, "such a rap on the shins with a saucepan"
that the philosopher "in huge pain *lectured* Sara on his bois-
terousness." Coleridge allowed that Hartley was somewhat too
rough and noisy," but "the cadaverous silence of Godwin's
children" seemed to him "quite catacombish," and he felt
oppressed by thoughts of their dead mother.

His failure to pursue his success as a political journalist has
been held as an instance of his shiftless incapacity for perseverance, but he never regarded his engagement by Stuart as more
than a temporary accommodation necessary to relieve his financial
position. Condemned to servitude for the winter, he laboured
hard, with an assiduity worthy of Southey, to purchase peace
of mind to enjoy the coming summer in the country. But
Stuart laid a straw too many on his back when requiring him
to report parliamentary debates. "I shall give up this Newspaper business; it is too, too fatiguing," wrote Coleridge to Southey
after attending two debates, one keeping him "twenty-five
hours in activity," the other from ten in the morning till four
the next morning. On the second occasion Pitt made a long
speech in justification of the war's continuance, and "I reported
the whole with notes so scanty, that—Mr. Pitt is much obliged
to me," said Coleridge: "he never talked half so eloquently in
his life-time. He is a *stupid, insipid* charlatan, that *Pitt*." Poole
was so impressed by the improvement on Pitt that he asked,
"Wherefore deck out the minister in this way?" Coleridge
thought Fox "a great orator," with the "eloquence of a man of
clear head, clear heart, and impetuous feelings." He allowed
the "elegance and high finish" of Pitt's rhetoric, but "he
argues but so so, and does not reason at all," and "nothing is

rememberable of what he says." All the other speakers he heard he described as " mere creatures."

He gave notice to Stuart of his decision to quit the *Morning Post* in the middle of February, but continued to write articles while he remained in London. Justifying himself to Josiah Wedgwood, he thought himself—" considering that I have newspapered it merely as means of subsistence, while I was doing other things "—very lucky in having been able to write on subjects " important in themselves, and excellent vehicles for general truths," like the new French constitution appointing Buonaparte first consul, the subsequent peace proposals, and, the union with Ireland. With reason, he declared, " I am not ashamed of what I have written." He continued to work " from morning to night, but in a few weeks I shall have completed my purpose, and then adieu to London for ever."

When Sara and Hartley left at the end of February to stay five weeks at Stowey with the curate and his wife before going to her mother at Bristol, he went to share Charles Lamb's lodgings at Chapel Street, Pentonville. Describing himself as " living in a continuous feast," Lamb felt all his former love for Coleridge revived. " The more I see of him in the quotidian undress and relaxation of his mind, the more cause I see to love him, and believe him a *very good man*." When he returned from his day at the East India office he found Coleridge in a dilapidated dressing-gown, industriously translating Schiller's *Wallenstein*, but very ready to lay down his pen and talk. " He tends me," said Lamb, " amidst all his own worrying and heart-oppressing occupations, as a gardener tends his young *tulip*." " Ferreting " him " day and night to *do something*," he was as full of suggestions of work for Lamb as for Southey. He " lugged " him to the brink of engaging himself to the *Morning Post,* and set him to forging feigned manuscripts by Burton of *The Anatomy of Melancholy*. Sometimes they enjoyed nights in the spirit of the old Salutation and Cat convivialities, and one Monday morning Coleridge felt impelled to apologise to Godwin for any rash expressions resulting from tipsiness caused by " punch, after the wine," on the previous night. He assured Godwin that he had

no headache, but " tipsiness has, and has always, one unpleasant
effect—that of making me talk very extravagantly; and as, when
sober, I talk extravagantly enough for any common tipsiness,
it becomes a matter of nicety in discrimination to know when
I am or am not affected. An idea starts up in my head," and
" the whole thinking of my life will not bear me up against
the accidental crowd and press of my mind, when it is elevated
beyond its natural pitch."

Lamb was in no hurry for Coleridge to finish his translating,
which would complete his work in London, but without waiting
to finish *Wallenstein,* Coleridge set off to see the Wordsworths
in their new home at Grasmere before joining Sara at Bristol.
He was still undecided where to settle. From Germany he had
written to Poole that he definitely could not continue in the
uncomfortable cottage at Stowey, and Poole had undertaken to
look for a more suitable house. During the winter he reported
a house at Asholt, near Stowey, which Coleridge declared entirely
satisfactory except its remote situation, for " Sara being Sara, and I
being I, we must live in a town or else close to one, so that she
may have neighbours and acquaintances." Explaining that the
society of his friends was insufficient for Sara, he said, " God
knows where we can go; for that situation which suits my
wife does not suit me, and what suits me, does not suit my wife."
Already hurt by Coleridge's acceptance of newspaper work
without consulting him and by his departure to London direct
from Sockburn, Poole fairly supposed that he was manufacturing
excuses to escape from Stowey and to establish himself near the
Wordsworths—a prospect unlikely to appeal to Sara, both on
account of her jealousy of Dorothy and the distance of Grasmere
from Bristol. He therefore warned Coleridge against under-
valuing himself by " prostration " before Wordsworth, while
Coleridge declared that neither Poole nor the Wedgwoods had
" ever entered into the feeling due to a man like Wordsworth,
of whom I do not hesitate in saying that, since Milton, no one
has manifested himself equal to him."

With sincerity he assured Poole that his affection for him was
undiminished, and that he would rather live in or near Stowey

than anywhere if a suitable house could be found. But Poole knew him too well to doubt that he preferred the society of " his god Wordsworth "—as Lamb called him—to his. Needing the moral support of a stronger personality than his own, Coleridge turned to Poole when he was estranged from Southey, but while Poole was a good listener, a sound practical adviser, and a more devoted friend than Southey or Wordsworth, he could compete with neither as an intellectual stimulus. Coleridge was not so wedded to Wordsworth that he would not have stayed at Stowey if Southey had joined him there. Wistful over happy recollections, on hearing that Alfoxden was still unlet, he suggested to Southey that they might share the house. But Southey's health required a holiday in a warmer climate, and he sailed in April 1800 on a second visit to Portugal. Till Coleridge left London he " supposed " that he would settle at Stowey, if for no better reason than that his books and furniture were there.

But arrival at Grasmere revived the delights of Alfoxden. There were long walks and talks, scenery in its majestic wildness as inspiring to the romantic imagination as the moorlands between Porlock and Lynton, and after a simple supper such reading and discussion as had engendered *Lyrical Ballads.* On 22nd April he sent off the last sheet of his translation of *Wallenstein.* It had been distasteful, " soul-worrying labour," and he nourished scant hopes of its success, but he felt with reason that he had proved himself capable of " Industry and Perseverance." Having for four months applied his energies exclusively to bread-and-butter work, he was free to begin his *Life of Lessing,* which would accord the Wedgwoods "some proof that I am *endeavouring* to do well for my fellow-creatures." With what better prospect could he engage on a task worthy of his powers than with the close companionship that had proved so stimulating at Alfoxden? And the Wordsworths wanted him. If Wordsworth's genius derived inspiration from his conversation, he fulfilled a duty to mankind by situating himself to supply it. There was no house available near Grasmere, but Wordsworth might move to Keswick at the end of his year's tenancy of Dove Cottage, and at Keswick the owner of Greta Hall offered Coleridge half of a house with such a prospect that " if . . . impressions and ideas *constitute* our being, I shall have a tendency to become a god, so sublime and beautiful will be the series of my visual existence."

After a month at Grasmere, he left on 4th May for Bristol, determined, " if I cannot procure a suitable house at Stowey," to settle at Keswick. There was no suitable house at Stowey, and argumentative scenes ensued with Sara and saddening arguments with Poole. " I parted from Poole with pain and dejection, for him, and for myself in him," he told Josiah Wedgwood after finally moving to Keswick. Acknowledging that he would have " given Stowey a decided preference " if there had been a suitable house, he admitted the force of Poole's plea that he was there " conveniently situated " among " almost all whom I love and esteem."

8. FATALITY OF THE LAKES

His arrival at Grasmere with Sara and Hartley on 29th June foreboded the fatality that the Lake District held for him, for he took cold from getting wet, spent most of a fortnight in bed, and swollen eyes prevented his reading. Ironical that history should have labelled him a " Lake Poet," whose inspiration was frozen and whose health was devastated by the prevailing damp of the Lakes! Two months of idleness and the cost of removal having placed him again in debt, he undertook, after toying with a notion of translating Blumenbach's *Natural History*, the distasteful task of preparing for publication his letters from Germany. Moving into Greta Hall on 24th July, he announced to Josiah Wedgwood that he had also started the *Life of Lessing*, the plan of which had now so swollen that the Introduction was to occupy the first volume and be ready for separate publication by Christmas.

Association with Wordsworth now proved a distraction instead of a stimulant, for Wordsworth was preparing a second edition of *Lyrical Ballads* and all projects were unimportant beside his own. He wanted Coleridge to finish *Christabel* for inclusion, so *Lessing* was laid aside and the second part of *Christabel* written. Every line was produced with "labour-pangs," for, as he wrote, he seemed, by complicating the plot, to be further than ever from the end. Possibly, if he had ever planned the story, he had forgotten its sequence. More probably he had begun with the vivid picture of Christabel and Geraldine in his mind, and trusted to his imagination to develop the tale as it progressed. His imagination failed him from inability to concentrate. His conscience was haunted by the neglected *Lessing*, the task intended to justify himself to the Wedgwoods, and by the necessity for earning money, for the burden of his expenses was increased in September by the birth of another son —named Derwent, from "a sort of sneaking affection for the *poetical* and novellish," disguised by the plea that his brothers had already appropriated all such simple names as John, James and George.

His state of mind was further harassed by Wordsworth's impatient urgings. On 15th September Wordsworth wrote to the printer, countermanding the printing of *Christabel*. Five days later, "for the sake of variety, and from a consciousness of my own weakness," he wrote that his friend had furnished him with "the long and beautiful Poem of *Christabel*, without which I should not have ventured to present a second volume to the public." On 4th October Coleridge arrived "very wet" at Grasmere, and the Wordsworths were "exceedingly delighted with the second part of *Christabel*." But he saw no hope of finishing *Christabel* in less than thirteen or fourteen hundred lines, a length which would dwarf such metrical tales as *Ruth* and *Michael*. So, two nights later, when Wordsworth read as much as he had written of *The Pedlar*, as *The Excursion* was then called, they decided to exclude *Christabel* from the present publication and print it with *The Pedlar*.

Coleridge was released from the harrowing task of completing his poem, but the effort of more than two months had so delayed "bread-and-beef occupations" that he was "sweating for it— Dunning letters, etc. etc.—all the hell of an Author." He resigned

himself to " abandon Poetry altogether—I leave the higher and deeper kinds to Wordsworth, the delightful, popular and simply dignified to Southey; and reserve for myself the honourable attempt to make others feel and understand their writings, as they deserve to be felt and understood." The modest self-imposed function, handsomely fulfilled after seventeen years in *Biographia Literaria,* was doubtless intended to find immediate fruition in an *Essay on Poetry,* which, though " an essay on the elements of poetry," was to have been " in reality a disguised system of morals and politics." This project, which would indeed have proved to the Wedgwoods his utility to mankind, was, he declared, " still more at my heart " than the *Life of Lessing,* but both were deferred by the need for money.

He has been accused of " lying " to the Wordsworths in attributing his difficulty in finishing *Christabel* to obligations to the *Morning Post.* But he prepared for publication in October some papers by Poole on the wartime trickery of the corn trade, *Monopolists and Farmers,* to which he prefixed an essay, besides additions and alterations. It is not surprising that such work, undertaken while driving himself to poetic composition, kept him up all night before setting off to Grasmere with the second part of *Christabel,* and all his contributions to the *Morning Post* have not been identified. As an inducement to reconsider his resignation from regular employment on the paper, Stuart had offered him shares in the *Morning Post* and the *Courier,* but he declined to be tied, insisting always that journalism was a necessary evil to purchase the leisure for work of lasting worth.

With " mortal pangs " he worked unwillingly on his letters from Germany, and news from Godwin, now one of his regular correspondents, that he was having a play produced, inspired the beginning of " an historic drama," *The Triumph of Loyalty.* With these two works completed, he planned to visit London in December, and there earn enough by a few weeks' work for Stuart to enable his paying a promised visit to Poole at Stowey. But the prevailing damp of the Keswick autumn irritated his rheumatic complaint to attacks more frequently recurrent than he had ever before suffered. " Coleridge, very ill," wrote

Dorothy on 14th November; on the 28th "very unwell";
on 1st December "Coleridge unable to go home" from Grasmere; on the 20th "very ill, rheumatic, feverish," and Dorothy
adds with unconscious significance, "Rain incessantly." Driving
himself to work against bodily lethargy and pain, unable to go
to London, he fretted as he had fretted over settling at Stowey
just four years before, and similarly painful, but more protracted, illness resulted.

Already he realised that the move from Stowey to Keswick had
been a tragic mistake. "I feel what I have lost," he told Josiah
Wedgwood, "feel it deeply—it recurs more often and more
painfully, than I had anticipated—indeed, so much so that I
scarcely ever feel myself impelled, that is to say, *pleasurably*
impelled to write to Poole." By such surrender to sensibility he
was to offend and alienate many friends in the future, to create
for himself an undeserved reputation for ingratitude, indolence,
and insincerity. Whenever sadness was associated in his mind
with a correspondent—whenever he despaired of explaining his
state of mind, or, rather, of convincing with his explanation,
of excusing a cause for disappointment or exculpating himself
from blame—his sensibility shrank as from self-torture. He
acquired the same attitude towards work, especially towards
poetry. So often he disappointed himself, so often he delayed
till his trend of thought had travelled too far from an objective
to be easily recalled, that he became hopelessly "entangled in
the old Sorites of the old Sophist, Procrastination—I had suffered
my necessary business to accumulate so terribly, that I neglected
to write to anyone—till the Pain I suffered from not writing,
made me waste as many hours in dreaming about it, as would
have sufficed for the letter-writing of half a life."

As he thought of happy hours in Poole's "great windy
Parlour," he reflected how well suited to each other they were.
"My animal spirits corrected his inclinations to melancholy;
and there was something both in his understanding and in his
affections so healthy and manly, that my mind freshened in his
company, and my ideas and habits of thinking acquired day
after day more of substance and reality." Sitting, wracked by

neuralgia, in the loneliness of his study at Greta Hall, the window-panes running with rain and the mountains dim through drifting mist, he wished with tears in his eyes that he could hurry through the connecting garden-gate to Poole's fireside, where the Wedgwoods, Cottle, Davy, or Estlin might come occasionally, while always with Poole would be Cruikshank and the devoted Chester.

Yet he could not see how he could have acted otherwise than by coming to Keswick. Musing, he would look " without seeing " from his study window, till the splendour of the scene— " the two Lakes, the Vale, the River, and mountains and mists, and clouds, and sunshine made endless combinations, as if heaven and earth were for ever talking to each other "—struck suddenly upon him, always with unfailing sense of novelty. His landlord, Jackson, a retired carrier, was " modest and kind," delighted in little Hartley's company, and had a useful collection of modern books; his housekeeper, " a good, affectionate motherly woman," was a comfort to Sara. A town's amenities were close at hand, and eighteen miles away Sir Wilfrid Lawson's " princely library " was at his disposal. To Wedgwood he did not mention his main inducement in coming to Keswick, and from delicate consideration of Poole's jealous pangs he " lied " with the elaborately casual remark that he saw Wordsworth " upon an average about once a month, or perhaps three weeks."

Actually he was making stays of three or four days at Gras-mere almost every fortnight. But the long intervals between visits left him with none but Sara's arid conversation, and he missed the easy convenience of escaping despondent moods by the short walk to Alfoxden. Nor did he find the same solace in Wordsworth's society. " His faculties seem to expand every day," Dorothy had written of Wordsworth to Mary Hutchinson after eight months at Alfoxden: " he composes with much more facility than he did, as to the *mechanism* of poetry, and his ideas flow faster than he can express them." At Alfoxden Wordsworth had learned much from Coleridge, not only of metre and rhythm —the " mechanism " of poetry—but of stimulating imagination by association of ideas. Unlike Coleridge, he had no inquiring mind, but an instinctive mental orderliness; having acquired a system of thought and composition, he concentrated on work according to his system. So he no longer depended on Coleridge's conversation for inspiration—a fact which his self-absorption made no attempt to disguise.

His sex repression induced hypochondria. "He writes with so much feeling and agitation that it brings on a sense of pain and internal weakness about his left side and stomach," wrote Dorothy: "His digestion is still very bad—he is always very ill when he tries to alter an old poem." As an early sufferer from piles, though habitually active in open air exercise, it seems that he paid the penalty for irregularity in his natural functions, and the nervous strain of composition immediately induced indigestion. When Coleridge came to Keswick, he promptly wrote for Dr. Beddoes' opinion of Wordsworth's complaint, but Wordsworth professed "*scepticism* concerning medicines" and neglected to persevere with Beddoes' prescriptions.

It is curious to contrast Coleridge's letters, full of intellectual speculation, metaphysical introspection, and suggestive thought, with Dorothy's, which detail commonplaces with the circumstance of historical portents. Everything in the Wordsworths' narrow life was magnified, and Wordsworth's dyspepsia assumed the dread dignity of malign disease. Apologising for delaying the printing of the second edition of *Lyrical Ballads,* Wordsworth declared, "I have been stopped by bad health," and he so played on Dorothy's nerves with his moods that her days were coloured according to whether William had worked successfully or otherwise. "Wm. went to bed, very ill after working after dinner"; "Wm. could not compose much. Fatigued himself with altering"; "Wm. very well. We had a delightful walk"; "William was not well, had laboured unsuccessfully." His moods were the barometer of her spirits, and seeing this, Coleridge could no longer derive the same delight from her company. He saw that, since Goslar, the relationship between brother and sister had morbidly deepened—that her affection for himself was relegated below her passionate devotion to Wordsworth. Though he accurately diagnosed Wordsworth's ailment, his loyalty—or, rather, his idolatry—never faltered. The corrections of Wordsworth's poems were in his hand, and all the transcriptions in Dorothy's. When Francis Wrangham wrote separately to each, while Wordsworth delayed three or four months before replying, Coleridge wrote immediately, making Wordsworth's excuses for him. Lamb could be touched by such generous attentions " amidst all his own worrying and heart-oppressing occupations," but Wordsworth accepted them and—in the dark days ahead for Coleridge—forgot them.

Walking to Grasmere a few days before Christmas, Coleridge arrived wet through, and though he changed immediately, was next day confined to bed with rheumatic fever. After nearly a fortnight, when his temperature dropped, he was conveyed home in a chaise, going straight to bed and suffering " most excruciating pain on the least motion." By February he declared himself convalescent; the fluid was nearly absorbed, and he was able to sit up for short intervals before pains in his back drove him again to lying. But, suffering frequent " relapses," he continued ill and in pain during the ensuing months, and by the spring, the prospect of such another winter seeming intolerable, he spoke of seeking health in a warmer climate. Anxiety over inactivity retarded his recovery, for all the time he worried over inability to work. " It presses upon me with a painful weight that I have not evidenced a more tangible utility," he wrote in December. And seven months later: " Nausea and giddiness are far worse than pain—for they insult and threaten the steadiness of our moral Being and there is one thing yet more deplorable than these—it is the direful Thought of being inactive and useless."

When swollen eyes permitted reading, he plunged into metaphysics, and in March informed Poole that he had " overthrown the doctrine of association, as taught by Hartley, and with it all the irreligious metaphysics of modern infidels—especially the doctrine of necessity." Though his book of letters from Germany was " nearly done," he disliked the publishing of personal gossip for curious amusement, justly condemning it as " *beneath me,*" and as a " money book " for Longman he thought of exposing the defects of Locke, Hobbes, and Hume " as a *pioneer* to my greater work." Intensity of thought interfered with his sleep, and his dreams being of ideas " little different from the operations of reason," the sleep he secured brought no refreshment. To Josiah Wedgwood he wrote three letters " of prodigious length " (unpublished, but so described by E. H. Coleridge, who saw them), embodying the result of his studies, prefatory to his proposed work and pathetically proving that he was not wasting his time.

During the winter Sara was ill with an ulcerated throat, but the Wordsworths found her " in excellent health " when they spent eight days at Keswick in April. With all her domestic capabilities, she was, in Dorothy's opinion, " a bad nurse for C." Dorothy thought her " much to be pitied, for when one party is ill-matched the other necessarily must be so too. She would have made a very good wife to many another man, but for Coleridge!! Her radical fault is want of sensibility, and what can such a woman be to Coleridge? " Always at Stowey Coleridge had been doing something, so Sara was buoyed on continual hope that suddenly his genius would be generously recognised and her dreams realised of receiving the homage of reflected celebrity. But his return from Germany empty-handed apart from debts incited an attitude of querulous criticism, which intensified during these barren months of illness. She was incapable of understanding how he could put aside his travel book " because the thoughts which had employed my sleepless nights during my illness were imperious over me; and though poverty was staring me in the face . . . it seemed to me a suicide of my very soul to divert my attention from truths so important." Harassed as he was by conscience, her petulant reproaches goaded him to agony, and from this time want of sympathy became antagonism, which with Coleridge's sensitive temperament soon developed into definite aversion. Truly she was pitiable as a stupid woman; sympathy in affliction would have won Coleridge's readily grateful response, but her nagging finally undermined the frail foundations of their marriage.

Sarah Hutchinson had been a guest at Grasmere during the

autumn, and as she was generous in sympathy and cheering in conversation, Coleridge's tenderness for her deepened. Her brother George had left Sockburn for Bishop's Middleham, near Durham, where Sarah was his housekeeper, Mary Hutchinson acting in a similar capacity for another brother, Thomas, at Gallow Hill, near Scarborough. In July Coleridge went to Durham to pursue metaphysical research in the Dean and Chapter's library, and stayed at Middleham. At Durham he dined with " a large parcel of priests " from the cathedral, all " thoroughly ignorant and hard-hearted," and had difficulty in obtaining permission to take a few books from the library to Middleham. The librarian, who had never heard of Leibnitz, said superciliously, " We have no Museum in this Library for natural curiosities," understanding Coleridge to have asked for " live nits."

Walking the eight miles from Durham to Middleham, he was taken ill, his left knee swelling " pregnant with agony." The doctor having prescribed horse-exercise and warm sea-bathing, Sarah rode with him to her brother Tom's at Gallow Hill, which was handy for bathing at Scarborough. The treatment affording relief, he stayed about three weeks, thus spending five weeks in Sarah's company. As a result, he recognised the impossibility of continuing married life on present terms, and on his twenty-ninth birthday in October, he summarised the situation in a letter to Southey. His health was " sadly shattered," the " least agitation " brought on " bowel complaints " and vomiting, " and Sara—alas! we are not suited to each other." Proposing to spend the winter in London working for the *Morning Post*, he determined to devote the months of absence to " *self*-discipline," returning to make a final effort " to draw her nearer to me." He would go " believing that it will end happily—if not, if our mutual unsuitableness continues, and (as it assuredly will do, if it continue) increases and strengthens—why then, it is better for her and my children that I should live apart, than that she should be a widow and they orphans." When first discussing pantisocracy with Southey, he had defended marriage as an institution necessary in the current state of civilisation; Godwin's advocacy of its abolition as a pillar of the property system

supplied a ground for his argument that Godwin legislated for
" a future state," impracticable under current conditions. He
was still " convinced of its indissolubleness," his unstated reasons
arising mainly from consideration of his wife's condition. " When
I least love her, then most do I feel anxiety for her peace, comfort,
and welfare," he wrote: " Is she not the mother of my children? "
He could not bring himself to hurt her by leaving her for another
woman, for he must have known that she lacked the sensibility
to feel the deeper humiliation of his preferring loneliness to life
with her. He felt, too, the obligation of contributing all he could,
without subtraction by a second establishment, to the upbringing
of his children. But not even delight in his children (during his
months of illness, odd, precocious little Hartley had been a
solitary sunbeam, inspiring a rare excursion into poetry in the
lines beginning

> " A little child, a limber elf
> Singing, dancing to itself,"

published eventually as a pendant to *Christabel*) could reconcile
him to the twilight repression of unhappy married life. " If I
separate," he said, " I do it in the earnest desire to provide for her
and them, that while I live she may enjoy the comforts of life
and that when I die, something may have been accumulated that
may secure her from degrading dependence."

He wrote thus to explain to Southey any domestic discord he
might have detected during his first visit to Greta Hall and the
self-imposed reticence that had prevented his full enjoyment of
Southey's company. He did not then know that Southey had
to face a similar problem of incompatibility.

9. EPOCH OF *DEJECTION*

After fourteen months in Portugal, Southey returned to
England in June 1801. He had finished *Thalaba*, collected
material for his *History of Portugal*, and begun another epic, " in

metre Thalabian, in mythology Hindoo," called *The Curse of
Kehama*. Regarding it as "thrashing straw" and committing
murder on his intellect, he renounced the law, but contemplated
accepting a diplomatic post through his friend Wynn's influence.
If a married man was eligible, he would accompany the new
ambassador to Constantinople. Having persuaded himself that
Coleridge's complaint was "gouty," that "good living is
necessary, and a good climate," he suggested that Coleridge should
accompany him to the Mediterranean.

Coleridge was talking of wintering in the Azores to regain
health, but needed at least fifty pounds for the purpose. With
incredible lack of tact, Wordsworth wrote to Poole, proposing
that he should lend Coleridge this sum, and even adding the
terms which "I should propose to him myself, if I could do it
with any propriety." Already resentful of Wordsworth's influence as responsible for Coleridge's removal from Stowey,
Poole naturally regarded his approach as impertinence. He
replied to Coleridge, asking him to show the letter to Wordsworth, "as it will prevent my troubling him with a letter,"
and offering to lend him twenty pounds—but "let Wade and
one or two other of your friends do the same." He also wrote
a statement of the matter to the Wedgwoods.

During the five weeks spent with Sarah Hutchinson in Durham
and Yorkshire, Coleridge postponed the painful task of replying
to Poole. He then deplored Wordsworth's letter, excusing his
writing without knowing Poole or his circumstances. After
assuring Poole (as he had, in fact, written before Wordsworth's
letter) that he had no intention of asking a loan of him, he told
him that he "ought assuredly to have written" to Wordsworth
instead of to himself, and reproached him for broaching the
subject to the Wedgwoods, who might be inspired with "a
feeling of disgust, and a notion of *troublesomeness*." Poole
responded in heat and some dismay, but Coleridge's counter
blended dignity with affection. He proposed to visit Stowey
after working in London and to accept any small loan for four
months that Poole could contribute towards his debts. He had
"very particular Reasons" for not anticipating any part of his

Wedgwood annuity, which he meant to preserve intact for Sara's use in the event of separation.

Reputed dampness of climate inspired abandonment of the Azores scheme long before Wordsworth's irritation of Poole was mollified. Coleridge momentarily entertained the idea of accompanying Southey to Constantinople, till, hearing that the ambassador, one Drummond, had translated Persius, he warned Southey against becoming " secretary to a fellow that would poison you for being a poet, while he is only a lame verse-maker." Seriously he told Southey that it would not suit him " to be under any man's control, or biddances," and if he became a consul, " 'twould fix you to one place, as bad as if you were a parson." Instead he suggested an idyllic emigration to St. Neot's, " the most lovely as well as the most healthy island in the West Indies," where Wordsworth's Bristol friends, the Pinneys, had an estate, with " a country house situated in a most heavenly way," which he had reason to believe would be at his service, with other material advantages. He and his family, Southey and Edith, Wordsworth and Dorothy would go together and " make the Island more illustrious than Cos or Lesbos." With pathetic persistence in his belief that Wordsworth reciprocated his own loyalty, he was convinced that " Wordsworth would certainly go if I went."

But with Southey remained no remnants of pantisocratic ambition. Though Ambassador Drummond apparently objected to a married secretary, Southey thought the West Indies plan " a vile one," preferring to visit Italy preparatory to another stay in Portugal, where he needed to make more researches for his history. He came to Keswick, and leaving Edith with his sister, went to Wales for more local colour for *Madoc*. At Wynn's home he received an offer to become secretary to the Chancellor of the Exchequer for Ireland, accepted, and after a call at Keswick, departed to Dublin. As the Chancellor's duties required his residence in London during the winter, he soon returned, and his arrival in London coincided with Coleridge's on 15th November. Daniel Stuart took " a first floor " for Coleridge in King Street, Covent Garden, the house of his tailor, whose wife, " a cheerful housewife of middle age," would nurse him as her son. Coleridge was so " miserably uncomfortable " that, he informed Godwin, his stay was likely to be short. But he remained, writing for the *Morning Post*, reading in libraries for his " curious metaphysical work," and seeing much of Lamb and Godwin, till Boxing Day, when he travelled to Bath on top of the coach through an unseasonable thunderstorm, arriving at Stowey on 28th December.

The war having ended with an armistice in October, preparatory to the Peace of Amiens in the following March, Coleridge talked during his three weeks at Stowey of visiting France with Poole and Davy. Back in London, he attended Davy's lectures at the Royal Institution, and however much he helped himself by work for the *Morning Post*, he was active in helping others. George Burnett, having resigned his Yarmouth ministry, was continually losing opportunities afforded by friends through assuming the eccentricities of misunderstood genius. He engaged in hack journalism, undertaking the *History of Poetry* which Southey had declined as a bookseller's job, and Coleridge recommended him to the *Morning Post*. Stuart promised to employ him, but at present " a Lion was in his foot-path ": while Coleridge was available, Stuart had no use for Burnett. From Stuart, Coleridge also obtained work for Lamb. " But," said Lamb, " Coleridge from ill health and unsettlement having hung an Arse, as the saying is, I gradually got out of favor." Stuart remarked that Coleridge repeatedly pressed him to settle Lamb on salary, but " of politics he knew nothing . . . and his drollery was vapid, when given in short paragraphs fit for a newspaper." Having already allowed himself to be bound as guarantor for five hundreds pound on behalf of his young brother-in-law, George Fricker, Coleridge now apparently tried to settle him through Lamb's influence at the East India House.

His health was better, and as the " dank and chill and foggy " weather had been against him, he attributed the amendment to a " more tranquil state " of mind and " to the cheerfulness inspired by the thought of speedily returning " to Sara " in love and peace." It was his " frequent prayer " and " almost perpetual aspiration," he told her, "that we may meet to part no more, and live together as affectionate husband and wife ought to do."

But when he left London at the end of February, he travelled to Yorkshire to see Sarah Hutchinson, staying a fortnight at Gallow Hill. He left there on 13th March, and after a few days at home, walked through pouring rain to Grasmere on the 19th. Dorothy was "much affected by the sight of him"; his eyes swollen with the wind, "he seemed half-stupefied." Evidently, after scenes with Sara over his stay at Gallow Hill, there had been another over his eagerness to visit Grasmere.

How far the Wordsworths confided in him is doubtful, but he had written from London to Sara that "Wordsworth will marry soon after my return, and he, Mary, and Dorothy will be our companions and neighbours." After the armistice, frequent letters came from Annette, and Wordsworth, despite his dislike of letter-writing, had to reply. Dorothy recognised the arrival of a crisis. The notion, accepted when she first heard at Forncett of the liaison, that Wordsworth must remain self-doomed to celibacy till he could make amends to Annette, had prevailed during the war years. But while, at Forncett, she had visualised as perfect happiness the prospect of sharing her brother's home with Annette, she could now no longer contemplate complacently the intrusion of a stranger upon their intimacy. Knowing that his morbid moods arose from sex repression and that he must marry, she wanted for him a wife to satisfy his sexual and domestic requirements without being likely either to disturb his way of life or supplant herself as his intellectual confidante. Mary Hutchinson was admirably eligible. She was her friend, capable and complacent, unimaginative and unassuming, already accustomed to their domestic habits, appropriately respectful of Wordsworth's genius, and attached to him as a companion and friend. She would always be a self-effacing third party, silent and smiling, as she had been on many excursions and visits in their company.

Whatever was confided to Coleridge, on the day after he left them on 21st March, when William was "very poorly," they "resolved to see Annette, and that Wm. should go to Mary." Dorothy began as she meant to go on. Two days later, on

K

receiving a letter from Mary, she "made a vow that we would not leave this country for Gallow Hill." After a week at Keswick, Dorothy went to stay with their neighbours, the Clarksons, while Wordsworth departed to propose marriage to Mary. No suspicion occurred that she might refuse him, and she did not. He wasted no time in dalliance. Having parted from her on 12th April, he wrote four days later to Coleridge, "Poor Creature! she would have an ugly storm of sleet and snow to encounter, and I am anxious to hear how she reached home." Reminiscence arises of Samuel Pepys and "my wife, poor wretch," but Wordsworth was neither yet married nor writing in a secret diary.

To endow respectability with some titillation of romance, the Victorians decided that Coleridge, overwhelmed by the contrast between his friend's approaching bliss and his own mental and domestic unhappiness, went home and wrote *Dejection: An Ode*. The ode was conceived and drafted on the evening of Sunday 4th April 1802—the last night of the Wordsworths' eight-day visit to Keswick. Coleridge had come to know Mary Hutchinson well, and felt affection and esteem for her; he was glad that Wordsworth was to marry her, believing that her unselfishness and common-sense would assure the tranquillity essential to the poet's work. But he had written from Germany that "dear Wordsworth appears to me to have hurtfully segregated and isolated his being," and he also deplored the idolatry of Nature that Wordsworth substituted for religion. So he feared that Wordsworth's reserve and self-absorption might hamper his domestic happiness, and wrote a warning in the lines:

> " O William! we receive but what we give,
> And in our life alone does Nature live."

"Joy," he said,

> " is the spirit and the power,
> Which wedding Nature to us gives in dower,
> A new Earth and new Heaven,
> Undream'd of by the sensual and the proud—
> Joy is the sweet voice, Joy the luminous cloud—
> We, we ourselves rejoice! "

And he ended his poem with the prayer,

> " *Brother and friend of my devoutest choice,*
>   *Thus may'st thou ever, evermore rejoice!* "

The main theme of the ode was his own loss of joy in life.

> " *There was a time that, tho' my path was rough,*
>   *This joy within me dallied with distress,*
> *And all misfortunes were but as the stuff*
>   *Whence fancy made me dreams of happiness:*
> *For hope grew round me, like the twining vine,*
> *And fruits, and foliage, not my own, seem'd mine.*
> *But now afflictions bow me down to earth:*
> *Nor care I, that they rob me of my mirth,*
>   *But oh! each visitation*
> *Suspends what nature gave me at my birth,*
>   *My shaping spirit of imagination.*"

As he sat by his window—looking out on the moonlit landscape, watching flitting flakes of clouds, the stars, the new moon itself—the natural beauty of the scene failed to excite in him the old responding exultation, and he cried in anguish, " I *see*, not *feel* how beautiful they are! " It was the poetical expression of a lament that had lingered with him anxiously for many months—that, as he had written to Godwin more than a year before, " The Poet is dead in me."

In accordance with the fashion to deride or disparage De Quincey, critics have discarded his theory—sometimes, in ignorance of facts, on the grounds that Coleridge was not yet a drug addict; sometimes through their lacking personal knowledge of " the pains of opium " which De Quincey alone, of all commentators, possessed—that Coleridge's sufferings, " and the death within him of all hope—the palsy, as it were, of that which is the life of life, and the heart within the heart—came from opium." Always Coleridge had taken laudanum to relieve his rheumatic pains, and increase of illness increased resort to the drug. During his sufferings at Keswick he apparently took doses as large as eighty or a hundred drops. In January 1801 he asked Humphry Davy for details of a drug to alleviate pain without inducing the " after fatigue " of opium. After he confided in Tom Wedgwood as a fellow-sufferer in the autumn of 1802, describing his only medicine as " an universal and regular stimulus," he declared that brandy and laudanum made him well " during the first operative; but the secondary effects increase the cause of the disease." Evidently, therefore, De Quincey accurately diagnosed Coleridge's case in supposing that " the sufferings from morbid derangements, originally produced by opium, had very possibly lost that simple character, and had themselves reacted in producing secondary states of disease and irritation, not any longer dependent upon the opium, so as to disappear with its disuse."

Opium alone was not the origin of Coleridge's " dejection," his physical lassitude and incapacity to concentrate; it was only the irritant and intensification of two root causes—ill-health and mental distress. During life few of his friends, and after death fewer of his critics, recognised the effect of bodily suffering on his career. A post mortem examination of his body revealed a dropsical disease, which " had its commencement nearly forty years before his death," and two generations later, expert medical opinion emphasised the pain he must have suffered and marvelled at his intellectual achievements as a " triumph of mind over body." Aware that he ailed something beyond the knowledge of contemporary science, Coleridge was particular in describing his symptoms, but everybody conceived that he exaggerated his ailments to excuse his indolence. He was deeply hurt when Poole doubted " if your disease be really bodily, and not the consequence of an irritated mind," and even Davy, one of the most imaginative scientific minds of his time, reported of him that " his will is probably less than ever commensurate with his ability."

Poole had reason to be dubious, for Coleridge had never suffered at Stowey the agonies afflicting him at Keswick, whereas Poole had frequently seen him driven to distraction by mental distress. Easily moved to emotion, sensitive to the slightest reproach or note of discord, he suffered agonies from excessive sensibility, and the peevish nagging of his wife's jealousy and discontent excited unbearable agitation. Failing to satisfy his own or his friends' hopes of his powers, he slumped ever deeper into dejection, proportionately increasing his inability to make amends. Taking everything to heart, he worried over shadows till they loomed as phantoms to haunt his troubled sleep and waking thoughts. Underestimating the deleterious effect of his physical ills, he attributed the loss of his poetic faculty to preoccupation with metaphysics, and worried over this fancy while convinced of his intellectual duty to pursue his philosophical studies. And likewise, despite his determination on settling at Stowey to retire and live aloof from a world of fools and knaves, concentrating on his individual development, he continually felt compunction for apparent failure to make "the Light . . . stream to a far distance from the taper in my cottage window."

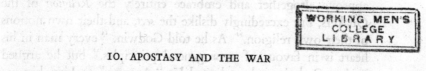

10. APOSTASY AND THE WAR

In later life, though Southey alone of the three became an active political partisan, he, Coleridge, and Wordsworth, from their avowed enthusiasm for the principles of the French Revolution, were condemned as apostates, and since the trenchant Hazlitt was foremost among the condemning democrats, so posterity has equally and indiscriminately deemed them. Southey and Wordsworth avowed themselves democrats in youth, but Wordsworth, with his aptitude for single-mindedness, abstained from politics when the unpopularity of his opinions threatened danger, while Southey, after losing faith in the power of revolution to produce reform, became an advocate of practical reform while jealously upholding the existing fabric of authority. Coleridge, on the other hand, never believed in democracy as an immediate political expedient. His expostulation to the Master of Jesus that he was "not a democrat, but a pantisocrat," generally regarded as an amusing undergraduate conceit, was a

statement of fact. In his first Bristol lectures, he had pointed out
the fallacy of democracy in demanding equality " of *rights*, not of
condition," and he saw no prospect of improvement in presenting
the ignorant with the symbol of equality in the shape of a vote,
to be used in favour of the first plausible liar who came along.
He disliked democrats—as in the case of his personal antagonism
to Holcroft—because they preferred destructive deeds and words
to constructive thought, because their grievances were inspired
by envy, and if they achieved positions of authority, they were
likely to be more despotically oppressive than aristocrats bred to
the responsibility of government.

Demagogues he despised because they misused their eloquence
to incite mob emotion to violence. With Godwin, he deplored
all manifestations of violence, and in his *Watchman* period, when
he wrote *Fire, Famine, and Slaughter*, he inclined to Christian
pacifist views. As late as December 1802, he told Estlin that " I
approve altogether and embrace entirely the *Religion* of the
Quakers, but exceedingly dislike the *sect*, and their own notions
of their own religion." As he told Godwin, " every man in his
heart is in favour of your general principles," but he argued
against Godwin and meditated his " Answer " to him, because
he legislated for " a future state," advocating a system impossible
in current conditions. But while he converted both Southey and
Wordsworth to his objections against Godwin's philosophy, he
adopted Godwin's attitude of remaining aloof from political
activity. And he did so mainly from dislike of association with
democrats and from detestation of Pitt's reason for war with
France—the fear of French revolutionary doctrines spreading
to England, which he derided as extravagant, since the English
democratic advocates of violence were a discredited handful of
men without distinction.

Southey and Wordsworth adopted his attitude of detachment
as convenient to their chosen careers. After failing to finish
his reply to Bishop Watson, Wordsworth prudently avoided
expression of political opinions; concentrating on poetry he lost
all interest in politics, contenting himself for many years in
expressing agreement with Coleridge's views. Southey sank his

ideals with the ship of pantisocracy. During his first visit to Portugal, he saw " a woman carrying a heavy burden of wood on her head, which she had cut herself, and spinning as she went along—a melancholy picture of industrious wretchedness." Such a sight in France excited in Wordsworth a reformer's indignation. From Southey it evoked the assurance that " I have learned to thank God that I am an Englishman; for though things are not so well there as in Eldorado, they are better than anywhere else." Yet, on his return home, when his conventional friend Bedford protested that " we had the essence of liberty in England," he could retort, " Then it was the *volatile* essence, for it had all fled away." Like Coleridge he scoffed at Pitt's pretext for war. " The old systems of government I think must fall," he wrote in 1798, " but in this country the immediate danger is on the other hand— from an unconstitutional and unlimited power."

After the Reign of Terror, all three, along with most other intelligent thinkers, lost faith in the French Revolution's potentiality for good. " I have still faith enough in God, and hope enough of man, but not of France," wrote Southey in 1801. " Freedom cannot grow up in that hot-bed of immorality; that oak must root in a hardier soil—England or Germany." He mistrusted all the forms of government in France after Robespierre, writing to Coleridge in December 1799, " These cursed complex governments are good for nothing, and will ever be in the hands of intriguers; the Jacobins were the men, and one house of representatives, lodging the executive in committees, the plain and common system of government. The cause of republicanism is over, and it is now only a struggle for dominion." Alone of the three, Southey approved the Jacobins. Wordsworth had inclined to the more moderate Brissot faction, and Coleridge, always following an individual line, had included Jacobins in his dislike of democrats in general.

In *Biographia Literaria* Coleridge wrote: " To this hour I cannot find reason to approve of the first war, either in its commencement or its conduct." In his Bristol lectures and in the *Watchman* he had boldly opposed the war and the government waging it. But when he told Thelwall, " I am not fit for public life," he retired with relief to Stowey; he, whose heart warmed to appreciation, had not enjoyed " the horrible Conspiracy " against him, of " Mobs and Mayors, Blockheads and Brickbats, Placards and Press gangs." Too sensitive for dirty political warfare, he was wounded to the heart by the slanderous attack in *Beauties of " the Anti-Jacobin"*. The affair of the spy at Stowey, the persecution of Thelwall, and the pother over Wordsworth's taking of Alfoxden, testified to the dangers of active opposition to the government and confirmed him in his attitude of detachment.

But, unlike Southey and Wordsworth, he could not concentrate on his chosen pursuits with equanimity in detachment. Continuing to read all important political pamphlets, he kept in close touch with affairs, as appeared in his articles for the *Morning Post*. Though he condemned the " extravagancies " of Godwin and Condorcet, he did not think that Malthus's *Essay on Population* confuted them. He confessed himself " more than ever sceptical concerning the possibility of universal plenty and wisdom," but his doubts rested on other grounds than Malthus's. In despair of enlightenment, he speculated to Josiah Wedgwood on whether " the march of the human race " was " progressive or in cycles." To Poole he wrote from his sick-bed in Keswick of the " heart-gnawing melancholy " with which he contemplated " the state of my poor oppressed country." The poverty and starvation to which the working classes were reduced by the war wrung his heart. " God knows it is as much as I can do to put meat and bread on my own table, and hourly some poor starving wretch comes to my door to put in his claim for a part of it." He was indignant at the anti-democratic propaganda that publicised " croaking " accounts of America by English emigrants—" the society so bad, the manners so vulgar, the servants so insolent! "—all the stereotyped sneers to be repeated thirty or forty years later by Mrs. Trollope, " Cyril Thornton " Hamilton, and Dickens. Why, he asked, did not the emigrants " seek out one another and make a society? " He was outraged that people should compare unfavourably a land where there was " no poverty but as a consequence of absolute idleness ".

with England, "where the laborious poor are dying with grass in their bellies." Foreseeing the evil consequences of the industrial revolution, he declared, "It is our pestilent commerce, our unnatural crowding of men in cities, and our government by rich men, that are bringing about the manifestations of offended Deity." Southey later saw the same evils, and thirty years later was ironically attacked, as a Tory, by the liberal Macaulay for execrating the vicious banking system and deploring the neglect of agriculture while the peasantry were herded into busily growing cities as slum-dwelling factory workers.

In despondent moments Coleridge still entertained thoughts of emigrating as late as 1801—"not on any romantic scheme, but merely because society has become a matter of great indifference to me. I grow daily more and more attached to solitude; but it is a matter of the utmost importance to be removed from seeing and suffering want." But when his mind was busy with schemes to justify the Wedgwoods' confidence in his capacity for bene-fiting mankind, his conscience was afflicted by his failure to influence the trend of political thought. Seeing Southey, still impatiently indignant, but cynically shrugging his shoulders while concentrating on building a career, and Wordsworth, so successfully detached that he achieved self-absorption, he re-cognised in regretful retrospect how far in a few years they had travelled from their burning romantic ideals. Appalled by the possibility that all their hopes and plans for human improvement should dissolve as idle dreams of fast passing youth, he appealed to Wordsworth on his return from Germany: "I do entreat you to go on with *The Recluse;* and I wish you would write a poem in blank verse, addressed to those who, in consequence of the complete failure of the French Revolution, have thrown up all hopes of the amelioration of mankind, and are sinking into almost epicurean selfishness, disguising the same under the soft titles of domestic attachment and contempt for visionary *philo-sophers.*" So *The Pedlar,* to be published in 1814 as *The Excursion,* was begun by Wordsworth, who himself sank utterly into that "almost epicurean selfishness" under precisely the disguises Coleridge described.

After the armistice of October 1801, by which Addington accepted terms of peace far less advantageous than Pitt could have had two years before, Coleridge told Poole that " We, i.e. Wordsworth and myself, regard the peace as necessary, but the Terms as most alarming." The terms in themselves, requiring England to surrender all her conquests in the course of the war except Trinidad and Ceylon, seemed fair enough. But their acceptance ratified the preceding harsh treaty with Austria, giving France virtual control of Italy and therefore rendering the independence of Malta, though guaranteed by the six principal powers, at the mercy of French caprice. It was the just reward of an unjust war—a peace, as Sheridan said, " which every man ought to be glad of but no man can be proud of."

Buonaparte's triumph was the main cause for alarm. His brilliance as a general in the field had excited admiration, and Fox's followers, in disapproving of the war, were glad that Pitt's minatory aggression had invoked French victories. But his emergence into politics and appointment as First Consul awakened Southey's and Coleridge's hatred of military dictatorships, and they wished he had fallen in his disastrous Egyptian campaign. " Why had not the man perished before the walls of Acre in his greatness and his glory? " exclaimed Southey. " I *was* asked to write a poem upon that defeat, and half-tempted to do it because it went to my very heart." Declaring that " the French are children " and " 'tis an infirmity to hope or fear concerning them," Coleridge wished " they had a king again, if it were only that Sieyès and Bonaparte might be *hung*. Guillotining is too republican a death for such reptiles."

Thanks to Pitt's criminally stupid reactionary policy, the tables were turned. In 1793 England's reactionaries had refused to recognise republican France and gone to war to prevent the spread of democracy through Europe. As a result, in 1802, England ironically identified herself as the last stronghold of democracy in Europe and felt impelled to resume the war to save Europe from a military dictator. Forgetting Godwin's warning that, " to render despotism auspicious and benign, it is necessary, not only that the sovereign should possess every human excellence, but that all his officers should be men of penetrating genius and unspotted virtue," Southey inclined to the Fascist ideal, wishing that there had been " a Lycurgus after Robespierre, a man loved for his virtue, and bold and inflexible, who should have levelled the property of France, and then would the republic have been immortal—and the world must have been revolutionised by example." Coleridge had no faith in the possibility of a super-man. He believed that " property will some time or other be modified by the predominance of intellect, even as rank and superstition are now modified by and subordinated to property . . . but first those particular modes of property which more particularly stop the diffusion must be done away, as injurious to property itself; these are priesthood and the too great patronage of Government."

During the summer of 1802—while still suffering in health, making determined efforts to live happily with his wife, translating German verses, writing *The Picture*, the *Hymn before Sunrise*, and other verses for the *Morning Post*, and entertaining Charles and Mary Lamb for three weeks of August—Coleridge apparently found time for much meditation on politics, for in September and October he contributed to the *Morning Post* a series of papers on *Comparison of the Present State of France with that of Rome under Julius and Augustus Caesar*. Describing Buonaparte as " the new Caesar," he considered his character as comprising the good and bad traits of all the first three Caesars. " In courage, splendour of military fame, in military success and conduct, and the love of science," he recalled Julius as he resembled Augustus in " his close application to public business, and his encouragement of the liberal arts and great public works," but he had " likewise the imperious, irritable, and ostentatious mind of the former, with the constitutional coldness and politic craft of the latter." Further, " if reserve, if darkness, if the employment of spies and informers, if dread and hatred of all political discussions, if vindictive hatred of all bold political writings, if an indifference to all religions, except as instruments of state policy, with a certain strange and dark superstition respecting fate, a blind confidence in his destinies "—if these were in the

Chief Consul's character, then he recalled " the name and history of Tiberius." Warning Buonaparte against the fate of each and the fate of Rome, Coleridge had " no hesitation in predicting, that it is impossible that France can ever realise her ambitious dream of universal sovereignty." Though the unsubjugated powers were " called upon to suspicion, watchfulness, and prompt and firm courage," he saw " much to alarm us, nothing to terrify." With a back-handed slap at Pitt, he concluded: " Happy it will be for Europe, if her governors shall at last perceive, that the more free a nation is, the less she will be disposed to conquest; that the absurd principles of demogogues are mere effects, and not causes, and will, at all times, die a natural death; but that, if opposed by violence, they may become indeed pernicious; not by their own proper action, but by the facility which they afford to the levying of armies, whose political fanaticism is soon transmuted into a passion for military glory. A noisy republic is interred; and an iron-handed empire rises out of the grave, its ghost, and its avenger."

It was a wise, clear-sighted thesis, like all his earlier writings. But he knew that " suspicion " and " watchfulness," allied with the accumulating armaments which politicians demanded even as they signed the peace treaty, must engender war. He knew, too, that the war would prove the longest and bloodiest, the most prodigal of misery for the common people, yet recorded by history, and that, by its fostering of the worst human instincts, it would postpone for generations even rudimentary realisation of " the republic of God's own making," which had been the romantic ideal of his crusading years. Recognising this, he discarded his own doctrines, as he had disparaged Godwin's, because they dogmatised for " a future state." Compromising for practical purposes, he crashed suddenly from the pedestal of his romantic ideals, and a further series of articles argued from a historical parallel with Charles II's restoration after Cromwell's usurpation that the situation in France was ripe for the return of the Bourbons!

" Bad as we may be," he wrote, " we assuredly are the best among nations," from which position of compromise, he considered that constitutional monarchy like England's was the best condition immediately realisable for France's fresh start towards a better destiny. Anything was better than military despotism, and reconciled to discarding his ideals and accepting the ruin and misery of war, he concentrated loathing on the cause of his changed attitude. When Fox visited Buonaparte and accepted honours at his hands, Coleridge did not consider the humanity of the statesman's motives in seeking to avert the misery of millions. Horrified at such truckling to the militarist impeding the march of human progress, he boldly attacked Fox in two articles that set all London talking. Pacifism and veneration for Christian doctrine alike forgotten, he became fervent in determination to rid the world at all costs of a blight. " We will tremble at the possible punishment which our national crimes may have made us worthy of, from retributive Providence," he wrote to his brother: " Let us be humble before our Maker, but not spirit-palsied before our bloodthirsty enemies." When invasion threatened in 1803 after the war's renewal, he felt few of the noble sentiments expressed in *Fears in Solitude* of 1798. " The Invasion must be a Blessing," he told Poole, " for if we do not repel it, and cut them to pieces, we are a Vile sunken race, and it is good, that our Betters should *crack* us—And if we do act as Men, Christians, Englishmen—down goes the Corsican Miscreant, and Europe may have peace."

His apostacy from his former principles was as sensational as Burke's twelve years before, and achieved an effect only less impressive. Even Southey, whose thought travelled a similar course, thought he went too far in attacking Fox. Coleridge could argue that he was condoning war only in preference to a greater evil; that it was an expedient imposed upon England by Pitt's criminal folly in forcing revolutionary France to become a fortress; that he had consistently deplored Pitt's policy, but must now join in suffering its consequences; that England, with all its faults, still offered more fitting material than France for a better future, and therefore, if the choice was death or survival, England should survive. But he was too clear-sighted to suppose that he was condoning " a war to end wars." He knew that he had succumbed to an expedient; and the effect was to enhance the disturbance of his mental peace. Delighted by the increase in circulation accruing from the sensational articles, Stuart renewed offers that would have raised Coleridge to affluence. But, repeating his refusal to be tied, he remained silent on political affairs for six years after the spring of 1803. For politics, as for poetry, his inspiration lost its spark, and for the same reason—that the tinder of imagination was damped by despondency, disillusion, frustration of hope.

11. PARTING OF THE WAYS

The year of suspended hostilities enabled Wordsworth to visit France. In August 1802 he and Dorothy crossed to Calais, where they met Annette and her small daughter Caroline. No record remains of the arrangements concluded, but on their return, the Wordsworths stayed in London, where Lamb was " their guide to Bartlemy Fair " (whence Wordsworth derived the impressions incorporated in *The Prelude* as belonging to his nonage) and they interviewed their brother Richard on financial matters. Lord Lonsdale having died in the previous May, his successor agreed to settle his debt to the Wordsworths' father with accumulated interest, and Wordsworth and Dorothy eventually received nearly four thousand pounds as their share. Thus assured of an income commensurate with simple comfort, Wordsworth married Mary Hutchinson on 4th October 1802 from her brother's house at Gallow Hill.

Dorothy had her way, and their home remained Dove Cottage. She did not attend the wedding ceremony, but when two men came running with the news that " it was over," she flung herself on her bed and " lay in stillness, neither hearing nor seeing anything," till Sarah Hutchinson warned her, " They are coming." " This forced me from the bed where I lay, and I moved, I knew not how, straight forward, faster than my strength could carry me, till I met my beloved William, and fell upon his bosom." The bride's conduct during this affecting scene is unrecorded; presumably she smiled complacently. The honeymoon consisted of the two days' journey from Gallow Hill to Grasmere, and Dorothy accompanied the nuptial pair. She began as she meant to go on.

Their life proceeded the same, and for five years Wordsworth continued the prolific poetical fecundity begun when Coleridge attracted him to Alfoxden in the summer of 1797. With Mary as housekeeper and bedfellow, Dorothy as companion and secretary, he achieved completely such detachment as Coleridge had intended and desired. Untroubled by cares, unfettered by responsibility, he was free to live his inward life and concentrate on composition. But his inspiration had flourished on self-immolation as well as isolation. He was now no longer tortured by the possibly impending intrusion of Annette, now no longer sex-repressed—whatever her intellectual limitations, Mary was domestically adequate as wife and mother. Her comfortable complacency came to pervade their home with a snug warmth, lulling to drowsiness, and wrapt in its blanket, Wordsworth's always sluggish imagination lapsed into torpor. Defeated by the detachment he had invited, he became preoccupied with the petty and trivial; his mind grew like Dorothy's journals, a receptacle for the commonplace. As his children grew around him, he became querulous, doting, so obsessed with the preservation of his own security that he mistrusted every inevitable change of passing time, and ironically troubled so habitually over the sordid business of life he had formerly despised that, as Landor said, he had one eye on a daffodil and the other on a canal share.

Coleridge continued to sing his praises and eventually sealed his recognition in *Biographia Literaria*, but by then he was already degenerating into Edward FitzGerald's " Daddy Wordsworth." When Lamb ventured to remark on passages in the second edition of *Lyrical Ballads,* he " received almost instantaneously a long letter of four sweating pages from my Reluctant Letter-Writer," saying he was " compelled to wish " that Lamb's " range of sensibility was more extended." When Sarah Hutchinson criticised *The Leech Gatherer,* Dorothy wrote, " When you happen to be displeased with what you suppose to be the tendency or moral of any poem which William writes, ask yourself whether you have hit upon the real tendency and true moral, and above all never think that he writes for no reason but merely because a thing has happened—and when you feel any poem of his to be tedious, ask yourself in what spirit it was written—whether merely to tell the tale and be through with it, or to illustrate a particular character or truth etc. etc." This irritability under criticism swelled to an overweening vanity repellent to all save lion-hunters like Crabb Robinson and doting adorers like Miss Fenwick, and he became notorious for his disinclination to bestow a word of praise on another writer's work. By the time he became Poet Laureate, he was well fitted for the dignity of a court functionary, though a more appropriate office might have been Gold-Stick-in-Waiting.

Southey soon resigned his appointment as secretary to the Chancellor of the Exchequer for Ireland, and settled again at Bristol. "You are happy in your marriage and Life," wrote Coleridge to him; "and greatly to the honour of your moral self-government, moralities and manners are pleasant to, and sufficient for, you to which my nature is utterly unsuited: for I am so weak that warmth of manner in a female housemate is as necessary to me, as warmth of internal attachment." Edith Southey had a character similar to her sister's. In the winter of 1801–2 Lamb found her "considerably improved, and she will talk if she is talked to, but she bitterly complains that when literary men get together, they never speak to the women." Both retained the mental outlook of the provincial suburb in which they were born. Southey had not outlived his eager enthusiasm, and retained enough of his adolescent attachment to resort to his wife's society as recreation and relaxation from habitual diligence. He had therefore scant sympathy with Coleridge, and when at length he was persuaded to come to Keswick in the autumn of 1803, he settled happily in the house from which Coleridge longed to escape.

At Greta Hall he lived for the remaining forty years of his life. *Thalaba* had not enjoyed the popular vogue of *Joan of Arc,* but it was a *succés d'estime*, as were its successors, *Madoc, The Curse of Kehama,* and *Roderick*. They consolidated his reputation, and when Walter Scott declined the Laureateship in 1813, Southey was the obvious choice. By that time he was the main prop of the *Quarterly Review,* the Tory counterblast to the *Edinburgh Review,* and his poetical repute was equalled by his celebrity as a fluent writer of lucid prose.

Till the finely tempered mechanism of his brain broke down under strain four years before his death, his life at Keswick was devoted to literary labour with the rarest remissions. His visits to Landor at Llanthony in 1811, Como in 1817, and Clifton in 1836, three continental and two Scottish tours, were almost his only formal holidays in forty years. Visits to London infrequently interrupted his routine. "My days among the dead are past," he wrote in his best-known lyric, and the life of seclusion in his study, "conversing with books rather than men" and "communing with my own heart," he regarded as "the greatest of all advantages" to a poet. It nevertheless contributed to an absence of psychological understanding evident alike in his biographies and personal relations. Incapable of sympathising with the complexities of Coleridge's temperament, while he ungrudgingly assumed responsibility for the upbringing of Coleridge's children, he condemned his infirmities as moral frailty. Recognising Coleridge's incompatibility with his wife, he could not realise the intolerable torture he endured in daily contact with her, because he himself demanded no intellectual affinity in a wife. Southey's wife "sympathizes with nothing, she enters into none of his peculiar pursuits—she only loves *him*," wrote Coleridge; "she is therefore a respectable Wife, but not a Companion. Dreary, dreary, would be the Hours, passed with her." Seeking no spiritual solace from a wife, Southey devoted all his intellectual energy, as Coleridge remarked, to "unceasing Authorship, never interrupted from morning to night but by sleeping and eating." Like Philip Quarles in Aldous Huxley's *Point Counter Point,* the idea of intimate relationship "made him uncomfortable" in threatening his solitude— "that solitude which, with a part of his mind, he deplored (for he felt himself cut off from much he would have liked to experience), but in which alone, nevertheless, his spirit could live in comfort." From doubt or dissatisfaction he shrank, but their intrusion upon his thoughts appears in his advice to Landor on marriage, " Find out a woman whom you can esteem and love will grow more surely out of esteem, than esteem will out of love." And again, when warning Caroline Bowles of the danger to a young woman friend, " lest some one with as much romance in his heart and head as there was in mine when I began life as a poet should fall in love with that sweet countenance of hers." Like Quarles, " emotionally he was a foreigner." At twenty-five he wrote, " I have a dislike to all strong emotion, and avoid whatever could excite it." He never succeeded in subduing his emotions; Carlyle found him in his latter days " a serious, human, honest, but sharp, almost fierce-looking, thin man, with very much the militant in his aspect—in the eyes especially was visible a mixture of sorrow and anger, or of angry contempt, as if his indignant fight with the world had not yet ended in victory, but also never should in defeat." Hazlitt, too, sensed the inward struggle of prudence urging reason to subdue instinct, remarking " a hectic flush upon his cheek, a roving fire in his eye, a falcon glance, a look at once aspiring and dejected." This self-discipline enabled concentration on his daily routine of bread-and-butter work, the compromise with conscience that purchased the peace he desired. But it sapped his poetry of spontaneity and his political thought of strict integrity.

Coleridge departed in search of health to a southern climate soon after Southey came to Greta Hall. He returned, more than ever derelict, dreading re-union with his wife yet hesitating to hurt her by the drastic step of separation. At last, having exhausted the patience of the Wordsworths as well as Southey, he drifted out of her life. He merely went to London, and did not return. Years of physical pain and mental agony lay before him, while he struggled with slavery to opium and with the persuasion that his life's mission lay in evolving an improved system of philosophy. His fascination and his eloquence lasted his life. " I think his essentials not touched," wrote Lamb in 1816, when recording that " his face when he repeats his verses hath its ancient glory, an Archangel a little damaged." The famous phrase fairly describes him in his later career. In spite of compromise and dereliction, he still retained the semblance of his former self and the shadow of that integrity which departed utterly from Wordsworth and partially from Southey. The romantic ideal lingered in his mind, and though he left his work fragmentary and unresolved as his life had been, the legacy of his thought has yet to be fully valued for probate.

As a potential force among contemporaries the first romantics abdicated with Coleridge's declaration of support for the war against Napoleon. Their ideals next flamed in Shelley, to expire with him in the waters of the Mediterranean. Fitfully they have flared since—in the Pre-Raphaelites, in late Victorians like Wilfrid Blunt and Cunninghame Graham, in some of the realistic novelists, in soul-scarred survivors of the first war with Germany. At the close of the twentieth century's second calamitous war, there have been signs of the flames flickering again. Unless these flames are fanned to brilliant illumination, there can be no hope that the world has not once more suffered desolation in vain.

BIBLIOGRAPHY

(In addition to the main source-books, the following list contains books quoted or referred to, and also a few other books to which the interested reader may be recommended.)

COLERIDGE

Letters of Samuel Taylor Coleridge. Ed. E. H. Coleridge, 2 vols., 1895.
Unpublished Letters of Samuel Taylor Coleridge. Ed. Earl Leslie Griggs, 2 vols., 1932.
Thomas Poole and His Friends by M. E. Sandford, 2 vols., 1888.
Letters from the Lake Poets . . . to Daniel Stuart, 1889.
Biographia Epistolaris. Ed. A. Turnbull, 2 vols., 1911.
Minnow among Tritons: Mrs. S. T. Coleridge's Letters to Thomas Poole. Ed. Stephen Potter, 1934.
Essays on His Own Times, by Samuel Taylor Coleridge. Ed. by his daughter, 3 vols., 1850.
Anima Poetae. Ed. E. H. Coleridge, 1895.
Biographia Literaria. Ed. J. Shawcross, 2 vols., 1907.
The Friend. Ed. H. N. Coleridge, 4th ed., 3 vols., 1844.
Poems. Ed. E. H. Coleridge, new ed., 1940.
Letters, Conversations and Recollections of S. T. Coleridge. Ed Thos. Allsop, 2 vols., 1836.
Life by James Gillman, 1938.
Early Recollections by Joseph Cottle, 2 vols., 1837.
Reminiscences of Coleridge and Southey by Joseph Cottle, 1847.
Coleridge by H. D. Traill, 1884.
Life by Hall Caine, 1887.
Samuel Taylor Coleridge by James Dykes Campbell, 1894.
Coleridge by Richard Garnett, 1904.
Coleridge and Wordsworth in the West Country by W. Knight, 1913.
Coleridge at Highgate by Lucy E. Watson, 1925.
Samuel Taylor Coleridge by Hugh I'Anson Fausset, 1926.
Coleridge: The Sublime Somnambulist by John Charpentier, 1929.
Coleridge as Philosopher by J. H. Muirhead, 1930.
Coleridge's Shakespearian Criticism. Ed. T. M. Raysor, 2 vols., 1930.
The Road to Xanadu by John Livingston Lowes, 1931.
Coleridge: Studies by Several Hands. Ed. by Edmund Blunden and Earl Leslie Griggs, 1934.
Coleridge's Miscellaneous Criticism. Ed. T. M. Raysor, 1936.

Samuel Taylor Coleridge: A Biographical Study by Sir E. K. Chambers, 1938.
Life of S. T. Coleridge: The Early Years by Lawrence Hanson, 1938.

DE QUINCEY

Writings, 7 vols., 1851.
Works. Ed. David Masson, 14 vols., 1889–90.
De Quincey by Malcolm Elwin, 1935.
A Flame in Sunlight by Edward Sackville-West, 1936.

GODWIN

Enquiry Concerning Political Justice, 3rd ed., 2 vols., 1798.
William Godwin: His Friends and Contemporaries by C. Kegan Paul, 2 vols., 1876.
Life of William Godwin by Ford K. Brown, 1926.

HAZLITT

Complete Works. Ed. P. P. Howe, 21 vols., 1930–4.
Life of William Hazlitt by P. P. Howe, new ed., 1928.
Born Under Saturn by C. M. Maclean, 1943.

HUNT

Autobiography of Leigh Hunt. Introd. Edmund Blunden, 1928.
Leigh Hunt: A Biography by Edmund Blunden, 1930.

LAMB

Complete Letters of Charles and Mary Lamb. Ed. E. V. Lucas, 3 vols., 1935.
Life of Charles Lamb by E. V. Lucas, 2 vols., 1935.
Charles Lamb and the Lloyds. Ed. E. V. Lucas, 1898.
Works. Ed. Thomas Hutchinson, 2 vols., 1908.

LANDOR

Works. Ed. T. Earle Welby and Stephen Wheeler, 16 vols., 1927–36.
Savage Landor by Malcolm Elwin, 1941.

ROBINSON

Diary, Reminiscences and Correspondence of Henry Crabb Robinson. Ed. Thomas Sadler, 3 vols., 1869.

Blake, Coleridge, Wordsworth, Lamb, etc.: Selections from the Remains of Henry Crabb Robinson. Ed. Edith J. Morley, 1922.
Correspondence of Henry Crabb Robinson with the Wordsworth Circle. Ed. Edith J. Morley, 2 vols., 1927.
Life and Times of Henry Crabb Robinson by Edith J. Morley, 1935.

SOUTHEY

Life and Correspondence of Robert Southey. Ed. by his son, 6 vols., 1849–50.
Selections from the Letters of Robert Southey. Ed. J. W. Warter, 4 vols., 1856.
Correspondence of Robert Southey with Caroline Bowles. Ed. Edward Dowden, 1881.
Letters from England: by Don Manuel Alvarez Espriella. 3 vols., 1807.
Poetical Works. 10 vols., 1837–38.
Southey's Common-place Book. Ed. J. W. Warter, 2nd ed., 4 vols., 1850–1.
Poems. Ed. Maurice H. Fitzgerald, 1909.
Southey by Edward Dowden, 1880.
Early Life of Robert Southey by W. Haller, 1917.
Southey by Jack Simmons, 1945.

TAYLOR

Life and Writings of William Taylor of Norwich by J. W. Robberds, 2 vols., 1843.

WEDGWOOD

Tom Wedgwood by R. B. Litchfield, 1903.

WORDSWORTH

Early Letters of William and Dorothy Wordsworth. Ed. E. de Selincourt, 1935.
Letters of William and Dorothy Wordsworth: the Middle Years. Ed. de Selincourt, 2 vols., 1937.
Letters of William and Dorothy Wordsworth: the Later Years. Ed. E. de Selincourt, 3 vols., 1938.
Letters of the Wordsworth Family. Ed. W. A. Knight, 3 vols., 1907.
Journals of Dorothy Wordsworth. Ed. Wm. Knight, 1925.
Journals of Dorothy Wordsworth. Ed. E. de Selincourt, 2 vols., 1941
The Prelude. Ed. E. de Selincourt, 1926.
Prose Works. Ed. A. B. Grosart, 3 vols., 1876.

Poems. Ed. Nowell C. Smith, 3 vols., 1908.

Poetical Works. Ed. Thomas Hutchinson, new ed., revised E. de Selincourt, 1942.

Memoirs of William Wordsworth by Christopher Wordsworth, 2 vols., 1851.

Life of William Wordsworth by Wm. Knight, 3 vols., 1889.

Wordsworthiana. Ed. Wm. Knight, 1889.

Wordsworth by Walter Raleigh, 1903.

William Wordsworth: His Life, Works, and Influence by G. M. Harper, 2 vols., 1916; revised ed., 1929.

Early Life of William Wordsworth by Emile Legouis, trans. J. W. Matthews, 1921.

William Wordsworth and Annette Vallon by Emile Legouis, 1922.

Dora Wordsworth: Her Book by F. V. Morley, 1924.

Dorothy and William Wordsworth by C. M. Maclean, 1927.

The Lost Leader by Hugh I'Anson Fausset, 1933.

Wordsworth by Herbert Read, 1930.

Dorothy Wordsworth: The Early Years by C. M. Maclean, 1932.

Dorothy Wordsworth: A Biography by E. de Selincourt, 1933.

Wordsworth's Anti-Climax by Willard L. Sperry, 1935.

INDEX

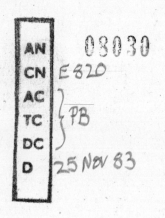